DEATHBOUND
SUBJECTIVITY

Studies in Phenomenology and Existential Philosophy

DEATHBOUND SUBJECTIVITY

ALPHONSO LINGIS

INDIANA UNIVERSITY PRESS
Bloomington and Indianapolis

Manufactured in the United States of America

Library of Congress Cataloging-in-Publication Data

Lingis, Alphonso
Deathbound subjectivity.

(Studies in phenomenology and existential philosophy)
Includes index.
1. Subject (Philosophy) 2. Death. I. Title.
II. Series.
BD223.L56 1989   126   88-45450
ISBN 0-253-31660-X

1 2 3 4 5   93 92 91 90 89

CONTENTS

INTRODUCTION   1

Part I. THE IMPERATIVE IDEALIZATION

   I. The Origin of Infinity   11
  II. Images of Autarchy   38
 III. The Vicious Circle of Mastery   59
 IV. The Work of the Masters   87

Part II. THE SUBJECTION

   V. Deathbound Thought   109
  VI. Face to Face   135
 VII. The Sign of the Subject   156
VIII. The Other Death   176

NOTES   193
INDEX   205

DEATHBOUND
SUBJECTIVITY

INTRODUCTION

Contemporary technological civilization is characterized, according to Martin Heidegger, by the absence of finalities in its thought, which is essentially mathematical, a calculation of equivalences, and by the absence of finalities in its praxis, which is essentially technological, transformation into the equivalent. It now no longer represents the objective universe as a multiplicity of objects, identities posited by their own contours before empirical observation, but as an electromagnetic field whose transformations can be calculated in advance. Nature as a whole has been cast as a pure fund or stock of raw material or energy-quanta subjected to a ceaseless transformation now on the brink of being driven by the quasi-infinite energy exploded from the infinitesimal, atomic constitution of the given. The unrestricted power of nuclear technology for transformation and destruction appears to Heidegger as the ultimate avatar of the civilization that in Greek antiquity conceived the mathematical idea of infinity to extend infinite space-time dimensions about the quanta of its rational calculations. Natural man no longer figures in this civilization as the cognitive monad whose substance supports all the predicates with which nature is objectified nor as the will that determines transformations in nature in view of its own finalities. The human psychophysical nature is itself represented as a stock of physical and psychic energies, genetic material, in principle calculable and in principle technologically transformable. The staggering quantity of nuclear weapons this civilization has now stockpiled—the explosion of less than ten percent of them could now reduce the human species to extinction—individuates each speaker of language and each participant in a civic order, through which this arsenal is maintained, in an unprecedented way. Even if the present stock of weapons were destroyed by common consent, the science and the technology that produced them cannot be destroyed, and the power to reduce the human species and the whole history of its works to radioactive ashes lies in the hands of any outlaw nation or group, almost in the hands of any individual.

In these times of the obsolescence of the concept of human subjectivity in our sciences and our postmodern philosophy, the reduction of subjectivity to cybernetic circuitry, and the reduction of human initiative to the power to precipitate nuclear extinction, this book searches in the thought of six philosophies for the principle of subjectivity. It seeks to know the subject not so much as the generator of meaning but rather as a locus of order. The Enlightenment philosophy of subjectivity was a project to emancipate subjectivity, of its own nature spontaneous; but this philosophy also found in subjectivity legislation: Subjectivity orders—it organizes its experiences, it executes on the outside the

1

decrees of its autonomous will. In the contemporary antisubjectivism of continental philosophy, subjectivity has been denounced for playing, in Husserl's
phenomenology, a false role, that of being the origin and source of meaning,
which it would invest, with spontaneous acts, into the verbal material of a
language, into kinship relationships, into the exchange of values in an economic
system, into the effects of power in social institutions. Structuralism, in linguistics, in anthropology, in political economy, and in psychoanalysis, has thus
presented itself as antisubjectivism; it has proclaimed the death of man or the
absence of a subject from the strata of culture which function as systems of signs
and of values. In the the midst of this major deconstruction of subjectivity in
our time we have set out to locate and promote the imperative that constitutes
our subjectivity, that orders it to order.

The Idealization of Subjectivity

Our project was conceived with the conviction that the extraordinarily illuminating polemics against the meaning-constituting function in which
Edmund Husserl's phenomenology located the absoluteness of subjectivity has
not exhausted the rich investigations of major continental thinkers into the
subject as ordinance and responsibility. Indeed, the role of the subject of
discourse has to be completely reformulated in the light of what linguistics and
the fields of anthropology, political economics, and psychoanalysis recon-
structed as semiological disciplines have shown us: The relationship between a
subject and that subject's usage of the resources of a signifier-system—whether
it is linguistic, gestural, or ritual, or one of kinship identities, politico-economic
values, or erotic signs—is not that of a relationship between origin and product,
constituting act and constituted term. The subject can operate in a signifier-
system only by himself being formed by that system; one can enter into speech
only as an element of language; the subject that issues signs is himself a sign.
The subject that assigns libidinal and politico-economic values to bodies,
forces, and goods is himself a depository of genetic material, an economic
resource, an element in multiple micro- and macrosystems of power which
dominate because the representation one could have of them conceals their
operations and their finalities.

Yet subjectivity operates on its own sign. It idealizes itself. In a phenomenological account the ideal is that which transcends the *hic et nunc* in which
the real is actualized. It is that which recurs, showing itself in each *hic et nunc* to
be the same. Subjectivity idealizes itself by identifying itself across the passage
of its states and acts. Theoretical subjectivity, which was impelled to idealize
also its affectivity and its practice, was, according to Husserl, idealized from its
origin in Greek antiquity by identifying itself on a dimension of infinite time.
The idea, or ideal form, of infinity first emerged in Greek mathematics, with its
idealization of space, and in Greek, Platonic, philosophy, with its ideal of

absolute truth, that is, a truth that can be evident to the open series of all lucid minds. The idea of infinity is *the* theoretical idea, the idea with which the theoretical attitude is constituted. Theoretical subjectivity structures its own temporal order as an infinite succession of nows, which recur the same in form as their content passes. With the axis of infinite time space can be extended beyond every limit that a panorama has within perception; truth can be subject to unlimited confirmation. Theoretical cognition locates in this infinite time the panorama of idealized, infinitized space in which the objective world is to be represented. And it locates itself, idealized as a theoretical subject that recurs the same, at any moment of infinite time. It identifies itself as the power to reproduce ad infinitum the form of the present in which truths with which the infinite space of the objective universe is represented can be evident.

It is then the idea, or idealizing form, of infinity that orders the layout of the space of the objective representation of the universe and that orders the axis of infinite time in which theoretical subjectivity locates itself. The idea of infinity is the orientation and the ordinance that, Husserl explains, makes Western, theoretical culture historial, makes Western theory, desire, and practice teleological. But is the idea of infinity itself a spontaneous product of subjectivity? Does it get reiterated simply by force of the lure it represents for subjectivity? For Immanuel Kant all understanding is obedience; an order weighs on understanding. Subjectivity is constituted in subjection to alterity; the subject that orders is ordered to order. That which orders the objective representation of the universe and that which orders subjectivity's representation of itself on the axis of an infinite time is categorically imperative. Kant interprets this imperative, in terms derived from formal logic (that is, from the formalization of the ordered signs with which nature is objectively represented), as an imperative for the universal and the necessary. This imperative works on the cognitive mind to command a representation of the universe synthetically grasped in universal and necessary laws. It is an imperative that the cognitive subject make itself, in its acts of understanding but also its acts of feeling and its stances and operations among things, into a pure exemplar of the universal and the necessary. The cognitive subject is to transform its composite human nature so as to live as a purely rational agency, one that realizes the universal in each particular situation. It is imperative that the subject use its rationally energized will to actively suppress in itself all that is particular in its wants and desires, its sensuous appetite, and its sensuous will. It is to subsist as the pure locus where the universal and necessary is, in the space of a consciousness, transformed into a willed legislation. Subjugating the irrational impulses of its particular sensuous nature, it will make itself the agency where the universal law of all nature is promulgated. Suppressing its sensuous dependency on the contingent lures of particular environments, it makes itself an end unto itself. It is by the incessant reiteration of the universal and the necessary in every particular situation that it idealizes itself. Idealization is not simply a project; it is enjoined by a categorical imperative.

Friedrich Nietzsche's antiidealist program is a positivist operation working to naturalize humanity, but the nature in which he situates life is a nature projected on an infinite time of cyclic recurrence. Life is production of excess force, self-affirmation and self-overcoming. This affirmation is to be intensified, taken to the limit, to the point of affirming, loving, infinitely, all that one has ever willed and all that one shall ever have willed. To affirm life and to bring life to its unrestricted self-affirmation, Nietzsche diagrams that life on a dimension of the infinite time of nature. To affirm unrestrictedly the now that discharges its forces and passes is equivalent to willing the eternal recurrence of its transience. The Husserlian idealization was projected on a time-axis of the ever-possible recurrence of the selfsame subjective identity; the Nietzschean idealization is projected on a time-axis of the recurrence of the selfsame transience. It is the production of excess force, the joy, which Nietzsche identifies as the positive essence of life, that compels this theoretical projection. Zarathustra discovers the unrestricted affirmation of all he has ever willed and all he shall ever will, the will for their infinite passing and their infinite recurrence, as the law of his own master nature. But this subject that eternally recurs is so entangled, ensnared, enamored with every other event of nature that every particular in nature recurs with it. This most singular law, discovered in uncovering the imperative of his own nature, is at the same time the law of all nature, the most universal cosmological ordinance. The modern transcendental, and the ancient, cosmological, forms of philosophy meet and are revealed to be subject to the same law.

The Law of the Universe and the Singular Law

Husserl distinguishes the cosmic format of time, in which nature is objectively represented, from the internal time of subjectivity, which can represent the passing events of nature because it retains and anticipates its own past and future phases. But the time-form of subjectivity, as Husserl then describes it, is a mirror-image of the external time of the events of objectified, idealized nature; it too has the form of a reproduction of the form of the now selfsame ad infinitum. This idealization depends on Husserl's metaphysical separation of the form from the content of a time-phase of experience. To decisively disengage subjectivity as locus of order from metaphysics, we shall then have to recommence the analysis of the form—or forming—of a moment of presence in consciousness, of a field of the past, and of a horizon of the future. Beneath the idealized time of a reproduction of the form of the now ad infinitum we shall exhibit the lived experience of natural time where the form of the present dilates and contracts with the content and where the time that passes veers into a level by alteration both of its content and its form. We shall find in the past of natural consciousness an irreversible, irrevocable, definitive fatality that weighs on the present; we shall find in the future of consciousness an axis which already assigns it position, direction, force, form. The idealizing consciousness that is conceived to arise by itself, without commitments, without a mission, is a transcendental illusion of metaphysics. We shall argue that it is constituted in a circular movement by which a theoretical consciousness idealizes its own time by conceiving it as the mirror-image of the time of external nature, which it represents using the idea of infinity it derives, by formalization and idealization, from the extension of its own natural time. Beneath the imperative idea of infinity with which theoretical subjectivity locates itself in cosmic time, we shall look for the singular law that destines the subject that orders to the fatality and destination of a time of its own.

We shall similarly separate, in the Kantian practical philosophy, the *fact* of the imperative that weighs on understanding from its properties of universality and necessity. We shall argue that there is a circle in deriving the properties of the imperative for law from the logic that is formalized from an inspection of the principles with which speculative reason has constituted the world as one nature. This will suggest that external nature is not merely an illustration of a law-governed totality but is an original locus where the a priori force of the imperative acquires a specific form. We shall argue that the ideal republican state where each citizen is both legislator and subject of the laws, upon which the Kantian concept of subjective autonomy depends, embodies also a concept of law derived from the formal logic of scientific dynamics. This argument makes possible the search for a singular—and singularizing—law that orders our authentic existence and our responsibility.

Nietzsche seeks this singular and singularizing law in infinity—in the infinite time of eternal recurrence. His avowedly antiidealist philosophy thematizes the *physis* of a universe of forces and events beneath the physical nature objectified in terms of selfsame entities that recur and, beneath the metaphysico-the-oretical will for self-responsibility and abiding selfsameness, uncovers in the affect of joy a will that extends a time of the unending transience of all its own forces and events. The image of all nature in eternal recurrence functions to imperatively bind a will to the succession and sequence of its own singular life; the Nietzschean mastery is produced by this imperative. The life that has mastery does not order the succession and sequence of nature and its own nature but consecrates the non-teleological, Dionysian, movements of all nature with the worth of eternity. Nietzsche deliberately conjoins the most universal cosmological law with a law that formulates how a life makes itself a sovereign singularity, a law now formulated as a certainty in the first person singular. Contemporary science has not confirmed Nietzsche's affirmation that its representation of the finite universe is inscribed in infinitely recurring time. It is true that Zarathustra does not, and cannot, discover this most universal law, ontological law of the universe in becoming, by empirical observation of its cyclic recurrence; he discovers it as the imperative of his own most singular joy. The representation of all nature in eternal recurrence is not a phantasm pro-duced by, but an imperative image that produces, a will that affirms itself unrestrictedly. One believes and one must believe one's joy. But how can belief in the eternal recurrence of one's joy be possible unless one can believe in its truth?

The Imperative Mortality

For Heidegger every idealization of one's existence in a horizon of infinitely recurring nows is evasiveness before the mortality that constitutes the essence of that ex-istence. Heidegger's doctrine of authenticity is the project to convert the passive passing of one's time into an active synthesis, to convert the fatality of ending into a teleological destination—a dying that is an obligation. This conversion, worked in the way one appropriates one's time as a whole, converts dying from a law of nature into a categorical imperative that precedes and makes possible every veridical appropriation of the events and the time of nature. It also makes possible the conversion of our existence itself into a singular seat of responsibility not for an idealized universe but for indwelling in our earth and skies and with hands open to the divine, the conversion of our anonymous existence into the autonomous executor of our own destiny which is a good for others who are not bound by the same law, the conversion of our practical existence into not the excesses of the essentially gratuitous Nietzschean artistry but a poetry of care.

Heidegger's thought reflects this conversion into a dialectics which converts the most negative experience, the experience of nothingness itself, into the most positive, positing, experience, which sets forth one's existence as one's own. His concept of the world—pure clearing which is also the abysses of death, reservoir of possibility constituted in the region of impossibility—is the ambiguous locus of this dialectical conversion. It is true that death is *extase matérielle:* one dies in and into the world. The life that advances resolutely unto its own singular termination determines itself and posits its singularized existence in the world. But dying is also taking leave of the world. Beyond the death toward which I advance resolutely and take hold of in advance, there is the death that comes of itself, to take me. Is not this *other dying* an event that does not confirm and embrace the resolute enactment of one's dying as one's own, but abruptly closes the interval for any act and dissolves the resoluteness with which any I stands? In thematizing this other death, that comes of itself, that is in each moment imminent, that is not internal to the essential ecstatic constitution of our existence but is absolute exteriority, do we not touch the limits of every authenticity and every responsibility?

The nothingness that terminates our existence and that determines the possibilities of the world positioned about us is not a destination and does not destine. The imperative that constitutes our existence as a subject that orders is exterior to our existence and exterior to its dying, an alterity *otherwise than being, otherwise than nothingness*. This alterity Emmanuel Levinas shows in the other that faces—that is, that appeals and demands. Language becomes indicative and informative through the vocative and imperative force with which it is addressed to me, and this vocative and imperative force is the very alterity with which the other approaches and faces. The demand the other that faces puts on me is not the weight of his positivity; the appeal he addresses to me is not a negativity that shows through his surfaces. Appealing, contesting the course of the posited world and its transience made determinate through and passing into nothingness, the alterity of the other is the material imperative that singularizes one's subjectivity as a subject that orders. The imperative I respect in the other is not a universal form I recognize because I know it already within myself as the law that a priori binds my own understanding. Levinas refuses the Kantian separation of the universal form and the particular sensuous substance in the figure, the ethical "type," of the other; for him it is the wants and needs that imperatively appeal to me in the face of the other that is the law. In the needs of his moral substance weighs the alterity of an imperative that appeals to me as a subject that orders and that contests the imperatives I issue. Levinas thus uncovers beneath speech as the exchange of signs with the other a relationship of proximity with his face which is ethical—a relationship of contact with the appeal and the contestation addressed to me by his sensuous vulnerability, his mortality. The subject that is a locus of order is a singular responsibility.

But does not the one that speaks to me speak in signs, and is it not true that he cannot enter into speech except as himself an element of language? Does he not give himself a sign? In presenting himself to me, and in my presenting myself to him, as a sign, do not I and the other idealize ourselves inevitably as soon as we address one another? For is not every sign constituted as a sign by instituting a *meaning*-relationship with a term that recurs the same; is not every sign a *semiotic value* by being equivalent to and interchangeable with other signs?

We than shall elaborate a *genetic analysis* of the meaning and the value of the sign of the subject. We shall draw especially from Jacques Lacan's interpretation of the Oedipus complex of psychoanalysis as the structure by which an infant *(in-fans)* life, libido, enters into language, passes from the infant, insignificant and unexchangeable, contact gratifications into the infinitely extended field of the symbolic gratifications of its desire. We shall see how the infantile eroto-genic surfaces acquire an idealized phallic identity. But identified with the sign of the phallus, the Oedipal child's life-libido is constituted as a vocative and imperative rather than indicative sign: All his libidinal cathexes address them-selves to the other, put a demand on the other.

This metapsychoanalytic theory unearths a source of idealization and val-orization of the subject not first in its theoretical project (Husserl), nor in its practical application to a field of essentially teleological and essentially inter-changeable implements (Heidegger), nor in its affect of joy (Nietzsche), but in its libidinal essence. It shows how the subject enters language and the field of the symbolic objects of desire by itself acquiring a sign—the master-sign of the phallus. Is not then the idealized and valorized subject revealed to be essentially virile? Is not this virility itself a castrated and castrating project in a naturally bisexual nature? Will not the *other death*, that which advances of itself and invades the aging and vulnerable body of the father, voice of law, reduce this virility? Will it not make heard again the infant body of primary-process libido, the laughter and tears, the blessing and cursing beneath the phallic mask with which it had covered itself? Will we not hear the laughter, weeping, blessing and cursing with which the infancy that returns encounters the real other beneath the uniform of mother and that of father—the deathbound flesh of the other?

In the final chapter of this book we shall seek then—beneath the signs of the language with which we, presenting ourselves in and as signs, communicate with one another, and beneath the relationship with the face, the appeal and the demand, of the other—a relationship with the dying of the other. In the face-to-face communication of speech, in the handshake with which the collaboration of labor is initiated, in the pledge with which participation in a civic order is enjoined, the other takes up a stand apart from us; the touch that the consoling hand extends to the dying one touches an alterity beyond contestation and beyond appeal. Here the one that dies departs in his most strange and singular alterity and the one that remains, singularized not by production or auto-production or by idealization but by birth, reaches out with the most extreme distention of his existence. Here forms the order of what Maurice Blanchot has called community, the ordinance that weighs on our coexistence in communication and in collaboration. Our mortal community, our community in mortality more fundamental than every commonplace established by understanding, every productive collaboration and every civic existence we can constitute, every work we can externalize, is ordered by the imperative to render present the concern for the other at the abysses of his or her dying.

Part I

THE IMPERATIVE IDEALIZATION

Already I have thought:
hell's clemency
has given me
those years in my hands,
glittering and
infinitesimal.

Heaven is not the earth
made anew:
it is the ruins of the earth
gazed on
compassionately.

—Montri Umavijani

I

THE ORIGIN OF INFINITY

The incurable disquietude, the self-perpetuating tumult which forces the West to be world-historical (which destines its history to be the one history of the world, destines the West to become the world) results, according to Heidegger, from its nihilist essence, from the absence of finalities in its thought, which is essentially mathematical, a calculation of equivalences, and from the absence of finalities in its praxis, which is essentially technological, transformation into the equivalent. It is just this absence of any term that makes it interminable; Western history is a movement without ends and therefore without end. The idea that what it pursues is power, mastery over nature, the subjugation of nature to human nature, is an interpretation that Heidegger judges to be completely awry; this bad infinity cannot be subordinated to man, that finite structure. Natural man figures in this history as but another fund or stock comprehendable by rational or calculative thought, a fund or stock of physical and psychic energies transformable by the technological process for its own interminable dominion.

How exorbitant, then, when we turn back to it, seems the confident exaltation in Edmund Husserl's doctrines! For Husserl if the West has a historical mission, if the Western world is historically destined to become coextensive with the world, that is because Western endurance alone is really a history, the West alone has ideas and ideals, it alone has a destiny, it alone has finality that is non-relative. The Western mind is the highest form of spirituality; it alone promotes subjectivity, in its history subjectivity pursues its absolute form, becomes the absolute form of being. Not only is personal existence an ideal in the civilization that practices rational philosophy and science, but the person as an ideal form of being emerges only in the pursuit of rational philosophy and science. If one must not say that mastery over nature, the subjugation of nature to the needs of human nature, is the essence of Western theory and practice, that is because the pursuit of Western theory and practice effects a metamorphosis of human nature itself, making this nature a responsible personal existence, in which spirituality is made absolute.

That these two declarations of what the essence of the West consists in are

polar opposites is all the more striking when we recognize that both philosophers agree that such a thing as an eidetic insight into the central, and
invariant, core of Western spirituality is possible, that it would not be a mere
speculative interpretation, and both agree in identifying what must be taken to
be the essential forms of Western life. Both agree in taking Western spirituality
to be essentially historical and in locating its birth in the same place, in the
same decisive moments: in the mutation the idea of truth undergoes in Platonic
philosophy and in the mutation the idea of reality undergoes when space and
time come to be studied through ideas—that is, mathematically.

What to Husserl was decisive was the emergence at that conjuncture of a
telos—indeed, of telos. He devoted his last work to understanding this event.
Just what was the finality that emerged, in Greek antiquity, and that was to be
decisive for the Western world and for the world? What form of spirituality, what
structure of consciousness did this objective, this term, determine? In what
horizons of activity did this telos operate?

For Husserl the West is the direction history pursues. But the West is not
seen to be a movement in lives that are purposive in a particular way, that
pursue a distinctive set of ideals and therefore have the form of a historical
development. For the West takes shape as the one world that, in the strong
sense, has finality, is teleological; Western life alone, in the strong sense, is
purposive, Western history alone is really historical. The teleological analysis
elaborated in his last work was not set up in order to be able to analyze
methodically and apodictically any particular telos; it is an analysis of the
historical emergence of finality—and thus of the very inauguration of history.

The precise loci where teleology emerged are Greek philosophy, specifically
Platonic philosophy, in the setting up of the philosophical idea of truth, theoretical truth, and Greek mathematics, in the setting up of an ideal representation of space-time. The space whose properties are grasped in ideas is the total
space, which can be represented, however, only in a dimension of infinite time.

From the beginning Heidegger's thought set out to establish the essential
finitude of truth, opposed to the theoretical idea of absolute truth. And to
rethink being in the horizon of time meant for him to show the finitude, the
mortality, of authentic time, in opposition to the mathematical idea of infinite
time. According to Heidegger, it is just because the idea of theoretical truth was
forged in Platonic philosophy and the idea of ideal, infinite space-time was
framed in Greek mathematics that the West was launched not into the pursuit
of the ideal but into an interminable wandering in the dimension whence
nothing comes and nothing is promised, where the spirit was not decisively
destined to its absolute form but rather alienated from every possibility of
acquiring a form of its own, a significance of its own, a destiny, and where
subjectivity will be therefore subject to transformation without end and without
ends.

Husserl's teleological analysis is designed to reveal the dimension of infinity
in which Western reason represents its objects and formulates its truths. His

transcendental phenomenology is designed to show how infinity is generated in the inner time-structure of rational consciousness. Husserl's late work can then be seen as the last and most lucid promotion of the infinite time-horizon of Western ends. Or, of Western endlessness.

1. The Idea of Infinity

It is striking that the overarching unifying finality Husserl discovers in Western history is purely formal, not a material goal such as the satisfaction of needs, the greatest possible happiness for the greatest number, or the humanization of nature. Europe—the spiritual destiny to be known as the West—was born the day that the idea of infinity emerged in human consciousness. It is infinity that the West pursues. Western cognitive life is not distinct from the wisdom of the East or that of the savage mind in that it holds to different concrete doctrines but in that it and it alone is in pursuit of an essentially infinite truth. Western praxis is distinctive in that it is not yoked to the satisfaction of needs, which are always finite, but, continually able as it is to produce new needs, it is able to give itself infinite tasks. Western ethical life is the production not of concrete types but of ideal norms. The West's God has infinity as his sole positively understood property; Western religion is the worship of the infinite. The Western expansionism, its imperialist ambitions, has its ratio not in climatic or biological factors that would explain the vigor of the European races, but in the spiritual format of Western culture which must transcend all simply finite goal-structures.

The idea of infinity is not an idea of something, is not a concept, does not contain a content. Infinity is only as an idea or as an ideal; the idea of infinity is the idealizing form of ideas. Infinity cannot be given, actual; it can only be ad infinitum. It is only as aimed at; it indeed is the pure form of a telos. It is by becoming through and through aim, intentionality, that Western consciousness pursues infinity.

The idea of infinity will have this decisive role in Western cognitive life because it is not another concept which can be judged as to its truth; it is the decisive constituent of the philosophical idea of truth. And it is not something that can be taken as a reality among other realities; infinity is the decisive constituent of the idea of the universal characteristic of mundane reality, extension. The extension whose forms and properties are studied by mathematics, that is, no longer by empirical measurements but by ideas, is infinite extension. The idea of extension is the idea of infinite extension.

The idea of theoretical truth was posited in the Platonic reaction to the skeptical doubt of the Sophists. Over and beyond all existent truths, theoretical truth is the ideal of a truth for everyone, for all possibly lucid or mental beings, even for gods, for all beings who can be convinced by evidence, by the visibility of being. And theoretical truth is unconditioned truth, a truth that no future or conceivable test will belie or adjust; it will stand through the infinite series of all its possible confirmation-tests.

Such an idea of truth supposes that being is of itself clear and distinct, is clarity, phosphorescence or evidence. If this unrestricted visibility is limited, what limits it is the particularity, the finiteness, of subjectivity, which, precisely, is always *an attitude*. But the freedom of subjectivity, its real mobility and its free imagination, virtually infinite, will make it adequate in principle to the unrestricted visibility of being.

Infinity is not only thus in the subject; it is also in the objects. Scientific reality is idealized reality, infinitized reality. Each real object is identified by an idea; it is posited as a unity that contains an infinity of aspects, by which it is related to the infinity of points in the infinite space-time in which science situates real nature.[1]

Science begins in the study of the forms and properties of extension by studying not the empirical givens but the ideas of those forms. There is an infinity involved in the idea of each form of *continuous quantity*. One finds in nature the round; by an imaginary infinite adjustment of the round, one produces the idea-limit of the circular, which is only as an ideal, result of an idealization of the round. Idealization is also involved in the constitution of *discontinuous quantity*. By pushing the sense of similarity to the limit, one reaches the sense of the identical, which yields the idea of the unit, that is, of a magnitude that could be seen—at another moment, in another place—to be identically the same. But if ever a magnitude could recur once and prove to be the same, it would have proved to be unaffected by the difference in place and time and therefore could always recur. As soon as the idea of unity is posited, infinity, recurrability ad infinitum, is posited with it.

Infinite space cannot be intuited, in any attitude, but, given an infinite time, can be engendered ideally. Infinite time is the element in which nature infinitized can be objectified. If one measures time, mathematically, one is starting with the idea of a unit, a moment, that would be of a determinate extent and that could recur exactly the same; the very idea of a moment involves the idea of an infinity of such moments.

Idealization is the advance possession of an infinity of elements of aspects. The idealization of empirical units of measurement and of empirical figures in space was found to make possible the idea of a systematically coherent deductive theory that begins with "axiomatic" fundamental ideas and principles and that constructs, according to apodictic arguments, the totality of all possible spatial forms. This deductive format of a science—which would veritably contain knowledge of all the possible figures and relationships of its region of objectivity—was fixed as the ideal of all Western, rational sciences developed after Galileo.[2] It is the ideally infinite knowledge contained in its laws, rather than the really immense knowledge contained in its accumulation of observations, that sets apart Western science from the fund of observations amassed elsewhere in ancient or contemporary humanity.

Theory Is Theory of Infinity

Infinity is a theoretical idea; it is the determinative structure of the theoretical attitude. The theoretical attitude is formed by disengagement, disinvolvement, disinterestedness; it is a taking of one's distances from one's natural objects, it is indeed a taking of an infinite distance. The theoretical attitude seeking absolute truth opens upon infinite horizons. The theoretical attitude takes form in the measure that infinity is conceived. Theory as such is essentially theory of infinity.

The objects of the theoretical attitude are ever ideal objectives. An idea is an ideal object, a structure of factors or elements which cohere necessarily such that if any one of them is there, all are there; it is through and through in its object-position. It is an identity. If ever it should recur, it will recur with the same identity. If ever it could recur even once, exactly the same, it could recur at any time, anywhere. This repeatability is not a property that follows from its ideal essence, but constitutes it; for Husserl, who is not a Platonic substantialist, ideal being consists not in intemporal subsistence but in unrestricted recurrability. The form of infinity—the ad infinitum—enters into the constitution of every idea.

In addition every ideal term determines other ideas; the theoretical objects form a self-differentiating multiplicity. He who addresses himself to theoretical objects directs himself to a domain which prolongs itself ad infinitum. A theoretical object is not so much a term as a task.

The Disconnection of Nature

If theoretical consciousness, whose gaze is fixed on the interminable, is formed by a disengagement, a disinvolvement, it is not really constituted by a disconnecting from the practical and affective life; in fact theory immediately initiates theoretical praxis, and Husserl characterizes the theoretical attitude as a *passion* for infinity. Theoretical consciousness is rather defined by opposition to nature.

The perceptual orientation by which there occurs an intentionality directed straightforwardly upon objects of the world is the natural "attitude" of consciousness. Consciousness originates through this movement, which first gives it objects. An internal examination of every other "attitude"—recall of objects past, imaginative variation, abstraction, conceptualization, deduction, reflection—will show that each is formed by a reorientation effected on the basis of this primary station before the perceptible world. The transcendent correlates of natural consciousness are given by being closed, determinate, finite—determined presumptively. Conscious life needs such correlates in order to live; it is bound to them by the force of its vital interest. The givens that figure in the natural attitude are of finite extent.[3] They are vital to a certain nature, which, qua nature, is finite.

The theoretical attitude is defined by, is formed by, the suspension of natural interests. It suspends the presumptiveness of the natural attitude, which posited its correlates in reality despite the inadequacy of their presence. The theoretical attitude inquires after evidence for them in the total field and time in which it is offered—and finds that field and time to be without end. The givens of natural life, which were at hand, within reach, involved with life, now become *objects*, objectives that can never be anything but objectives, terms that remain themes and tasks and never become termini. An infinity of evidence is henceforth required for their adequate identification, their definitive objectification.

This search after theoretically confirmed objects can occur only as long as a life holds in suspense its natural ends and its natural needs. It really involves a loss of the natural, an alienation of life from its own nature, from the natural world given to it by virtue of its original and continual birth.

The loss of the touchstone of nature does not come then at some point in the development of technology nor at that point when the Greek science of forms, essentially contemplative, is replaced by a modern science of forces, essentially calculative; it comes at the beginning, with the first constitution of the theoretical attitude. The disconnecting of one's nature, the suspension of all natural involvements and interests, the deliberate and definitive forgetting of the quest for utilities and for happiness, is what produces the theoretical attitude.[4]

Nothing in the natural attitudes of life does or could motivate the theoretical attitude, which is in fact the neutralization of all natural interests. The theoretical attitude can only appear unmotivated by life.

Motivation is the link that connects together the phases of life into one stream. This linkage breaks when theory arises. The theoretical attitude is not engendered out of any development of vital interests and cannot serve them; it forms in discontinuity, it is gratuitous. It originates in a birth; it is a new life, a new nature. Once it appears its objects can never stop soliciting it, it can never exhaust its interests, it will engender its own movement. Theoretical life is a mutant, a new species of life—and not only, we shall shortly see, of cognitive life. It is as different from the cultured forms of life pursued in the natural groupings of humanity—family, tribe, nation—as that life is from the life of animals. For Husserl the brahminical thinkers who composed the Upanishads are closer to the stone-age aborigines of Papua than they are to the rational thinkers of Greece.[5] The theoretical life pursued in Athens is as different from the life pursued by the astronomers and engineers of Cheops as their life was from that of their camels and donkeys.

The Infinite World of Theoretical Life

Once this form of life is born, so singular and unnatural, unmotivated, unexplainable, even strictly speaking unintelligible as its appearance is, it nonetheless proves to contain within its structure the sources of its own subsistence and even a force of expansion that will finally prove quasi-irresistible. It grows in three dimensions.

First, the field of theoretical objects is itself an infinity of infinities. The theoretical attitude with regard to an object occurs when one notices the presumption involved in the natural attitude when it takes its correlate to be real, thus anticipating a course of evidence that extends ad infinitum. The field in which an object's aspects are recorded contains an infinity of sites. The conversion to the theoretical attitude does not abruptly confront one with such an actually infinite multiplicity; on the contrary, the theoretical attitude is always directed at an object, something definite. What is theoretical in that attitude is the motility in it that drives it to transcend the naivety or one-sidedness that is inevitably and necessarily involved in addressing itself to *an* object. An attitude then becomes theoretical, and lives, that is, extends itself throughout, or *into*, a time, by focusing on something naively and then transcending the naivety, by the attempt to grasp, conceive, comprehend, objects and the continual, never final, displacement of itself that this attempt requires and motivates.

This naivety or this one-sidedness makes of theoretical consciousness too an attitude. Its attitude-structure, the sense in which it too is a determinate intention in a determinate direction, in which it too occupies something like a position, is not explained by some theory of its corporeal underpinnings but rather by the infinity in, and of, its objects, which it nonetheless is out to determine, to objectify.

The Theoretical Intersubjectivity

Secondly, if theoretical life is—and must be—born as an individual life, individuating that life, isolating it from the human species, it immediately engenders an intersubjectivity, which is destined to a greater expansion than any natural community, destined to grow ad infinitum.

There is a structured gregariousness that is natural and that engenders families, tribes, nations, themselves segmented into functional associations. This structured coexistence has its ratio in the natural form of human interests, their natural coalescence and complementarity, their natural overlappings and conflicts. The one who converts to the theoretical attitude isolates himself, disengages himself from the common needs and interests of human nature. The theoretical attitude is consequently never pursued in order to serve the natural communities of men, family, race, tribe, nation.

But the theoretical attitude takes form, in an individual it isolates, by placing him in an ethical intersubjectivity. Its ideal of truth implicates others.

The stranger arrives in the city, finds alien ways of life, alien ways of thought, asks the citizens: Why do you do as you do, think as you think? They answer by appealing to the common heritage of their reasons, answering, in the end: because our fathers, our ancestors have thought so and have done so, because our rulers have taught us to think and to act so, because our gods have revealed this. The stranger is a stranger because he does not have the same ancestors, traditions, leaders, gods. Something entirely new begins the day someone attempts to offer the stranger a reason. A reason that he, the stranger, can accept. That he need merely be a man to be able to accept. At the limit, a reason that would be valid for any lucid being, capable of seeing the evidence, the visibility of what is. Valid for his demons or gods too, as well as for ours.

Such a praxis involves a recognition that there is a lucidity in the stranger, in any stranger, equivalent to one's own. That what is to be thought and what is to be done imposes itself equally on the stranger and on oneself. It is in this praxis that the idea of humanity, a spiritual humanity destined for truth, is constituted. For the concept of humanity is not acquired from empirical observation of the physical and behavioral similarities that can function to group us together by contrast with other animal species. Humanity is the intentional correlate of a certain exigency, that of answering for whatever one says, feels, and does and answering by an appeal to insight available to anyone. It is no accident that humanity is defined in terms of rationality—which in the classical sense is not so much the capacity to reckon as the aptitude to found one's thought on evidence, on insight.

In reality the theoretical attitude involves recognizing the stranger not as my equivalent but as my judge. It involves the resolution to impugn everything that seems evident to me if it cannot also be evident to another. There will be coexistence not in the mutual equivalence of opinions but, Husserl says, in mutual criticism. Here what interests me in the other, and what binds me to him, is not what in him is akin to me but the other in him, his status of being one before whom I must justify all I do and say.[6]

The one who resolves on this sort of coexistence with others contracts a specific sort of will—the will to give a reason. The will that agrees to answer every question that may be put to what one does and says. That agrees to supply a reason—and a reason for the reason. Ad infinitum.

This will produces science. For a science, in the Platonic sense, the Western sense, is an explanatory system, such that any fact can be explained by, deduced from, rational laws.[7] Science is built up by supplying a reason for the observed facts, and a reason for the reason. The reiteration of this exigency orders a body of statements hierarchically under more and more universal laws, deducible in principle from the absolutely universal laws of the universe. The will by which a subject sets himself up as a seat of answerability is realized in elaborating science in the Western sense.

This will to answerability is at the same time a will to sovereignty. The one who sets out to supply, out of himself, the reasons for all he says and feels and does is one who posits himself as an origin, one who has within himself the reasons for all he says and the motives for all he does. The will that generates science is indeed a will to mastery but not first a will to master external nature, to subordinate nature to human nature. It is the mythico-religious mind, Husserl provocatively claims, that is inhabited by a will to master all nature! All its speculative knowledge is meant to serve man in his human purposes so that he may order his worldly life in the happiest way possible and shield it from disease, from every sort of evil fate, from disaster and death.[8] Mythico-religious speculation is practical. The scientific will, which is theoretical, is first a will to exist in sovereignty. This will, Husserl writes, will be taken up by the naturally higher or dominant types, those less exhausted by the cares of life.[9] Universal rational science is the activity by which a subjectivity determines itself as absolutely responsible, free—spontaneous and autonomous.

The Life Engendered out of Theory

Thirdly, the theoretical attitude, which begins as a cognitive activity, tends of itself to take over the whole of life.

The passion for infinity necessarily becomes practical, infects all the operative wills of life. It does so by idealizing the goals of practical intentions. The practical objectives that shall henceforth subsist shall be set forth in normative ideas, posited not only as what is desired and desirable, correlates of de facto natural desires, but as what is unconditionally valid.

Thus the interruption of natural interests and life turns into a "universal critique of all life and all life-goals, all cultural products and systems that have already arisen out of the life of man, and thus also becomes a critique of mankind itself. . . ."[10] Far from the theoretical work functioning to serve human nature, the theoretical attitude initiates a first praxis which consists in the universal critique of all natural praxis. Nothing will emerge intact from this critique; every goal will be idealized. This critique does not simply subject life's objectives to tests; it transfigures them, it yokes life's impulses to ideals, to absolute norms. That this critique demands that finite practical life exhaust itself in the pursuit of infinite tasks is no argument against it; mere human nature is, as Nietzsche liked to say, no argument. In this "critique of mankind itself" the question is rather whether human nature is worth *anything*. The Vedic, Socratic, Zarathustran conviction that human nature is not something to be fulfilled, resolved, healed, consoled, or emended, that the task imposed by philosophy is to liberate oneself from human nature, is intrinsic to theory; the theoretical attitude is not set up without this consequence. Nothing is more remote then from the Husserlian explanation of the origin of theory than any evolutionism, pragmatism, or vitalism.

Such a life can no longer even be content with pursuing what has been already established, by prior theoretical inquiry, to be universally just, absolutely beautiful, genuinely good; it must itself possess, in personal lucidity, the reasons and the justifications that render its goals universally valid. This terrible exigency follows from the fact that the transformation of the impulses of life that is demanded is formal and not material. It is not a question of assigning different content to the will, on the basis of rational insight into human nature that would make clear that some spontaneous impulses attach themselves to the wrong goals, or that not all impulses can be satisfied simultaneously, and that consequently an ordering, a hierarchizing, of the will is necessary. It is rather a matter of changing the form of the will in its entirety, of idealizing every possible goal, and of changing the relationship of the will with its goals such that between the will and its goal an interminable theoretical task is inserted. The final outcome is the production not of a lucid humanity that would de facto will proper and realistic goals but of a humanity absolutely responsible for all the moves it makes.

Absolute, Personalized Subjectivity

The theoretical attitude, and the science and practice in which it is elaborated, must be seen as a new, unnatural species of life. Western science and practice are not to be understood as an instrument that serves humanity; they do not exist for the sake of human nature. Theory may arise out of that combination of disinterested free-floating curiosity and astonished sense of differences which is the philosogenic *thaumazein*, and all theoretical insight into essences, including the apodictic insight into one's own subjectivity, may well rely on natural imagination, which belongs to the nature of consciousness, and in which the reality thesis is already neutralized and there is already a certain infinity in the unbounded power to objectify forms. But the theoretical attitude itself is contracted only upon the constitution of the idea of infinity, which no nature could yield. It will henceforth use all the elements of life as so much material employed in its own infinite quest.

The pursuit of Western science and practice eventually transforms nature, to be sure, but first it transforms human nature. There emerges a new form of subjectivity—the person. The person is an ideal, a task, not a natural given. Western spirituality is the production of personal existence.

For rationality, Husserl says, is a "shaping oneself into a true 'I'" in the striving to be true to oneself, to remain identical with oneself.[11] This being true to oneself, this remaining identical with oneself, is not realized by substantializing oneself: that the things alone can manage. The spirit can exist only in passing. It can hold on to itself in retaining not the actual force, the actuality of a past phase, but possessing still the sense of that passage, being still able to produce the reasons for it. And those reasons it can possess inalienably only if it can maintain them against every possible contestation of them, only if it would not have to give them up when it encounters others. Remaining identical with oneself, striving to be true to oneself—the very shaping oneself into a true "I"—is realized by still being able to produce the reasons, the true reasons, that is, not only the genuine reasons, but the valid reasons, for all the phases and moments of one's intentional life.

Personal existence, then, has the form of rationally valid existence, totally responsible existence. Adequate self-reflection, or absolute consciousness, is the element in which such an existence is brought about. Personal consciousness relates to its existence as to what it itself has to answer for. Answering for itself absolutely, it is on its own, free and autonomous, absolute. This integral rationality in self-responsibility is the telos that inhabits all the acts of the ego; it is "that which man qua man, in his innermost being, is aiming for, that which alone can satisfy him, make him 'blessed'. . . ."[12]

The production of personal life, of an ego in this self-responsibility, is the sovereignty Western spirituality pursued always.

The person is a form of subjectivity utterly individual and intrinsically universal. It is an identity, not because it possesses some distinguishing property that would make it identifiable from without, nor because it forms itself as a variant on some nuclear constant which is transpersonal, but because it identifies itself in possessing the ratio for all its moves and phases. It determines what it is and determines itself as a subsistent entity by remaining true to itself. Its ratio or its essence is exhausted in this set of reasons it itself possesses and maintains in force; its essence is the correlate of this actual operation of maintenance, this practice of answering for itself always.

Yet it is intrinsically universal, answering to any and every other possible subjectivity for its deeds, ready to immediately abandon whatever cannot belong to anyone, virtually occupying every other possible point of view in the universe, ready to change places with anyone.

Such a subjectivity, existing of and by itself, positing itself incontestably and universally, is the absolute form of being.

2. The Infinity of Time

Husserl's genetic teleological analysis reveals, as the entelechy that assembled the Western world and the blessedness that it pursues, a project of absolute self-responsibility, consequently of complete autonomy and freedom, lived in horizons of ideal norms and infinite tasks. Husserl's transcendental analysis will reveal that theoretical subjectivity produces out of itself the infinity that it incorporates into the world. The infinite space in which theoretical subjectivity situates the world and the infinite series of witnesses for which absolute truth exists are engendered in a horizon of infinite time. And the infinite time of the world is constituted in the inner temporality of subjectivity itself. The living present of an actual consciousness has infinite horizons before and behind it. Husserl's phenomenology seeks to contribute to the Western spiritual project not only by making clear how infinity teleologically commands it but also by exhibiting the inner constitution of the subjectivity that pursues infinity.

Just why does consciousness, reflecting on its own form of duration, intuit it as infinite in extension? *Because this reflection is formal.* At least it is in Husserl.

The Form of the Present

Reflection makes consciousness itself the object of intuition. The presence of its objects and the presence of that presence—the acts and orientation by which they are envisaged—are seen, immediately and adequately, apodictically. By a certain shift of thematizing focus, reflection can see consciousness as having the form of phases which succeed one another—a temporal form.

What is given to such an intuition is the living now of consciousness. An actual moment of consciousness is produced with an impression, with something given. This content of itself clarifies; it illuminates a sphere, distinguishes itself from what is indistinct, the non-present. To clarify, in the fundamental sense, is always to bring to presence, to make present; it is the immediate presence of being, and not discursive operations of the mind, that clarifies.[13] In the living now the content is also "close," in a relationship of proximity, to the actual, active ego.

Yet it is not the content, the clarity and distinctness of content, and the proximity of content, its presence or immediacy, that decisively defines the living now; it is form. There is something the same, incessantly reiterated as any given content, and all content, passes—the form of the present. "The actual now is necessarily something punctual";[14] it marks a limit, inscribes a boundary. Every present impression marks an edge delimiting the actual experience from the content to come and determines a boundary where its fullness terminates and "sinks into emptiness."

This formal definition is distinctive to Husserl. One could conceive of defining the present not by its borders but by its internal constitution, not by its selfsame and invariant form but by its internal diagram, or process, or movement. One could try to define the movement that enacts the present—the presenting of the present. This is what Heidegger does when he conceives of the movement that presents our existence to its world, and makes its world present to it, as a projective, ec-static transport. He is putting the emphasis on the act involved in actualizing a moment of presence; the presenting of the present is active synthesis, or ecstasis, or ex-istence.

The now has a fullness that the past and the future do not have; it suffices to itself, is an absolute; the past and the future depend, for their existence, on it. Levinas for his part emphasizes this immediacy of the present and conceives of the movement involved in its realization as an involution; for him it is not the active synthesis of the definitive and the possible that makes the scope of the present, but the unmediatedness, the intensity of the sustaining content.[15] He conceives of the present as an instant, that is, a stand in itself, an intensity, an insistence, rather than as an ex-istence.

But for Husserl the internal movement that produces the present is the *forming of this form*. The form of the now forms itself spontaneously.[16] This imposition of itself on itself is the insistence in the instant.

Modalized Forms of the Present

The delimiting operation which forms the boundaries of the present also gives form to the past and the future.

Husserl conceives of the present and the non-present with the concepts of primary experience and its modification, its modalization. The living now, the present that actively presents being, passes. This passing Husserl conceives as a sinking away—a sinking away from fullness into emptiness. Also as an increasing "distance" from the ego. But neither the content nor the form is altered by this modification; every past is a past moment of content with the form of the present, a past present. It subsists in the modified form of an appearance for, retained by, the actual living now that is realized in its stead. The plenitude of the living now is the "source-point" of the intention that retains the appearance of the now it displaced, a now which still retains, with change neither of content nor of form, the appearance of the now it had displaced.

And the living now is the source-point of the now that succeeds it. The transformation of the living now as it passes from something "present in person" into an appearance of itself anticipates another now of the same form to hold it. The form of the now contains a protention of the form of the moment that bounds it and that is to come—coming from distance and from emptiness into bounded, formed plenitude.

Each past moment is retained, in its place and order, because it is retained by the form of the moment that succeeded it. The past extends back moment *through* moment. Similarly the future—moment anticipating moment.

The present then is the anchorage, the substrate, the absolute; the extension of passed moments is retained by it, and the succession of moments to come is extended by it. We are not to conceive of the form of time as a given a priori ideality which the living reality of a life has to pass through. Rather we have to see a certain form, the form of the present, realizing itself spontaneously in the sphere of consciousness, bounding a certain content, which sinks away into emptiness along with the form that formed it. But the form of the present, of the now, reproduces itself forthwith, to form the same or new content, for which the now that sinks away is an appearance. Life is the spontaneous production and reproduction of the form of the now; it is this temporalization of impressions. Consciousness qua life consists in the actuality, and the act, of the living now.

But, we can ask, are past and future indeed extended by the actuality, the presence of consciousness? Are they but the correlates of its retention, its protention? Are they correctly conceived in their own essences when they are conceived with the concept of form, which served to define the present, and the concept of "distance"?

Is there not an indetermination as to form that is essential to the future? And is not this because first the content of the future could not be conceived with the terms with which the content of the present is conceived: this content is not just a presence, a plenitude, a givenness "at a distance"? Is not the future rather, as Heidegger thought, a possible, a real and not only conceptual possible? Whose possible reality and possible impossibility weighs on, afflicts the present, and is not only a form contiguous with it?

Likewise, where Husserl conceives of the past as a form whose content is retained by the present as an appearance while sinking into emptiness, Heidegger and Levinas conceive of the past through its specific content, as force. The passing of the past is not a sinking away into emptiness or a passing into nothingness; what comes to pass is what comes to be, definitive and irrevocable. The past is then not behind my act, an appearance of a presence in person I maintain at a distance; it is in my act, as what retains, sustains, upholds, and gives its resources to my act. Such concepts of the content of futurity and of the past make us conceive of the horizons of the present as fields or depths; against them Husserl conceives of internal time as an infinite succession of moments with the form of the now.

The Intuition of Infinity

Just why, if past and future are made of moments of the form of the present, must past and future be conceived as without end? How indeed could an endless totality figure in a philosophy that limits itself strictly to what is given in intuition and posits nothing whatever by discursive reasoning? How could an infinity be intuitively given? Yet Husserl's grounds are intuitionist; he explains that a scrutiny of the way the living now is intuited leads us to see that it could be intuited only as a phase of an infinite series of nows.

Whereas Heidegger's analysis is dominated by the idea that we grasp "internal time" as a whole by its limits, its boundaries—that existential time is disengaged from mundane time and apprehended by apprehending its birth and its mortality—Husserl's thought is commanded by the idea that we grasp *the moment* as such through its limits. "Every perceived time is perceived as a past which terminates in the present, the present being a boundary point."[17] The present as such is a form, and this form is a limit. "A now is always and essentially the edge-point *(Randpunkt)* of an interval of time."[18]

A determinate moment of time is formed, then, by its edge-point, its boundary. A boundary between what? Between the primal impression and something—another experience, which also has the form of consciousness, of a living present, though now temporally modalized by the actual consciousness. Thus "every experience in its fresh beginning has necessarily been preceded in time by experiences, the past of experience is continually filled with content." Similarly "every present moment of experience has also, and necessarily, an after as a limit, and that also is no empty limit; every present moment of experience, be it even the terminal phase of the duration of an experience that is ceasing, passes off into a new 'now,' and that necessarily filled with content."[19]

Husserl is arguing that the idea of a determinate present requires that it be bounded by something, something full and not emptiness, another moment of time, itself determinate. No moment of experience can be apprehended that would not be experienced as preceded by another moment, as no moment of experience can be grasped that would be experienced as not followed by another moment. The time-horizon of consciousness has to appear to itself as infinite, an order of nows without end as without beginning.

The present not only receives its contours from the content that bounds it, but it gets its orientation, structure, direction, and form from the whole stream of moments of which it is a part; Husserl says "no concrete experience can pass as independent in the full sense of the term."[20] Thus there has to be some insight into the whole as such, even though this whole is infinite in extension, and even though all its moments but one are not present. There must be an intuition into the totality of consciousness with the intuition of the now and in the intuition of the now. And must not this immanent intuition be adequate, apodictic, like the intuition into the living now itself?

This would be possible only if the whole, the past and the future, are contained within the form of the living now. The intuition into past and future then would take the form of an intuition into the retentions and protentions which are actually operative now. "Retention itself is not an 'act' (i.e., an immanent unity of duration constituted in a series of retentional phases), but a momentary consciousness of the phase which has expired and, at the same time, a foundation for the retentional consciousness of the next phase. Since each phase is retentionally cognizant of the preceding one, it encloses in itself, in a chain of mediate intentions, the entire series of retentions which have expired."[21]

It is the properly Husserlian concept of an *intuition of the horizon* that will be brought to play to explain how there can be an intuition into the unending stream of consciousness. An intuition of the horizon of an object is an intuition of the same level as the intuition of the object; it is essentially different from intellectual intuition or eidetic insight into universals. Past and future form discrete temporal "objects" which surround the actual living now in the way the potential objects of the spatial field surround the actually given object. In conceiving the past and future as horizons, Husserl will think of them as indefinitely open, potential for temporal objects without limit.

These potential temporal objects on the horizon of the living now are not merely juxtaposed to it in a continuous gradation of distance; they form the implications, the developments of the living now. The future is the *und so weiter* of the present, not only the extension or the reiteration of the form with new content, but the ramification of what is seen already involved in the present. It is not going to be just anything; its content shall fit in with, develop, or contrast with the present. In seeing the present well, we already foresee the general lines of the future. Likewise the past is implicated in the present; the point of view of the present, the orientation, the attitude taken in the present, is motivated by the moments passed.

Husserl's understanding of how a life forms a singular individual, singular and individual in each of its acts and phases, is immediately connected with his understanding of how a life intuits itself as a whole. There are no two streams of consciousness that are identical, because each is a singular unity of different contents, and no two particular experiences are the same, because each one is woven into a different context. "*[N]o concrete experience* can pass *as independent in the full sense of the term.* Each 'stands in need of completion' in respect of some connected whole, which in form and in kind is not something we are free to choose, but are rather bound to adopt. . . . That two perceptions essentially identical in respect of this uniqueness should also be identical in respect of context-determination is in principle impossible, for they would then be individually *one* perception. . . . Every experience influences the (clear or obscure) setting of further experiences."[22]
The particularity of a given phase of consciousness thus devolves from the fortuity of the content which is given in it and from the order and succession of the acts which preceded it and are to follow.

The intuitionist exigencies of Husserl's philosophy require that one be able to turn an immanent reflexive gaze over one's whole consciousness, across all its phases. This is required for the adequacy of the intuition into the living now— which, as he says, is not an independent object. But in exactly what way can one's whole stream of consciousness appear before one's intuition? How can the absent—past and future—moments be intuitively given?
What one really sees, Husserl says, is the "limitlessness in the progressive development of immanent intuitions." One can adequately intuit the content and form of the living now, but one also intuits with it its lateral retentional and protentional intentionalities, and through them retentions of retentions and protentions of protentions, *und so weiter* ad infinitum.
To fix this peculiar sort of intuition Husserl constructs the concept of an *intuition in the form of an idea in the Kantian sense.*[23] One sees, adequately, apodictically, that one is seeing, and one also sees that one was seeing a moment ago and foresees that one is about to see still in the next moment. One sees that the present actual seeing implicates, calls for, requires, is structured so as to issue in, this continued seeing. One sees, in seeing how one sees, that this seeing will be developed along certain lines. Likewise one sees not only that

the form of the now implicates a certain form of the prior moment but that its content too is motivated by the content of the prior moments. Through the intuition of this motivational bond one intuits still the motivating content of the past.

There are difficulties in this solution. The concept of an idea in the Kantian sense, idea-limit or ideal idea, was introduced to distinguish between ideas of essences disengaged by abstractive intuition—morphological essences—and ideas of essences formed by a further operation performed on those abstracted essences, an operation of perfecting them in the direction of ideal selfsameness, an operation which is performed on imaginative material and is only ideally effectuatable. Because of this constitutive role of the imagination (which is in fact only imagined to be put into play) such essences are given through ideation and not through immediate intuition. The exact essences of mathematical eidetics are produced when, for example, the morphological essence "round" intuited in abstraction is subjected to an imaginative variation aimed at producing an unvarying circularity, an elimination of deviations which one imagines carried out to the limit, ad infinitum. The resulting essence is not posited with a thesis of reality.

But now Husserl compounds this idealizing ideation with intuition to produce a concept of the operation which intuits the actual infinity of conscious life. There is no doubt that this present looking I am enacting is a phase of a larger whole, a stream of life, which in all its phases past and to come is indubitably mine and immediately seen to be mine. They are mine because all are immediately seen to be involved in the living now immediately and adequately intuited by me.

This amounts to intuiting the ramification or the implication as such, that is, to intuiting something like a motive or a principle which makes one moment a consequence of another. To push this to the limit would be to grasp the unifying principle of all these ramifications. On the analogy of producing the exact essence "circle" from the morphological essence "round," it would be done by supplying imaginative material with which to imagine that the infinite prolongation of life in both directions would go through all imaginable variations of the living now. Such a process would produce the ideal essence of infinite life. But it would not produce the insight into my own actual life in its concrete flux and totality. Thus even if idealization could count as intuition, it could not comprehend that singular history which is my singular ego.

This discordance between what an "intuition in the form of an idea in the Kantian sense" could yield and what the a posteriori insight into the empirical singularity of my life once it has elapsed yields is in fact the same as that which Husserl is forced to acknowledge between the empirical knowledge of life as limited and mortal and the transcendental sense of life as infinite and immortal. Husserl, it is true, does set out in the manuscripts to define death phenomenologically, that is, to say what death means to consciousness. And he defined it in terms of the inner structure of consciousness, that is, in terms of the time-structure of consciousness. That consciousness dies would mean that there would be a moment to come that would not be followed by another moment. Death can only appear to consciousness as a fact. Not a fact among facts of the world, since it would be a fact affecting the transcendental stream in which the apparition of the world is constituted. It would be a "transcendental fact."[24]

Death then befalls consciousness, a fact breaking into, breaking up, the transcendental order. A fact, death is individual and contingent; it is not integrated into the essence of consciousness. Husserl does not, and cannot, offer any account of why we die, any account that would exhibit the inner essence of subjectivity in such a way that dying would be an integral part of that subjectivity, that the movement of dying, of casting oneself into the void, would be one with the very movement by which subjectivity *is*. To show that was the originality of Heidegger's existential hermeneutics. For the first time since the inauguration of the metaphysical form of thought Heidegger conceived the essence of life in such a way that our life dies of its own nature, dies with all its own forces, dies by virtue of its own auto-constitutive and world-constitutive movement.

For Husserl "transcendental life and the transcendental ego cannot be born; only man can be born in the world. The ego as a transcendental ego is eternal; I am now, and to this now belongs a horizon of the past, which can be unfolded back without end. And that means: I am eternal.

". . . Again it is unthinkable that the transcendental ego cease. It is easily understood that this does not mean to say that man has lived and will live eternally, and that birth and death, the entry of man into nature and the disappearance of man from nature, through creation or annihilation, are compatible with the transcendental infinity of life. The soul of a living being is not immortal in principle, that is, it is not necessarily to be conceived as immortal, and it does indeed really die according to everyday experience. But every human ego harbors in itself in a certain way its transcendental ego, which does not die and does not arise; it is an eternal being in becoming."[25]

3. Ideal Infinity

We will now argue that this infinite time, allegedly intuited apodictically in an intuition in the form of an idea in the Kantian sense, idea-limit, or idealizing idea, is in fact the product of an idealization. And that there is another format of internal time consciousness to be disengaged beneath this structure.

Our exposition will be based on a distinction between openness and infinity. We propose that we have to distinguish between horizonal openness and infinity in general, between horizonal open-enddedness and unendingness (*Unendlichkeit*, infinity) in the time of subjectivity in particular.

This distinction is fundamentally inspired by Husserl. Husserl teaches that the idea of infinity is proper to the Western world, that it is what characterizes Western thought, feeling, and praxis, that it arises in and is constitutive of the theoretical attitude as such. But then the theoretical attitude has to be contrasted with the natural attitude, upon which it is founded, out of which it emerges by conceiving for itself the idea, or idea-form, of infinity. The theoretical attitude and the life founded on theory are, in Husserl's forceful formulation, entirely unnatural, cultural, precisely characteristic of, formative of, European culture as such.

What then about the natural attitude? Its objects, which are always presumptively objects, never definitively determined, are open-ended, open to an indefinite exploration. They are situated in a space opening in horizons. What is this open-endedness of its objects and of their horizons—and how is it to be distinguished from infinity?

The idea of infinity is constituted with the concepts of unit and of the *und so weiter*. The horizons of natural experience shall have to be conceived in other terms. Merleau-Ponty wrote that Husserl's term horizon has to be taken to designate what had no name in any prior philosophy.[26] Husserl had formed the idea of a horizon with the concept of potential; the horizon about a figure is not the zone where being stops and non-being begins; it is where the actual turns more and more completely into potential. But if we conceive of the potential as a manifold of potential terms, units, the passage from object to horizon is only a change of sign, a factor of negativity. Yet the horizon is not simply derivative, privatively, from the unit; it is not only an *und so weiter* of the posited, positive figure. The horizon has a role to play in making the actual objects actual; it holds them in place, situates them, gives them their orientation, signification, and the very force of their actuality.

The concept of sensorial level will help give us a positive sense of a horizon. A particular sound, in music, is a contrast. It has the pitch it has and the force and the volume it has in virtue of its situation in the field of the melody, by virtue of the extent to which it diverges from the level established. The level is not itself conceptual; it is fixed by a sound, which can be sounded. But it does not persist in its functioning by being sounded anew each time; to hear it along with the actual sound would rather give a chord. The level is a distinct type of sensorial reality, with a general and latent subsistence.

A level has its own kind of definiteness and its own kind of givenness. The hearing has to first locate the level audibly, in order to be able to discern the melody from the mass of other sounds in the environment; one has to listen in a certain way, with a certain focus, a certain threshold. Finding the level is finding an axis which makes the melody possible, a sonorous dimension about which the variations form a field. The level is an openness in the sense not of an audible vacuity around the audible tone, but of a matrix of divergent sound qualities, a positioning axis of sonorous particulars. The light according to which we distinguish color values opens a field of the visible in this way. The zone of light opens the field not by counting for nothing for sight—and not by prolonging the centrally illuminated particular with an infinity of potentially visible particulars—but by subsisting as a visual base-line against which sight discerns gradients of contrast.

Perhaps this concept of horizon understood as a level can help us to conceive of the relationship between the living now of actual consciousness and the dimensions, the past and the future, upon which it is set. As a sound once heard can subsist as the key of the melody that follows, so a moment once present in a life can pass into a level. The "now I am awake," "now I am alive," "now I am well," is not bounded by an antecedent now of the same form, but rather with something that contrasts with it, and is perceived with it, with the same kind of reflective intuition as it—something that is time, like it is, but time generalized, latent, a schema of time, there as something that gives rise to variations, that is functioning through the variations.

Husserl, however, *identifies* the unit of time. The living now is something that is identifiable, that recurs the same, that passes but is constantly reiterated. In identifying the living now Husserl has already conceived it as what recurs the same ad infinitum.

The means for this identification of the unit of time is the distinction between matter and form. The present can be identified as recurring the same not in its content but in its form. There is continually fresh content, but the form of presence does not change; it is then ideal. It is even ideal in the most fundamental sense: it is not only recognized to be the same each time it recurs, but it recurs without cease, and it is because it recurs without cease that recognition of things temporal and intemporal is possible. Nothing whatever could be recognized to be the same, and thus to be ideal, if it did not recur within the confines of consciousness which re-cognizes them—recognizes itself—to be the same.

Wherever, whenever there is consciousness, it is now. The present re-presents itself without end. Consciousness is presence, is the form of the present producing itself "by spontaneous generation,"[27] and reproducing itself as it passes. Consciousness is the incessant, infinite power to reproduce the form of the present, producing a moment of living presence.

The form of the present is in fact the edge *(Randpunkt)* of a given impression. The actuality of consciousness is the act which accepts the givenness of some content. The impression, however, of itself passes as soon as it comes. The hold on the content then immediately gets strained; it strives to hold on to something which from the first is already sinking into emptiness. The primary experience, a presentation, is at once a re-presentation, an effort to retain a presence that is sinking away into emptiness and absence. A reiterative impulse is already in the simplest presence imaginable. This explains why a perception has from the first an intentional character, the character of an aiming at, and not that of a coinciding with. And it explains why Husserl can say that every experience is open to reflection by virtue of its essence.

Consciousness then is reiteration in two senses. It is the incessant or infinite power to reproduce the form of the present, and, on the other hand, there is in the intuition of every object a power and an effort to retain, to re-present or reinstate the content presented. The reinstatement of a content that passes is, to be sure, not possible without the power to reproduce the form. But we think that the reproduction of the form is also made possible by the power to retain a content.

This is to argue that the separation of matter and form, making possible the identification of the form, its constitution as a unit, is the result of an idealization. The identification of a form of time that recurs the same was produced by an imaginative equalization of moments whose form has first been abstracted from their content. What Husserl takes as an intuition of the internal, temporal, form of consciousness in fact constitutes that form through an idealization.

4. The Natural Time of Consciousness

For natural consciousness there is not a form continuously reproduced, which is filled with matter indifferent to it. The present is the realization of a presence; "now" is always "now that. . . ." It is sensed not through its form and delimitations, but through the inner movement of the moment, the surge of life solicited by the presented content, arising to receive what is given and impressed. The sense of the present is something like a vibrancy, a simmering of life, over an expanse of reality that surfaces.

This moment of the now is, in our terminology, given relief by the contrast it makes with the levels upon which it is set. But the contrast is not purely formal. The present contrasts with horizons of possibility and promise it seems to lead to. I feel I am alive now, health is resurging, initiatives are again possible. The scene presenting itself seems to me an overture to something; it is set on certain levels which are like axes along which schemes of duration are going to be generated. And on the other side, this moment forms in relief out of the fevers and delirium of the long night, which does not extend back now in discrete moments, but extends like the level from which this moment acquires its situation and its significance.

The now is not infinitesimal, instantaneous; it has a certain expanse. Husserl would no doubt admit that the span of the primary retention and protention are variable; the sentence from its first word, or the melody from its opening note, can be still retained by primary retention. But if presentation is retentional from the start, would not the span of the present be variable as is the span of primary retention? Every now is a "now that it is intermission," "now that the professor has stated his thesis," "now that we are together, ..." The span of the present has boundaries, no doubt, but these boundaries dilate and contract with the content they contain.

There are days that pass, leaving us with the irritated feeling that we are just losing time. The day that slipped away consisted in a succession of stretches of time, in which we occupied ourselves with whatever was on hand, reading the news at random, walking through town buying a few small things, talking inconsequentially with people who passed by. Each stretch of time which made up the field of the present came on the scene fortuitously, opened up nothing consequential, led to nothing in particular, just got dropped as we passed on. The days then seem to pass by without our seeming ever to have time for ourselves, for getting anything of our own done. There are also moments which are as long as one's life, moments in which all of one's past is retained, not as a discrete succession of moments but as one line of existence that has become definitive and irrevocable, moments too when all of one's future is anticipated, not to be sure in the distinctness of its order and succession but as a range of possibilities nonetheless circumscribed, isolated out of the profusion of possibilities that are for others. Such perhaps would be the hour of the raga Ravi Shankar is improvising this evening, delineating on his sitar with extreme patience and application the resonance of all the movements he feels in this temple courtyard after the sacrifice, among these worshippers, on the banks of the cosmic river Ganges whose celestial extension he sees flickering above him in what Europeans call the Milky Way, falling on the lofty Himalayas as it snows, coursing across the great plains along which the most ancient continuous civilization has flourished for five thousand years, bearing the ashes of millions of Hindus back to the primal oceans from which all life comes—his raga capturing the cadences and eddies of this moment in the night of the universe with all the powers and responsiveness he has assembled in his body in the fifty years of his life, with all he has learned and suffered and understood and been baffled by, reserving nothing for tomorrow, such that when the raga finds its end and he walks back through the night, emptied and resolved, he could die now. Such are no doubt also certain movements of thought which are unutterably one's own, such that they could have been conceived only by the one who thought all the things he thought thus far in his life and such that all that he will ever think thereafter may one day appear to have issued out of this nexus. There are no doubt public and political moments of this kind, when the historical actor commits everything, all his acquisitions, all his potentialities. And perhaps there are moments of passion of this character—moments, in lovemaking, when one has the certainty of having been born for this love, the nerves of one's organs and the recesses of one's brain made for this passion, moments when all the craving, abandon, hope, adoration one is capable of are emptied, moments when one reserves nothing for the morrow or for another lover, as though there will be nothing after, as though one could or would die in this transport.

The boundaries of the now are not a natural invariant. Here the content dilates or contracts the edges of the now; the content forms the form. The movement involved in the living now, the presentation in the present, is not only that of a form being impressed on a content; there is also a surging of the content into the mold of consciousness. The present—*prae-ens*—is being that draws near.

The moment passes, of itself, and its passing is irreversible. It does not suffice to say, with Husserl, that the formed content of the present passes from fullness into emptiness, from closeness to distance from the ego; what was an apparition to the ego is modified into an appearance for the ego. In becoming present something became definite; in passing it becomes definitive. What has come to pass has come to be, definitive and irrevocable. The past does not give place to the present by emptying out, by becoming an abyss of nothingness in which the present forms, by spontaneous generation, out of nothing. The past is the expanse of the definitive and the irrevocable—the fateful—from which the present does not spring free, for it gives its force to the present. The form that the present acquires inflects that force—the now is "now that the sickness is passing. . . ," "now that the school term is over. . . ."

The present also forms on a certain axis of futurity. Now is "now that I am awake. . . ," "now that summer is here. . . ," "now that I am married. . . ." Like a note that begins a melody, the now acquires a certain relief, a certain intensity, a certain pitch, by stationing itself in the field of a certain key. The present is solicited, menaced, oriented—destined—by the axis of futurity. The present opens upon the future as upon its field of potential.

As the past passes, of itself, so the future comes, of itself. It comes, Husserl says, from emptiness to fullness, from distance from to closeness to the ego. But what comes is not necessarily fullness. The potential of futurity is not simply a plenitude still distant; it is possibly nothing. This possible nothingness immanent in the future is not only a nothingness of content, which would leave the formative power of the present intact. If nothing comes, this nothingness comes of itself, affects the consciousness, disengages its formative operation, renders it impotent. Consciousness is not assured of having the power to give itself time without end.

5. Power ad Infinitum

What would be required for the time of natural consciousness to be transformed into an infinite succession of moments each variable in content but invariant in form? The conceptual disengagement of form from content is in fact based on a lived experience of the content being indifferent and recurrent. This could occur when it seems that nothing is decided, nothing resolved, in the moment, that the same pressures and the same signals recur. This inconclusiveness, this equivalence of content, empties it out, leaving just the form: a moment that passes, a day to be lived through, an hour to be used up.

There is no longer any fullness of time, any momentous moments, any great days, any days of wrath and any goodness of days. Such would be the existential equivalent of the abstraction that formalizes the inner experience of time. Husserl has in fact conducted his reflection on moments of laboratory time, filled simply with an elementary sensation—a color, a word, a tone. He has not retraced the genesis by which the form of a unit of time is constituted. He has not seen the idealization already at work in the process by which one no longer takes one day to lead to another, to fulfill another, to climax another; one just takes each as it comes, and after the climactic day one takes the next day as equivalent, to fill up one way or another. Here is where there occurs an equalization of the days and, by extension, a making equivalent of the moments of living presence and, by a sort of passage to the limit, conceived in imagination, an equalization and an identification of the form of the unit of time.

The idealizing identification of the form of time is then not only an intellectual operation; it arises out of a way the subject can live his time. Heidegger called it dispersion and inauthenticity *(Uneigentlichkeit)*—one does not take over the moment specifically as one's own *(eigen)*. But in Husserl the idealizing identification of the form of time, giving oneself an infinite horizon of time, is the accession of the subject to its own power. This power is the power to give itself its own form and content and to release itself inwardly from fatality and destiny.

The content becomes indifferent and taken for granted—taken as given. The giving of the given, the presentation of what becomes present in a moment, is lost sight of. The constitution of the moment of time as such will be taken to be entirely a work that consciousness effects. Wherever, whenever, there is consciousness, it is now; the form of the present recurs, the same, in the sphere of consciousness. Consciousness is then identified as the spontaneous generation of the form of the now and the power to reproduce the form of the now ad infinitum. This form forms a content. By stamping a content with the form of presence, consciousness holds it in its sphere. The content is not only given; consciousness gives it to itself. This is involved in the idea that consciousness is intentional. It itself directs itself toward, focuses in on, takes up, or takes in, the given.

Intentionality is first of all temporal intentionality. The same power that forms the content of the living now reinstates, re-presents, the content that passes. But since the content passes as soon as it is there, the power that retains it is already at work in the power that forms it. Retaining a content as it forms it, consciousness itself presents the content.

The form of the now retains the form of the past now as its own boundary. The past is taken to be produced by this forming and this retaining which is a present work, a work of the present—a power of the actual consciousness. It is a result of Husserl's formal reflection that for him retention means that the form of the past is retained by the form of the present—and not that the content of what has come to pass retains the present. The definitive and irrevocable character that adheres to the past is lost sight of. The present as a movement situated, fixed, on the level of what has come to pass is lost sight of. The present born "by spontaneous generation" is freed from the fatality of the past.[28]

In its indefatigable power to reproduce the form of the present, Husserl sees consciousness giving itself a horizon of futurity, articulated in advance in its form. The future as a level is lost sight of. The present as a force aroused by a perspective, a movement which owes its significance, orientation, force, form, to a contingent level, is lost sight of. The formalizing abstraction frees the present from every destiny.

Now the present no longer takes on relief by varying a dimension of existence that is irreversible, irrevocable, definitive; it arises of its own power, by spontaneous generation. It no longer arises upon an axis of futurity which already assigns it position, direction, force, form. It arises by itself, without commitments, without a mission.

It is a subjectivity of this form that can conceive of absolute self-responsibility.

Its own form, its own formative power, is such that it can maintain itself in identity, can be true to itself, can "shape itself into a true 'I'." In the form of its presence, it can retain still the raison d'être of all its past phases, of the in principle infinite series of moments in which the meaning of its deeds has been constituted. None of them have definitively passed from its presence; in its absolute power to reproduce the form of the present, it possesses unrestricted power to reproduce the form of every content in which its presence has been realized. And in its ever-intact power to reiterate the form of its presence, it knows that no form of future existence to which it commits itself now overextends its actual forces. It can already now answer for every future position it will assume.

Such a moment of presence will indeed set out to so answer for every future position it will assume when it conceives the value of absolute truth. It idealizes, infinitizes, the space of nature and the aspects of every natural object in the infinite time horizon it has extended; it thereby subjects itself to an interminable task of cognition. The consciousness that retains the form of all its past moments and anticipates now the form of all its future moments possesses still and in advance not the content but the meaning of all that becomes present in the space of nature. In committing itself to supply a reason for every fact and a reason for every reason, theoretical consciousness draws all reasons out of itself. Its access to nature is henceforth governed by the geometrical, deductive ideal—of possessing within itself a priori the laws of all possible objectivity.

Thus the commitment to absolute theoretical truth is also a pursuit of one's own true being. "If man loses this faith [in absolute reason], it means nothing less than loss of faith 'in himself,' in his own true being. This true being is not something he always already has, with the self-evidence of the 'I am,' but something he only has and can have in the form of a struggle for his truth, the struggle to make himself true."[29] In undertaking to answer for itself always and to anyone, theoretical consciousness recaptures, retains, reinstates all its past, not in its force but in its meaning, in its validity. In committing itself to unconditional responsibility, it takes over in advance all its future. In undertaking to know a priori the laws of all nature, it comes to possess itself absolutely.

This subjectivity engendering itself ad infinitum, realizing its sovereignty in the exercise of unrestricted self-responsibility, in the infinite pursuit of knowledge, and in the pursuit of ideal norms, cuts itself free from natural fatality and from destiny. It has done so first in freeing itself from the form of its own natural time. The form of its present is no longer situated on an undecomposable level of definitive past time. It is not aroused and oriented by the vortex of time to come.

Infinity first emerged in the transcendent ideal of absolute truth, and in the idealized form of the space of the world. Husserl's genetic teleological analysis reveals that the theoretical subjectivity that pursues infinite truth in an infinitized nature pursues at the same time its own truth, in unrestricted self-responsibility. His transcendental phenomenology has disclosed an internal conversion when this occurs—an inner transformation of its own natural time, an infinitization of the power of the present. "Perhaps it will even become manifest that the total phenomenological attitude and the epochè belonging to it are destined in essence to effect, at first, a complete personal transformation, comparable in the beginning to a religious conversion, which then, however, over and above this, bears within itself the significance of the greatest existential transformation which is assigned as a task to mankind as such."[30]

In the idea of infinity—infinite truth, infinite space, infinite time—Husserl has exposed the conditions for a form of life that can conceive of absolute self-responsibility. But *must* it? Husserl has shown that once subjectivity conceives of the horizon of infinity, it shall never lack cognitive and practical tasks, it shall always be energized by object-objectives. And he has shown that the subjection to the cognitive ideal of absolute, theoretical truth with the practical subjection to norms in the elaboration of an objective, objectified, infinitized universe is the very form of sovereignty. Absolute sovereignty has the form of commitment to infinity. "What follows this is the *ultimate self-understanding of man as being responsible for his own human being:* his *self-understanding as being in being called to a life of apodicticity,* not only in abstractly practicing apodictic science in the usual sense but [as being mankind] which realizes its whole concrete being *in apodictic freedom* by becoming apodictic mankind in the whole active life of its reason—through which it is human; as I said, mankind understanding itself as rational, understanding that it is rational in seeking to be rational; that this signifies an *infinity of living and striving toward reason; that reason is precisely that which man qua man in his innermost being, is aiming for, that which alone can satisfy him, make him 'blessed'.*"[31]

The idea of absolute sovereignty in the form of absolute self-responsibility is a force, "the idea which represents the driving-force of life for the highest stage of mankind."[32] The commitment to infinity is for Husserl now a *fact*. It is the fact that ultimately renders all facts intelligible and all reasons comprehensible, for it is the factum that first engenders the theoretical attitude.

This fact is a fact of history. It is the fact that locates and dates the history of reason and of true humanity. Yet this fact is also a bond, an obligation. To conceive the idea of infinity is to be bound by it, to be subjected to it. What is this bond, which makes of an idea a "driving-force"? The reality of this bond, this obligation, this exigency, is not thematized in Husserl's phenomenology. The enigmatic original subjection of subjectivity to the idea, or idea-form, of the universal is the starting-point of Kant's practical philosophy.

II

IMAGES OF AUTARCHY

1. The Imperative a Fact. The Command to be Master

If there is an exigency intrinsic to us, it is for Kant entirely in our faculty of thought. Kant does not seek the sense of being directed and under obligation in the total composition of our nature, in its drive for satisfaction. His *Anthropology* had concluded the idea of happiness is empty; it is, in reality, forever but an idea, a transcendental ideal of the imagination, and no empirical experience gives it real content. What is worse, the woes of human history are above all due to the passions, especially the cold, rational passions, which pursue a figure of happiness in which the ideal whole is eclipsed by an intuitive part. The idea of a final end to which we would be bound has to be disconnected from the fact of obligation.[1] As soon as thought enters into exercise, it finds itself under law, subject to an imperative. We cannot intuit the comprehensive end, happiness, but we can understand the categorical imperative. It is laid directly on thought.

To understand the imperative of law is not to deduce it or elaborate it out of antecedent elements by the spontaneous synthesizing initiatives of one's mind. That the mind is subject to laws, to law itself, to validity, is a fact.[2] This given, this fact, is received not, to be sure, by the receptivity for data which is sensibility, but by the very spontaneity of the mind. Understanding—pure spontaneity—nonetheless finds itself affected by law. This receptivity in spontaneity, this intellectual feeling is the sentiment of respect—something like inclination, something like fear.[3]

When one understands the moral imperative, one does not simply understand that there is an imperative, but one understands that one is oneself under an imperative. The understanding that understands the imperative discovers that its very act by which it understands the imperative is bound by the imperative. It discovers that its act is commanded, that when it is realized, it is realized as an act of obedience. One has obeyed law before understanding it; one understands law—as one understands anything—by obeying law.

Our understanding is thus obligated to understand, obligated to be understanding, to be fully itself. The rational thought that understands the obligatory force of principle understands that it is itself commanded. It does not understand just the meaning of law but understands that law must be its own energizing principle. It understands that law must become effective, practical, determine the will, command. The command is a command to command. Our rational faculty must command our nature to act validly, that is, according to principles, and it is obligated to formulate principles that can be practical principles. The human nature in which the faculty of reason is found is obligated to become actively rational, to become nothing but a rational agency. Human nature is of course a complex in which other faculties besides that of reason enter. The moral imperative is then an imperative that man become something other than what he is by nature.

The moral imperative is understood as the principle that one's will ought to be determined on the basis of representations one oneself constitutes, by one's law-subject spontaneity, one's understanding. It is their law-character, their properties of being universal and necessary principles, that will mark them as rational principles and not empirically derived maxims. "So act that the maxim of your will could always hold at the same time as a principle establishing universal law."

Since the rational will is one that is determined by the faculty of reason in one's own nature, a rational entity is one that is self-determined. This self-determination is not, as in Heidegger (and in Heidegger's interpretation of Kant)[4] a project which the agent has conceived and affected himself with by virtue of his own existential structure. It is true that self-determination means being subject only to laws one oneself legislates. But this subjection is itself commanded. By the moral imperative one finds oneself commanded to be master.

Just as our thought, when it is coherent and consistent, understands nature in terms of universal concepts and laws, so our thought must understand our own nature as having to be governed by universal laws in its practical existence. When it is so governed, it determines itself in virtue of its own representation of itself, and becomes intelligible to itself. But the exigency of law is not for Kant an exigency a man would have within himself that his acts become intelligible to himself—though if they become law-governed they will be. It is not a necessity that a man comprehend himself, synthesizing all his own acts under intelligible principles, and thus have a synthetical hold on himself, on all his successive and dispersed acts (find blessedness, as Husserl put it, in the struggle to make himself true)—though this demand for consistency and for concordance with all instances of like acts will indeed make it possible for a man who acts out of principles to maintain himself comprehensively; the rational apprehension of law will be also an ontological appropriation of one's effective existence. But the moral imperative is first the demand that there be law. This demand is not something that can be deduced from prior principles nor derived from an end, from the telos it does bring about—an explanation that would itself have to be already subject to law in order to be valid. The imperative of law is a pure and transcendental fact.

Subjection to law is not an inclination of our nature—not even of our rational nature.[5] Rather, our rational faculty results from, constitutes itself in, acts of obedience to this imperative. The moral imperative comes first, and then comes rational self-determination, that is, freedom. A man finds he can act rationally because he must!

Subjection to law is the condition for there to be possible a world of experience which would be a genuine world, a cosmos and not a chaos, a world of genuine objects, recognizable unities and not inconsistent phantasms. But it is not that the understanding determines that our active, functioning nature ought to be conformed to law in general because it understands our human nature to be part of nature as a whole, which it first understands to be through and through law-governed. Rather, thought sets out to understand all things in function of law because it is itself an activity, a willful and discursive activity, and is morally bound to follow out law. The whole theoretical employment of reason, as mapped out and bounded in the *Critique of Pure Reason*, turns out to be an activity morally incumbent on us. What is decisive for theoretical reason is not, as for Husserl, the teleological passion for the infinite but the a priori subjection to the universal.

The movement in Kant is from the fact of the moral imperative, the fact that our nature ought to become totally rational, to the constitution of the rationally ordered world, as the context or field for such a nature to operate. Our own will is the locus where the exigency of law is first assumed. The world as a law-governed totality is a representation that theoretical reason must work out, because man must represent the world to himself in such a way that the moral imperative makes sense.

2. The Moral Imagination

What does the law command? It commands *me*. As a command the law enjoins me to make myself, in my actuality and activity, an instance of law, a law-governed particular. I must then be able to synthetically unite the purely formal universality and necessity of law with my own particular act. My act, for its part, is not something only intellectually apperceived; it is an operation in the world of appearances. A synthesis has to be made between the purely intelligible form of law and the empirical content of my act. It is by making such a synthetic representation that my will will be bound. What determines my will is not a pure concept of the form of law in general but an advance representation of my act formed by the form of law.

But the act of my will is an act in the world. In subsuming my act under the law I subsume the world—or, at least, the field in which my act is placed, under the dimensions of law. Thus whereas in Heidegger the meditation seeks to discern law—Creon, Dikè, Logos, Destiny—in the world-play, in an enlarged sense of the given *giving itself*, in Kant the movement is from the law to the world. Law is not first found in the world; rather the world is found in law.

The moral imperative commands the exercise of moral judgment. The faculty of judgment has to connect the principle with the intuitive particular which exemplifies it. Judgment is a talent of the mind. One cannot supply rules for its use, since its exercise consists in the applying of rules. Theoretical judgment is guided by an intermediary image, or "schema," which shares with the intuitive particular the property of being sensuous, and shares with the concept or principle the property of generality. Its sensuousness is produced by the reproductive imagination. Its generality is not true universality; it is the generality of an image formed by the imaginative memory by collating the recurrent traits of apparently analogous particulars. Such an image when produced to guide the judgment in the application of the moral imperative to actions Kant calls a "type." Whereas the "schemas" involved in the theoretical use of reason are generalized representations of the given particulars, the moral type is a general model of what must come into being through its efficacy. Here the universal, the law, precedes the existence of the particulars, the moral acts. The successive formulations given by Kant and taken to be equivalent to the categorical imperative articulate the particular "types" that render the imperative intuitive. They formulate not theoretical implications of the law, but rules for forming imaginative models for use in practical judgment.

While the sense of law itself falls directly and immediately, a priori, on the faculty of reason, it is not known in a conceptual synthesis. To understand law as morally imperative, as a command put on me, I must subsume myself, my empirical existence, as a case under the law, and I must do that by first forming a representation for the will which will determine the will to actually intuit itself, in advance, as a case realizing the law. Thus the formation of the "type" is the first thing the law itself commands.

The sense of law is in this complex experience, where the subject is simultaneously obedient, imaginative, and rigorously cognitive and where the law is simultaneously an immediate affliction of the faculty of understanding, a form imaged in the spectacle of the world, and a project one imposes upon oneself.

3. Physical Nature as a Type of the Moral Order. Kant's Problematic Determination of the Properties of Law

Law of itself is the pure form of universality and necessity, which must form a material content. An empirical multiplicity that would be formed by the form of law is a "nature." The moral imagination must produce an image of oneself as a moral nature. The "type" will be, like a schema in the theoretical employment of reason, constructed by an inductive and analogizing imaginative memory of sensibly given data.

Such an image cannot be taken from data drawn from our perception of our own nature—which is humiliated and pained by the incidence of the moral imperative.[6] It is then the representation of physical nature, as a totality determined by laws, that will supply, for the moral imagination, an analogon or symbol of a moral entity. One is to imagine the acts of one's own nature, which one is going to determine by one's own representations, according to the analogy with actions and reactions in the physical universe. "Act as if the maxim of thy action were to become by thy will a universal law of nature."

It is the material world as scientifically represented that is synthetically linked to the idea of the moral agent, in Kant's "type." Kant imagines the moral agent in such a way that Newton's conception of material nature, unified under a single set of laws, could function as an analogue for it. What is suspect here is not so much the analogy made with the material universe—the material universe being the only law-regulated totality we can be said to know. But the "type" retroactively reveals something questionable in the conception of the properties of law. Kant characterizes the moral exigency for law by the properties of formal universality and necessity. Has he really drawn these properties from an inspection of the moral imperative itself, as it weighs immediately on our faculty of understanding? Has he not rather simply taken them over from the logical concept of law? From a formal logic that is a logic of theoretical reason, that is, of reason at work in the scientific determination of the world?

For Kant the sense of moral command is not derivative of the law-regulatedness of the world of physics; on the contrary, the moral imperative is absolutely a priori, and does not derive from any empirical experience of the world open to science. But it should also be prior to the a priori principles for the theoretical employment of reason.[7] The objective world of natural science can only function as a symbol for the moral order, and it can do so precisely because one has first an idea of law itself, which is immediately evident in the moral imperative.

And yet what Kant has done is borrow the properties of law—the universality and the necessity and how they are to be understood—from the formal, the logical, calculus of the a priori principles of natural science. It is this that forces him to conceive of a moral being as analogous to the universally and necessarily regulated clockwork of objective nature.

Without doubt for our age the commanding sense of law is instantiated in the scientific representation of nature. We conceive of the optimum moral order in the human community with close attention to the scientific representation of human society—that is, to the sciences which, modeled after the sciences of physical nature and their mathematical modes of determination, conceive of the human community as ideally regulated by laws—economic, sociological, political, linguistic—as any other region of material nature.[8] Law for us means logico-mathematical principles.

But this was not the only sense of law. Heidegger has shown that in the presocratic age the sense of law involved in its first notions, the notions of Creon, of Moira, of Dikè, of Logos in the fragments of Anaximander, Parmenides, and Heraclitus, was not determined logico-formally. The sense of law was that of an imperative for the understanding and the action of men, its form was taken to transcend the structures of the empirical givens; it had its necessity and its universality.[9] This necessity and this universality were not that of the formal universality and necessity first instantiated in a formalized representation of nature and alone envisaged by Kant.

Yet for Heidegger if the sense of law is for us, for our metaphysical epoch, understood in formal-logical terms, this too is commanded. Our reason heard something like a logico-mathematical imperative first, and our representation of nature, as well as our representation of rational acts of will, are elaborated in obedience to that imperative. The properties of the imperative itself were not predicated by the spontaneous understanding; law and its properties rather exhibit the facticity of our spontaneity.

And so for Heidegger if our metaphysical epoch could only conceive of the human moral order in the image and likeness of material nature scientifically represented, that too was commanded. Heidegger's inquiries into other world-epochs, in which other determinations of the sense of law prevailed, both in the theoretical representation of nature and in the moral sense of the human community that ought to be realized, do not imply that such laws could also be our law or that we could freely select which form of law to follow. Their real purpose is rather to bring more forcefully into relief the exact nature of the logico-mathematical, rational, finally technological imperative to which we are subject.

For Kant the sensible "type"—here the pure sense of the moral imperative synthetically combined by the moral imagination with the representation of material nature—is only an illustration of the law, which immediately and directly affects the faculty of reason. Material nature can be taken as an analogue to typify the moral order only if one already has the concept of law. The mind does not rise from the intuitive representation of a law-governed nature to the idea of a moral law that ought to govern the world of men. It is just the reverse: it is because the faculty of reason is first subject to law, affected by the moral imperative, that it then sets out to synthesize its theoretical experience into a representation of a law-governed nature. For Kant the sense of the law does not come out of the world, and does not come out of the "type." It comes out of one's own rational experience of oneself, one's rational sentiment.

Whereas for Heidegger what Kant calls the type, the imaginative figure, is veritably the locus of disclosure of the law. When we put into question the sense in which the properties of law have been determined in Kant, we are forced to reopen the question of the locus of receptivity for law in the mind.

In fact the typology is not only part of the process of application of the law; it is part of the process of understanding the law. It is necessary to move from the pure rational sense of law to some intuitive content. This movement the law itself commands. The elaboration of the type is both the moral subjection itself, whereby the sense of law is directly and from the start a sense of law binding *me*, obligating me to become an instance of itself, the matter of the form it imposes, and an intellectual requirement, what is needed in order that the sense of law be a sense of something, not be merely an empty concept.

The passage through the imaginative type is necessary, because one cannot find any reliable empirical example of moral action, either in one's own states and actions (which the theoretical reason can, and indeed must, always link up causally to antecedent phenomenal states and processes) or in the human community at large.[10] Only the imagination, produced out of the pure rational sense of law, can be trusted.

This moral imagination is anticipatory, projective. It is in this sense a work of poiesis, a poetic composition, and not a simple reproductive imaging. There is then an essential poetic moment, an advance work of the productive imagination, involved in moral consciousness—even if Kant conceives the voice of conscience as speaking in prose, that is, articulating a sense of law identical in its form with the physical and mechanical principles that regulate physical nature.

4. The Setting up of an End in Itself, by Moral Command

The moral imperative commands that the will be determined by rational representations alone. But the will is a faculty, that is, one power among others in our nature. It is only the conjoint energization of all our faculties that could give happiness, or, more exactly, the sentiment of advancing in the way of satisfaction, which is the inevitable telos of our nature. The moral imperative thus thwarts the inclinations of human nature and produces pain.[11] But it substitutes for the infinitely remote end, happiness, the rational satisfaction of an immediately realized end. This end is the moral agency itself, set up, by the moral imperative, as of unconditional worth, an end in itself.

Kant's decisive distinction is between the determination of the will by the rational faculty alone and the determination of the will by sensuous inclinations. When the will is sensuously lured, the end proposed to it is something exterior, objects, inasmuch as they are presented as having worth. All objects which we could acquire have worth relative to something; they are desired inasmuch as they serve our needs and thus have market value or serve our pleasure and thus have fancy value.

Kant takes all sensuous things to affect one sole "life-force," either directly, giving it pain or pleasure, or indirectly, giving it pain or pleasure through their capacity to serve our needs. Pains and pleasures, however different the refined may seem from the gross, are for Kant really one in kind; they differ only according to their extent, duration, and intensity. What feels pain or pleasure is our general life-force, which is one and undifferentiated in itself; the difference between slight vexations and great griefs and between vague titillations and grand joys is only quantitative.

It is Kant's reduction of the receptivity for affective sensation to the singular "life-force" that justifies the reduction of all pleasures and pains to one single scale graded only quantitatively. If they do not differ qualitatively, they in addition do not differ in the kind of effect they have on the life-force. They reduce it or augment it. Pleasure is the consciousness of the causality of a representation to keep the subject in the state in which he is having this experience. This is true even of disinterested aesthetic pleasure. Pain is our consciousness of an effect that a representation has of making us try to, or wish to, change our subjective state.[12]

Thus pleasures and pains can be compared; the relative worth of things that fulfill our needs or please us is measurable. Since the particular value of a thing for our vital force is quantitative, it can be exchanged for other things of equivalent worth or for money. Any given sensuous thing is not an incomparable end, but a relative end, of desire; it is taken by the will as an end in fact because it happens to be in the environment rather than another of equivalent worth.[13]

The things which we can acquire are ends for our practical will, but they are so because they are means[14] for pain or for pleasure for our vital force. What gives them their worth and makes them ends are the particular desires contingently turned on them and the environment in which they contingently happen to be found and which is itself contingent.

What of those particular desires themselves? They do not posit themselves absolutely as ends but only as the momentary appetites turned to the objects that happen to present themselves with their capacity to give so much pain or pleasure. What of the core life-force, then, of which the particular desires are the momentary determinations? Does it not posit itself as the end, to be fulfilled by all these satisfactions? And does it not posit itself so universally, always, and in all circumstances? Is it not then an unconditional end in itself?

For Kant the answer is no. The life-force in general is the substantially one will for pleasure, for satisfaction, from sensuous objects. It is itself relative to the sensuous field and conditioned by it. Should it seem that the world no longer gives the life-force a quantity of pleasure and satisfaction at least equivalent to the pain, it could will to suppress itself.[15] Thus the crucial issue of suicide, which is the first moral problem Kant selects to test each formulation of the moral imperative—as though reason's most urgent concern were to prohibit suicide. As though he thought with Nietzsche that all moral thinking answers to the essential vital imperative to save the will, to make life will itself.[16]

For there to be an absolute end, it would be necessary to posit oneself, one's vital force, as an end in all circumstances and at all times. One would have to will with a will that would be utterly independent of the concrete environment that happens to surround one. Such is exactly the moral will: Here the representations that activate the will are not representations of this or that particular configuration of the environment, but representations of law, of principle, which is universal, always and everywhere valid.

What would that give? *A will that is always determined to will.* Such a will is what is in fact commanded by the moral imperative. It sets up my own existence qua purely rational agency as an unconditioned and absolute end. "Act in such a way that you always treat humanity, whether in your own person or in the person of any other, never simply as a means, but always at the same time as an end."

The will must be commanded to will itself! Heidegger said that Nietzsche identified the will to power, or life, with the will to will. Here for Kant the will is not a will to will of its own essence; our vital force can cease to will itself. That it become through and through will to will, it has to be commanded, morally ordered.

In Nietzsche will (Kant's *Wille*, not *Willkür*) does not mean desire, wanting; exercising will is commanding, ordaining, ordering. The will to will in Nietzsche is not a simple reflective circle, a Spinozist *idea ideae;* it names a structure by which life finds itself commanded to command, to be master. For Nietzsche only life can command; in the master the command is something life simultaneously takes on, obeys, and issues, creates. The very upsurge of life out of chaos pronounces the imperative to be master. In Kant the moral imperative, the command to will my own rational existence absolutely, is a command I receive and do not spontaneously give myself; it is a command to which I find myself, from the first, subject, before I have done anything, before I even took the initiative to turn to it and hear it. I was already subjected to it before I could assume it.

This command is for Kant a primordial and transcendental fact. An ideal fact: absolute and unconditioned. In Nietzsche this fact became problematic: It seemed contingent. There are those in whom the will to be master commands, but there are also those in whom the will to be slave commands or, rather, in whose nature nothing commands and who have to be commanded from the outside because they are incapable of commanding themselves. The whole problem for Nietzsche was to know how to produce the original command by which a life commands itself to be master. All of Nietzsche's thought experiments were wholly concerned with this portentous task.

5. The Production of, and the Image of, an Existent End in Itself

It would seem that every effort to determine the will by oneself in such a way that it would be determined to will itself would have to involve presenting that will with an empirical representation, a representation of an existence, which would fix for it an end.[17] It would be an effort to persuade the will that it must be master, in order that some end be realized. This end would be its own sovereign existence. One would have to produce a representation of that end, in order to determine the will. One would first have to activate a will to produce such a representation . . . But this line of conditions regresses without end.

Therefore what Nietzsche aims for is an image that is no longer an objective representation, would not be posited apart from the will, presenting an end to be realized, but that would obsess the will. An image that would be incumbent on the will, be its own affliction. A phantasm that would not elicit an option of the will but make the will not free not to will. Such an image would not simply illustrate the imperative of sovereignty, but would be the very form in which it is put on one. But does the will then have to produce such a phantasm? How could the will bind itself with a representation it itself spontaneously produces?

Kant for his part thinks that the will, in order to produce a representation of itself as an end in itself, is determined not spontaneously by itself but by the facticity of the moral imperative. The rational agency, as an end in itself, is not a practical telos; it is not an end removed from the action, whose worth would derive from the extent to which it serves that end. That action itself, rationally motivated, is the end and has non-relative "dignity." Each moral action has unconditioned worth—an instance of a rational agency that is an existent end in itself. The rational practical faculty itself, as an absolute end, cannot be sensuously represented; it is only something that affects the sensibility, the receptivity of one's very understanding, in the sentiment of respect. It is given then not first in a representation of oneself but in a feeling of respect for oneself. One feels one's own absolute worth as a rational entity, as something against which one must never act.[18] And yet the moral action does need an intuitive image of its position in the field of action so as to form itself.

Here Kant produces, to correspond to the pure concept of rational nature as an end in itself, the image of man as lord over nature.

The Promethean, Western, image of man as lord over nature is not in Kant an image from which one derives the concept of being an end in oneself inasmuch as one is rational. It is the reverse. The concept of being an end in oneself inasmuch as one is rational is a priori; it is the meaning of the moral imperative incumbent on us prior to all empirical experience. But the productive imagination has to produce a type to guide the faculty of judgment. What one has to imagine is a situation in which I am an end in myself and all the rest are ends relative to this one. That would be the situation in which all of nature about me really consists of entities that, in their very being, exist relative to me, such that if a thing were bereft of its property of being my property and my implement it would be "reduced to nought."[19] And that would be the situation if I imagined that the outside world consists of sensuous objects whose value as ends I appraise according to how they serve me—and if that image were metaphysical, if it depicted all nature as really created to serve me and I really created as an end in myself.[20]

Thus the Kantian image is not dependent on technological experience but on a theological postulate. The image of man existing as lord over nature takes the world specifically as creation. In Kant man's sovereignty, his de jure nobility, is a suzerainty under a postulated divine investiture.

It is then not that because man finds himself more and more, by determination of his own will, master over nature that he comes to think of himself as absolute end. It is that the image of man as master over nature is produced by the productive imagination—and produced on categorical command—as a guide in judging, so that he will judge in practice in such a way as to never violate the absolute worth of himself as a rational entity. That image is not produced by reflection on the growing technological triumph of man over nature in the West; it is produced from within, exclusively by moral command.

But is the image of man as lord over nature really the image that the idea of being an absolute end unto oneself demands? Does not the image of mastery over nature or even in nature still depict a practical objective[21]—and therefore something posited apart from the will's own reality, something it would then be being enjoined to use itself as a means to realize?

Are not then the Nietzschean phantasms of mastery constructed more rigorously in conformity with the austere exigencies formulated in Kant? The image that would be required would be one in which nature in its entirety, that realm of unending ends, is effaced—not obliterated but neutralized, made into sheer appearance, pure flux of incomparable and inexchangeable and un-measurable images. The line of transmission of finality is everywhere broken; each sensuous image the world-play momentarily offers is shut up absolutely in itself, is an end to itself, but not at all an end for us. The Nietzschean master sees the outside world as Dionysian flux of pure images, pure differentiation everywhere leading nowhere, achieving nothing, in utter indifference to him, where nothing out there is made to serve him. It is with such an image of nature that the master then must posit himself as an end in himself. The master is the one that enshrines himself as an artwork, making his existence in all its positions statuesque, Apollonian, and in all its movements Dionysian, a dance, stamping each moment with the worth of infinity. This existence is sovereign, needing nothing and wanting nothing whatever of the world and its gods, not wanting to treat the outside things of nature as means it would need, as though it needed something still, wanting rather to experience them as needing it, and concretely so experiencing that in pouring over them, gratuitously, squander-ing, the value of one's own existence, the gold, the heat, and the light, of its own value-endowing and meaning-endowing force. The phantasm of eternal recurrence—the oldest and also the newest, the most scientific, thought—depicting an eternal existence utterly without hope as without regrets, is the form of every such phantasm of sovereignty. It is finally a sacred and blas-phemous phantasm—as though one can command this life to be master only by afflicting it with the image of divine sovereignty. That would not be an image of what it must become; it has to be an image of what it already is. The image functions to mediate between the two and make them equivalent; it is the image of what one has to be in order to become what one is. And it has to be itself an image that one does not engender, since it will engender one; it has to be an image that afflicts one, produced as from outside all one's own initiative, as from the depths of anonymous and chaotic nature itself. If it is an image of a god, that is not because the Nietzschean master takes from religions the image of god and applies it to himself. On the contrary, gods are invisible, and if an image of divinity first arose, it was first produced in the masters and then taken from them, alienated from the heros and seers to be attributed to transcendent entities.

For Nietzsche this image is not produced by my own productive imagination because I already have the understanding of being an end in myself. To the contrary, this image first afflicts me, and it engenders the ideas I will form about myself being an existent end. It engenders the mastery in me, the sovereignty; the masters are produced by their phantasms. Whereas in Kant it is the moral imperative imposing upon me the concept of myself as an absolute end that brings me to engender the image of being master over nature. The master images are produced by master types—liege lords, under legitimate, divine, investiture, exercising dominion over nature and over their own nature.

6. Moral Autarchy

I am to imagine myself in action forming a dynamic system governed by universal and necessary laws, like a nature. And I am to imagine myself as an existent end in the practical field, field of means. To imagine now the nature I form and the end I represent not as given but as required by the law laid on me, I have to produce an image of my internal constitution. This image will have to be formed by analogy with the constitution of a State. A State exists on its own right and maintains itself as a law-regulated body because it itself sets up a legislative organ for itself and in its executive acts recognizes neither the forces that drive men in the state of nature nor the laws of other States.

Following now this type, I shall imagine myself to be a legislator—universal legislator, for the law is law by being valid for everyone, being universal and necessary. And legislator for myself, my own will having no other maxim than the universal law I lay down. This yields the image-type of autonomy. I must imagine my will as not simply subject to the law but "so subject that it must be regarded as itself giving the law, and on this ground only subject to the law (of which it can regard itself as the author)."[22]

It is in this way that I come to imagine myself not only as end of material nature but as sovereign. A will subject to nothing but laws it itself puts to itself is a will that has liberated itself utterly from all the allurements by which sensuous things attract and repel, with their promises of pleasure or pain. It is imagined free at the same time from the laws of the causal efficacy of sensuous nature and from its own natural inclinations. And it is imagined freed from the natural fixation of all its inclinations on the unimaginable idea of happiness, which could only become intuitive in the passionate investments of wealth, power, and status by which passionate men pursue independence—a fixation that subjects me to images proposed by their pursuits, while those pursuits in fact have despotic designs on me.

The idea of freedom is postulated to make the image of autonomy intelligible. Freedom is not found in an inward experience of unbound, creative, potential but rather in the image of a will that is unconditionally constrained but only by itself, by its own representation of law. The idea of freedom is not postulated to make responsible civil existence intelligible; rather the constitution of a State functions as the means to construct a psychological model for operations of will constrained by law. Freedom is postulated to justify that model.

For freedom in the specifically Kantian sense of a will that is unconditionally constrained, but constrained by a representation of law that it itself proposes to itself, is not an immediate datum of consciousness. The causality of the will on the phenomenal world and the determination of that causality by the representational faculty forever elude all experience, and can never be apprehended or understood.[23]

The Kantian image of autonomy is not a development of the apperception of spontaneity, by which, it is true, the mind compensates for its finitude by producing the objects of its own cognition and in which therefore Kant saw the image and likeness of God in the human soul.[24] It is true that because man imagines himself autonomous he has a sense of his sovereignty and his inviolable dignity.[25] But there is not some irreducible inward experience of that, which would be man's intuition into his own nature. Autonomy is an image, which we *must* produce. Not in order to explain the incidence of the moral imperative on us, which is given as a fact and as the first fact. In order to obey it.

External constraint constrains *me*, not when it determines the presence or absence of means to my ends or restricts the exercise of my physical or psychic capacities, but when it determines an end for my will. Thus a torturer can undertake to constrain *me*, and not only limit or suppress the exercise of my faculties, by attacking my core vital force, under the assumption that the universal end of human inclinations, happiness, binds my will. In order to obey law I have to imagine that the representation of happiness can be displaced within me, that my will can be determined by an end *immediately*, inwardly, an end which is not the end of my human nature. I imagine that the pure representation of law by the faculty of understanding in me can be enough to bind my will. So as to exercise the faculty of judgment, to envisage acts free of any subjective interest, I must produce this image of my will bound only inwardly. The production of the image of autonomy is then not an element of a project of theoretical reason—setting forth an intuition of my essential nature with a claim to cognitive validity; it is an element of the practical project to produce acts of obedience. The image of himself as autonomous sovereign is an image a man must produce in order to function as rigorous judge of his own spontaneity.

Thus the image of autonomy, or moral autarchy, is not that of authenticity—project whose structure is analyzed by Heidegger. It is not an image of a freedom which is conceived positively as power, self-engendering potential, and which, in being faithful to itself according to a law, appropriates itself, comes into and retains possession of itself.[26] It is true that subjection to law makes this auto-appropriation and sovereign independence, this *Eigentlichkeit*, existing on one's own, possible. But the intrinsic lucidity of a project of self-appropriation is not what, in Kant, founds the auto-imposition of law. Rather, it is in order to exist as the locus where the law obliges that we have to produce the image of a universal legislative function seated in our own representational faculty.

In order to believe that acts commanded in pure obedience to the a priori imperative could be efficacious in the mundane field where phenomenal changes are understood causally, we shall further have to postulate a creationist foundation for both the moral realm and physical nature. And in order to imagine our morally determined operation destined to be practically efficacious in the physical world, we shall have to imagine a "type" for universal teleology; it will be drawn by analogy with the teleological order Kant finds objectified in aesthetic contemplation. This elaboration does not serve to ground a sense of our own intrinsic dignity and sovereignty that we would have through an inward intuition of our own person. It is rather commanded—in order for us to be able to produce practical acts of obedience. The sole *fact* beneath all this intuitive content which is in reality produced by the imagination is the force of the moral command itself.

The word of the sovereign is law, each word and each move makes the law; sovereign existence is an existence entirely exemplary. It is an existence not only without particular, private interests but without privacy, an existence always promulgating, public. Acting morally precisely consists in not taking oneself as an exception.[27] The speech of the sovereign one formulates the universal and the necessary, formulates the essential for everyone. No word, no gesture, no move admits any divergence between its public meaning and its private intention. Nothing in his public existence is contrived to dissimulate. For to use one's manifest or public figure *(homo phaenomenon)* as a means for something non-manifest *(homo noumenon)* is the general formula for acting against oneself as a self-existent end.[28]

In his relation with external nature, the rational one is lord; the general name for slavish resignation to the goods of fortune, rather than dominion over them, is avarice or miserliness.[29] In his relations with others, the rational one requires that he always be treated as an end; depravity in social dealings is not identified as hard-heartedness or lack of compassion[30] but as servility.[31]

Autonomy has to function within the complex of human nature; reason is practical by displacing the sensuous representations with the representation of law. The anticipation of feelings of pleasure and pain from sensuous particulars is displaced by the sentiment of respect, which is the intellectual feeling of how the law affects the mind. Feelings are not simply inert states of being passive with regard to something impressed; they are responses in the direction of inclination or fear. The sentiment of respect for the law—something like inclination, something like fear—has a force. This force is felt, negatively, in the pain with which it blocks sensuous inclinations of life, humiliates them,[32] making "life and its enjoyment have absolutely no worth."[33] Its sway is felt with a feeling essentially different from the feeling of satisfaction of inclinations, which is pleasure; it is purely rational contentment. Moral self-satisfaction is not happiness or even the smallest part of happiness. It is not a *reward:* "satisfaction in the comforting encouragement of one's conscience is not positive (as enjoyment), but only negative (as relief following previous anxiety [over being in "the danger of being found culpable"])."[34] And yet it is blissful. A state of will which finds itself in act always, independently of what the contingencies of the world promises or threatens, it is the bliss of godlike existence.[35]

Autonomy first comes to reign through virtue—extending its legislative constraint through one's whole psychophysical constitution. When we obey moral law, we "do so without gladness,"[36] but under constraint. The weight of the inner obstacles to be forced measures one's worth. "Virtue is not to be defined and esteemed merely as skill and . . . habit" but as *virtus,* to be understood as fortitude, "the greatest and only true martial glory of man."[37] Virtue—"the capacity and resolved purpose to resist a strong but unjust opponent"[38]— imposes apathy. Not in the sense of indifference but in the sense of absence of all emotion, mind at rest, in all one's actions. One should not imagine that a vivid affective sympathy with good works is an aid to moral strength; on the contrary, emotion is intoxication and passion disease; "only the apparent strength of a fever patient makes the lively sympathy with good rise to an emotion, or rather, degenerate into it."[39] Sensuous enjoyment of living is to be neutralized by contempt;[40] the autonomous one henceforth "lives only because it is his duty, not because he has the least taste for living."[41] One strengthens the moral will not by adjoining to it lively sympathy with good but rather "through wonder at its inscrutable origin." Rational obedience humiliates and pains not only natural impulses of self-love but also natural enthusiasms for actions noble, sublime, and magnanimous.[42] "As submission to a law, i.e., as a command (which constrains the sensuously affected subject), it contains, therefore, no pleasure but rather displeasure proportionate to this constraint."[43]

Sovereignty consists in exercising dominion over all nature but not for the satisfaction of one's natural wants. It arises in first maintaining the force of constraint over one's own nature while legislating for all.

7. The Final Kingdom

The sovereign one sovereignly enters into relationship with others. This association already figured in the formulation of the second "type": Act in such a way as to treat humanity, in oneself as well as in others, as an end and not only as a means. I must act out of respect for law, represented by my own representational faculty and proposed to my will but represented by the representational faculty in others also. My bond with others is a subjection to the law in them. Respect for others is not respect for their innate human nature but respect for the law that rules in them.[44] Respect for a man of talent reduces to respect for the law to perfect one's talent, of which he is an example.[45] It is essentially distinguished by Kant from admiration for the force or perfection of the tangible human powers in another. Admiration is reducible to something like awe before the wild, lawless fund of force in another and resembles the sentiment of the sublime before physical nature.[46] The sense of the other as a person is the perception of the action of another as instantiating a law, which is valid for me also.

The others concern me, for the principles that govern their actions obligate me too. And it enters into the very meaning of my own sovereignty that the law that I propose as a maxim for my practical behavior is a law I legislate for everyone.

The multiplicity of rational agents constitutes a "kingdom of ends"—that is, a society in which the legislative power is seated in each citizen, in which each commits himself to the law of his own will, but to a law he has himself decreed.

The kingdom of ends is formed by internal bonds; it must not be conceived as simple coexistence of free and equal members, where the tangency of their spheres of sovereignty is "due to the roundness of the earth"[47]—as though "if the surface of the earth were an infinite plane men could be so dispersed that community would not be a necessary consequence of their existence on the earth."[48] The society of sovereign legislators must not be conceived as an association through mutual aid, for the gratification of wants is no longer the motivation of the will among them. It is not an association for mutual protection—although, it is true, civil society is first formed in order to guarantee to these lords over nature their sovereign possession of the earth and all its goods, against those who exist in a state of nature; they are indeed obligated to constrain all those in the state of nature to enter civil society, and presumably have at one point formed martial associations for this purpose. Yet this motive does not define the association of autonomous ones themselves. And their society should not be conceived as for production. If these rational agents no longer recognize their own happiness as an incentive, they shall also not associate for a productivity that endlessly produces new desires and wants—as in our modern industrialized and automated States, our bourgeois, economic, republics. The kingdom of ends is also not to be conceived after the model of artist communities, whether those which exist for the sake of producing artworks—Newari, Balinese, or Nuba societies—or those which make of themselves an artwork—the samurai, the Jesuit order, the Prussian military caste (Nietzsche's examples). In this kingdom the members are not means, not even for the creation of external splendor or internal sublimity.[49] And sociality does not consist in the circulation of goods, implements, women, and messages among these equal and free possessors. The kingdom of ends forms because each is a legislating sovereign, whose word binds all the others. Each one in acting not only commits himself unreservedly to the law he formulates but also promulgates it in the public sphere of coexistence in the universe. It is the coercive force of the essentially exemplary existence of the rational agent that associates. The kingdom of ends is a society whose inner *energeia* is not the circulation of information but the promulgation of decrees.

It is true that such a society also organizes the universe. The earth and all its goods are its property, nothing is a *res nullius;*[50] all external things are means, and means for rational men, the existent ends of the universe. But this rational appropriation of external nature is not for the sake of their own natural wants and inclinations; it is solely for the sake of the universal promulgation of their rational ordinances. "[T]he well-being of the state must not be confused with the welfare or happiness of the citizens of the state, for these can be attained more easily and satisfactorily in a state of nature (as Rousseau maintained) or even under a despotic government."[51]

The movement of goods is not to be depicted as a circulation which is maintained by a law of reimbursement with which the citizens bind themselves. For when goods are transferred within the social field the recipient is bound to gratitude. Gratitude is a specification of respect, a recognition of the law of duty out of which the benefactor acts. It is a kind of subjection of the recipient to the benefactor which is irreversible: "A person can never, by any recompense, acquit himself of a benefit received, because the recipient can never wrest from the giver the priority of merit, namely, to have been the first in benevolence."[52] The movement of goods is not a simple material circulation; relations with goods within society are always also relations with persons and occur in a field in which a member associates others to himself because he binds them with his own law. Field of legislators and not of equals, the social relationships remain assymetrical; even the return of equivalent goods does not equalize or neutralize the moral subjection to the first mover in a chain of movement of goods.

What is the concrete content of the legislation which the moral community exists to elaborate? What is the civil code of the kingdom of ends? To guide his practical judgment so as to make his daily acts publicly exemplary, each autonomous citizen needs a general image—a "type"—of its laws. The kingdom of ends is first an idea, for which the productive imagination has to produce an intuitive content.

Empirical history does not supply us with a perception of a rational republic. Economic, social, and political history are the history of the cold, rational passions of cupidity, vainglory, and ambition. Yet in the history of human coexistence reason has elaborated laws. Is not the juridic code the formula for the rational coexistence of men? In his disputes and conflicts with his fellows, does not each one appeal to the civil code for what is reasonable and what is just? Yet the empirical civil codes do not in fact represent a legislation worked out in view of guaranteeing the moral inviolability of each. Their decrees represent armistices in the war produced by rational egoisms pursuing passionate phantasms of happiness.

One then cannot envision the rational regulation of human coexistence as the term of the legislation elaborated in economic, social, and political history. One rather has to proceed from above, from the pure idea of an order of sovereign beings regulating themselves by law, to the image which has to be derived by analogy with a law-regulated sphere and not from a field of passions. Kant appeals to the notion of a dynamic system governed by the law of equivalence of action and reaction. This image, taken from physics, permits one to envisage the coexistence of alien forces in a field in such a way that the constraint of reaction is seen not to nullify the possibility of action.[53]

Kant conceives the civil order also as a field of constraints. Rational men are obligated to force men in the state of nature to subject themselves to such a system of constraints in order to guarantee property—the sovereign possession of the earth and its goods and usage rights over the non-sovereign spouses, children, and servants. Within the civil order justice is the employment of external coercion to counteract external acts which encroach on the exercise of the rational will of citizens. Justice is enacted not by producing goods or good will but by the inflicting of equivalent damages on him whose action has illegitimately coerced the will of his fellow citizen. The *lex talonis* is the very *energeia* of civil society.

Judicial sentences are never to be used as a means to promote some good, whether for the victim, the criminal himself, or the commonwealth; neither deterrence nor reformation is allowed as justification of civil justice. Civil society is conceived by Kant as a field of circulation of coercions sanctioning encroachments on the autonomy of others, that is, of punishments—and not as a field of circulation of goods or production of them. Or, one can say the good for which civil society exists is retribution by equivalent damage. Thus "even if a civil society were to dissolve itself by common agreement of all its members (for example, if the people inhabiting an island decided to separate and disperse themselves around the world), the last murderer remaining in prison must first be executed. . . ."[54] For "if legal justice perishes, then it is no longer worth while for men to remain alive on this earth."[55] Or, for that matter, in the hereafter: "if punishment does not occur in his lifetime, then it must happen in a life after death, and such a life after death is therefore explicitly assumed and gladly believed in so that the claim of eternal justice may be settled." "For the belief in a future life does not, strictly speaking, come first in order that penal justice may be seen to have an effect upon that future life; but, conversely, the inference to a future life is drawn from the necessity for punishment."[56]

The constraints the civil code imposes concern not the intentions of actions but only the external actions themselves. Yet the purpose of the constraints is really to discipline the will to assume the law as the sole incentive of its action. Internal constraint is not a means civil society induces in order to realize its goal of the regulation of external actions. The civil society exists for the sake of moral coexistence.[57] When its constraints are inflicted with neither the good of the coerced one nor the good of his victim nor that of the society but only the pure universality of the law taken into consideration, the criminal himself will be able to see that the damage he inflicted on the life, property, or dignity of another requires his own execution, destitution, or defamation and will rationally assent to it.[58]

Working from analogy with the dynamic field governed by the law of equivalence of action and reaction, Kant thus forms an image of civil society as a publicly articulated field of coercions and retributions. This image is not derived from the perception of existing civil codes; it is formed by moral imagination governed by the idea of the law, and its function is to serve as a guide in practical judgment. The interiorization of this external coercion by each autonomous citizen produces society as a kingdom or republic of ends. For, for each one to restrain himself from any action that encroaches on the sphere of the rational will of another is also for each one to make the maxim of his will that which can be a law for everyone.

Positively, action in the republic of ends is imagined as friendship. This friendship is not affection for others, still less that sensitive enjoyment of another's person which is affective love. Moral friendship is "the complete confidence of two persons in the mutual openness of their private judgments and sensations, as far as such openness can subsist with mutual respect for one another."[59] It is thus in its essence publicness *(Öffentlichkeit)*.[60] The kingdom of ends as a friendship of the autonomous masters consists in the reciprocally exposed or manifest life, promulgating each of its deeds as laws, not only in veracity but also in confident transparence to the others.

8. The Singular Law

> Is there not an element of profanation as soon as the lover thinks to himself: "It is not strictly speaking this beloved one I desire, but love"—is not every generalization of the goal sought a profanation? In fact even to say "I desire this beloved one" is crude and insulting—the language of passion wants only what is rare, irrecoverable, only wants signs and symbols. Already the act of naming the whole as a goal is in itself profaning.[61]

Existential philosophy formulates a refusal of the thought, proper to classicism, that equates the promotion in the subject of universality with the promotion to sovereignty. The existential protest is not a protest against the law. It is a protest against the universal form of law.

One of the sources of the critique of this sovereign universality is the discovery by existential philosophy of a base form of universality. Beneath the classical image of the sovereign one in whose representational faculty the legislation legislating all the universe is elaborated, existential anthropology finds a life that has no will of its own, no desire of its own, no representations of its own, because it makes itself equivalent to and interchangeable with another, any other, every other. Such a one knows what anyone knows, says what one says, wills what everyone wills, has eliminated all particularity in himself by making himself equivalent to and interchangeable with anyone else. Is not the sovereign universal subject of classicism—the one whose every word and deed legislates for everyone but that first forms his word or need such that it can be that of anyone—an idealization of this anonymous subject?

Existentialism argues, positively, that the individual and not universal subject is required for truth. For existentialism has a new concept of essence—to know the essence of anything that exists is not to know a set of properties duplicated whenever, wherever an entity of a certain family is found; it is to know the inner event by which ingredients and relationships are for a time assembled into a singular figure in the real entity.

And existentialism argues, positively, that the individual life, constituted in an individuating law, is alone capable of value and capable of producing values. The one that makes himself useful by making himself equivalent to and interchangeable with anyone, the one without a law and a destiny of his own, is without worth. What good is it to exist as another voice that utters what everyone says, as another mind in which the representations that circulate are reproduced, as another will that wills what anyone wills? Such an existence can have no value of itself; it does not exist on its own, it does not will to exist of itself; it exists only by contracting what takes form recurrently, anonymously. Such an existence has no value and cannot value, does not affirm anything on its own, does not first affirm itself.

Whence, for Nietzsche, every generalization of one's own will is already devaluation, profanation. A will contracts the commonplaces and the reactive motives, the resentments, that circulate freely because it has no law of its own. If there is a law that renders existence sovereign, this law can only be singular, and singularizing. Nietzsche's cosmology will set up as its emblem the law of eternal recurrence, which forces each will into an unrestricted affirmation of the singular line of fortuities and fatalities of its own life.

Nietzsche is affirming not so much that the individual alone is real as that the individual alone has value. And for him the individuality of the individual does not consist in being de facto given in a *hic et nunc* which excludes any other from occupying the same *hic et nunc;* it consists in being a force, productive and self-productive. The singular force of an individual counts, has value, for himself because it can affirm itself, and it has value for the universe because it can give what nothing but it can give.

Then the Nietzschean valuation of the singular individual over the universal subject of classicism is a valuation of life as a creative force over the subject as locus in which the order of the universe is reflected.

In fact there is a doctrine of creation that sustains the Kantian ethics. Unconditional theoretical and practical commitment to the law postulates a belief in an ultimate concordance between the moral order and the natural universe. The concept of creation expresses, ontologically, this a priori concordance. The concept of creation is postulated in Kant's system not to make intelligible the fact of finding oneself under the law—ascribing the law to a creative legislator[62]—but to express the postulated concordance between the laws regulating a community which has transformed itself from men into pure rational agencies and the laws in force in the physical nature in which these rational agencies are to act.[63]

Then the moral agent who makes himself the seat of cosmic law has transposed himself to the point of view of the creator. It would be the creative ordinance of the universe itself that alone is expressed in the representations his mind puts to his will.

Creation in Kant is conceived as ordinance; giving form to a chaos is giving law. Nietzsche conceives it rather as giving form to a nothing—Apollonian, dream, production—and as giving a non-teleological, musical, form to becoming—Dionysian transformation. Creative sovereignty is conceived by Nietzsche as artistry; it is force and superabundance, excess; it not only consolidates itself of its own force but discharges, releases its force. Sovereign creativity orders by a gratuitous release of its formative will. But the law that governs its own singular constitution is a singular law, as is the law that its will decrees in the environment upon which it acts.

What could be such a singular law imposing sovereignty? How could it be both imperative and itself a contingent historical event, not found in all men and at all times? How could it be imposed on the one destined to sovereignty— imposed, that is, come upon him from without, from universal nature enjoining upon him irreducible particularity? If a singular law could exist, how could it formulate itself such that its existence could be known?

III

THE VICIOUS
CIRCLE OF MASTERY

There is master morality and there is slave morality; the concept of mastery in Nietzsche is an ethical concept, not a political one. Master morality is the active form of morality; those in whom life is sovereign have invented all the ennobling words of language. For the value terms receive their sense in speech acts of the form "How happy we are! How fortunate, how gracious, how powerful, how healthy we are!"—speech acts which function neither to designate nor to discriminate but to consecrate the surge of force vibrant upon itself. The words, themselves forces, do not merely encode the life they consecrate; they intensify it.[1] "With sounds our love dances on many-hued rainbows."[2] Servile morality is comparative and built on a sense of evil—itself wholly reactive, produced by inversion of the sovereign sense of worth.

The feeling that thus consecrates itself gives itself the name master. For those who know the bliss of inner force are the ones who order, the ones in whom life has the power to first ordain itself.

1. The Ascetic Form of Ideals

Nietzsche's history of culture is not a history of artefacts and monuments but a history of man's self-cultivation. There is not really a history of man's self-civilizing—self-domestication. For the progressively accumulated utilitarian intelligence, pragmatic skills, and equipment which made possible the control and exploitation of the material universe is not accompanied by any essential change in the human type; the utilitarian species man makes himself only ever more numerous and ever more dependent—ever more essentially servile.

The epochs of man's history are defined by the production of a succession of *ideal types*—artists, philosophers (sages), saints, priests, scientists and historians, atheists, nihilists. The list is both chronological and evaluative. Arranging the dominating ideals in historical order is also arranging them in order of rank, for Nietzsche will show that the history of human ideals has been a history of devaluation, of degeneration. Each successive ideal type will be shown to affirm less of the forces in the human material. The artist is the most ancient ideal type. The Nietzschean thesis is that the original savage dispersion was first bound into a human dispensation not organized in view of defense and mutual aid, but, essentially festive, ceremonious, formed in view of glory, not by "social contract" but by men driven by an artist compulsion that "come like fate, without reason, consideration or pretext . . . as lightning appears, too terrible, too sudden, too convincing, too 'different' even to be hated."[3] Empirical scientists and historians embody the highest ideals of modern culture. Representing in its in fact purest form a metaphysico-religious faith thousands of years old—the faith of Plato which is also the Christian faith: that the truth is divine[4]—they wear the masks of unbelievers, atheists. They already prefigure the uncanny ideal of the integral nihilist, ideal type in whom all ideals are immolated.

Nietzsche's work means to proclaim the overman—the one worthy to be master of the earth, innocence and new beginning, the tempter and attempter,[5] that tries the experiment whether it is possible to live, to *embody*, the truth.[6] What is the relationship between this figure of integral affirmation and the history of master morality, which issues in fact in the ideal type of the integral nihilist?

The usual—and metaphysical—way of explaining human phenomena in general, and the forms that life contracts in particular, is teleological; they are explained by their purposes, by the ends realized in them. By what Nietzsche calls the directing force. These ends are identified by consulting the advance representation that an efficacious form of life gives itself of its purpose, in consciousness. But Nietzsche has learned—it seemed to him "to be one of my most essential steps and advances"[7]—to distinguish the directing force, the purposes, ends, the vocations, from the driving force. Behind the form, the identity, that life contracts, there is a quantum of accumulating energy that needs to be discharged. This force is not assembled or aspired by the telos; it first exists of itself as a nonintentional intensity, a chaos of force asserting itself, the excess life in matter is the compulsion to produce. The goal that fixes the direction it takes befalls it as an accident, serving as a match for its release. Ends and vocations are relatively random, arbitrary, almost indifferent in relation to the quantum of energy that presses to be used up somehow.

But, secondly, the Nietzschean discernment distinguishes between the directing force itself and its representation in consciousness. The representation is chosen for its beauty, and not for its truth. The representation of the telos does not determine the directing force; it is in fact a "beautifying pretext, a self-deception of vanity."[8] The personage is a mask, the vocation a masquerade, which the driving forces of the thus adorned life themselves believe in and indeed have to believe in.

Nietzsche's historical list counts women among vocations. In woman as an ideal there is an ingredient of asceticism and self-denial, "a touch of *morbidezza* added to fair flesh, the angelic look of a plump, pretty animal."[9] If consciousness were consulted as to the telos of femininity, one would be informed that woman's role is for the sake of the reproduction of the race, and for men, that feminine characteristics are contracted in view of women's vocation to be breeders and to be objects of sexual gratification. These ends are taken to require the asceticism. But the Nietzschean method prescribes that we first set aside this representation of the telos as a pretext and a piece of self-delusion. We should have to pass around this form, this appearance, and even the true direction it masks, to determine the driving force in it. We should have to get a *feeling* for that force, for its active or reactive structure and its affirmative or negative, sovereign or servile, quality. We would sense a will structured as a will to asceticism.[10] We should have to get a feeling for an original chaos of lubricious forces, the natural polyamorphous perversity, out of which there arises the formative female compulsion to castrate all that is phallic in oneself. This becoming feminine, this simplification, is experienced as an achievement, a triumph, and a pleasure. The femininity that is paraded is chosen for its dissembling artifices. "What makes up feminine charm and feminine beauty," wrote Baudelaire, whom Nietzsche copied into his notebook, is "that blasé look, that bored look, the vaporous, evaporated look, that impudent look, that cold look, that look of looking inward, that look of domination, the voluptuous look, that wicked look, that sick look, that catlike look, infantile look, nonchalance and malice compounded."[11] Those who are good at it are those who can believe it.

The difficult, the really Nietzschean, problem concerns the driving forces and their power or impotence to will themselves. Here the genealogist is neither observing forms and representations nor interpreting them. His discernment is essentially passionate; it is necessary to have something like a feeling for the forces in the representations. It is necessary to let oneself be affected, moved, troubled by the structure and quality of the field of exultant and malignant feeling life dissembles with its ideals. One has to be able to sense the pervert behind the female, to feel the force of that compulsive polyamorphous perversity behind the will to self-castration which takes the form of woman.[12]

What is confounding is that all the ideal types of human existence Nietzsche lists, from artists to philosophers to scientists, mask an ascetic will. All these types have been formed by a release of compulsions to bar certain forces in the chaotic fund of primal life. None of them is utterly affirmative and self-affirmative; each is determinate by virtue of a mortifying compulsion. Yet Nietzsche's typology has listed only the ideals that have dominated the successive epochs of culture; they are formations of power, the highest ideals men have been able to form, forms of dominance. The study hardly mentions all the millions that have no ideal at all, no real form of their own, those whose lives can be but a means for lives capable of setting themselves up as an ideal. Nietzsche discusses only the lives in which the life-negating compulsion takes form, represents an ideal, forms itself into a distinct figure of sovereignty.

To discover the perverse *logique du pire* by which the will to mastery engenders ideals in a progression in degeneration, we have to understand the procedures employed in the Nietzschean genealogy of culture. Each new form of power is vulnerable as it emerges and has to mask itself in order to survive—and needs faith not in itself but in its masquerade, which must persuade by its charm. But, more deeply, acts truly sovereign—"actions of love and extravagant generosity"[13]—exist only as self-expropriation and could not exist in a closed and controlled adequation of exterior apparition to inward force. Thus, unlike Leo Strauss, whose hermeneutics consists in exposing the esoteric convictions of the philosophers under the exoteric forms in which they are dissimulated, Nietzsche discovers that there is no philosophical sincerity and authenticity, that the philosophical form of life is constituted not in an oracular Know thyself or in the lucidity of the Cogito but in the belief in its own dissimulations.[14] Artists, philosophers, priests, scientists, historians—each is shown to be possible only through self-misinterpretation.

The second principle of the Nietzschean hermeneutics is stranger yet. Each type is shown to wear the mask not of a prior form but of a succeeding form. The representation is a true creation. The disguise does not presuppose, derive from, a sincerity. There was not first a veracity, a face, a form of life that coincides with itself, that then degenerates into dissimulation and mere appearance. But the representation is also not an advance presentation of a form that will be realized and a means in consciousness for that realization. It is not the necessity of determining an intention by an end that engenders ideals. It is rather the necessity that an emergent nexus of force gives a fresh interpretation, that is, subdue and dominate, even the force of the representation with which it disguises itself.[15]

Nietzsche will then show that the ideal representation with which each successive form of life masks itself is in reality a figure of less power, greater self-negation, than the instinctual figure dissimulated by it. The forces that engender the succession of ideal types are profoundly—and increasingly—self-negating, ascetic. They contend under more and more complex dissimulations that dissimulate their quality less and less. In the integral nihilist, ideal in which all ideals are sacrificed, an inability to dissimulate oneself further makes its appearance.

This logic of dissimulation only concerns the directive forces of life and their ideal representations. It is intended by Nietzsche to prepare for an exposition of a wholly different type—a physics of the driving forces. For it the question is: what does the ascetic will mean on the level of the driving forces of life?

The first cultivated form of man, the founders of human culture, are *artists*. The first—and the supreme—form of art is that worked with the most precious clay and oil, our own flesh and blood. No one is more easily corrupted than artists. "They have at all times been valets of some morality, philosophy, or religion, quite apart from the fact that they have unfortunately often been all-too-pliable courtiers of their own followers and patrons, and cunning flatterers of ancient or newly arrived powers."[16] When they are weak they wear the disguise of auxiliaries of rulers, economic powers, populace. But when they are strong they wear the mask of philosophers. The gratuity of their will to create is dissembled as augury. The prime example of the time is Richard Wagner, masquerading as a *maître à penser,* whose music in its technical innovations and essentially dramatic composition is possible only as the lyrical demonstration of Schopenhauerian metaphysics.

Philosophers are depicted by Nietzsche under maternal images and not images of intellectual expertise; a philosopher is not a guarantor of the conceptual foundations of the polis and its sciences but a conceiver of a new form of life. His visionary forces are not destined to resolve the crises in mental systems; to Nietzsche the conceiving force in a philosophy and not the conceptual forms is the essential. The position of one established in the self-certainty of the Cogito as in the first axiom of knowledge does not define the philosopher but masks him most completely. For a philosopher "is a human being who constantly experiences, sees, hears, suspects, hopes, and dreams extraordinary things; who is struck by his own thoughts as from outside, as from above and below, as by *his* type of experiences and lightning bolts; who is perhaps himself a storm pregnant with new lightnings."[17]

Philosophers first came into existence representing a form of life solitary, sterile, and destitute. In presocratic Greece as in India they built for themselves notoriety as terrible ascetics. They were thus seen as otherworldly, being in touch with supernatural powers, having divine or demonic insight into another reality. In fact the intellect apt for efficacity in knowledge, Nietzsche loves to show, has to be constituted out of deterritorializing, detribalizing, desacralizing, and desecrating instincts.[18] The ruthless power these men used over their own lives did not separate them from the mundane sphere but from the secular rabble. The people regarded these sage-magi with awe and fear—and left them alone.[19]

But there is also another asceticism—in the philosophical driving force itself; philosophers live lives uninvested, humble, and continent. This is not a matter of morality, the disposition of being a sacrificial animal. Sages are not interested in becoming useful to the community, the herd. The philosophical poverty, humility, and chastity express on the contrary the philosopher's contempt for the herd riches of investment, reputation, and domesticity. They express the will to make of one's habitat a desert—the lion will to be master in one's own desert.

The compulsion to withdraw becomes the driving force of the one consecrated, sacred. Among *saints* Nietzsche lists Lao-Tse, the Buddha, Sankya, Epicurus, and Jesus. Physiologically the saint is a hypersensitive, gifted with intense sensations of cosmos and microcosmos—as well as a hypersusceptibility to pain. Through instinctual exclusion of all antipathy, all hostility, all boundaries or divisions in man's feelings—an exclusion dictated by the pain produced in him by all resistance—the saint achieves a state of unrestricted Yes-saying, unlimited affirmation, love for the universe. (Such is Jesus riding into Jerusalem on an ass—the ass that always says Yes-Yuh, worshipped in the fourth book of *Zarathustra* by the higher men who are unable to achieve the Zarathustran affirmation, that which affirms even all boundaries, resistances, emnities, pain, and death.) The sainted love universal in scope is capable of turning every event into an occasion of immediate beatitude.

But the saint is masked—not only by a willfully misinterpreting milieu but by virtue of an intrinsic necessity[20]—as redeemer. The saint embodies "the deep instinct for how one must *live*, in order to feel oneself 'in heaven,' to feel 'eternal' "[21]; he is masked as a public mediator between the profane multitudes and the sacred—as priest. His visible, scandalous death, his corpse, will conceal his invisible diagram of life. His whole existence in a political order is seditious, and Jesus died for his own guilt ("That holy anarchist who summoned the people at the bottom, the outcasts and 'sinners,' the chandalas within Judaism, to opposition against the dominant order—using language, if the Gospels were to be trusted, which would lead to Siberia today too. . . ."[22]), but he was taken to have died for the guilt of others. The ignominious glory of his death before multitudes, which, inasmuch as it is assented to, affirms and demonstrates the forces of sacred inwardness, becomes a priestly intercession for multitudes. This death leads the multitudes to guilt, to the four sacred truths according to which their worldly existence is pain. His priesthood is his *barbarian* exegesis of his life.[23] Whereas the saint's way of life, for himself, is a way to live a heaven within, it represents itself to others as led in order to shepherd others into a heaven beyond themselves and beyond life; whereas it was produced for him as immediate inward bliss, it gives itself out as a means for producing in others a sense of being in need of redemption, being dependent, being guilty.

The *priest* comes to proclaim asceticism, the disposition of a sacrificial animal, as the supreme ideal, for everyone. Yet he himself is "will to power intact," prodigious artist who works with the human material composed of the masses of the weak and the suffering, with the malignant and explosive force of their sickness, this resentment. In his intact will to power rancor becomes creative. Creative of inverse, reactive values, of the servile morality built on the sense of evil.

The priest comes to the mass of the exhausted, those in whom the feeling of life is resentful, as their shepherd, to make them into a herd, giving them ideals made to their own measure, their own institutions, their church. Allegedly to protect them. But in reality, like all movements of concentration of the sick, this shepherding intensifies and spreads the contagion.

For the strong, the priest does the very best thing one can do for them: in setting up culture as the field of battle between the gregarious and the singular ones, he brings about the great division within the species. Gregarity itself devalues; baseness is produced in guilt and shame which spread through contagion. Nobility is produced in and by the pathos of distance.[24]

The priest comes to the sick as their physician and healer. His remedies are homeopathic; they consist in desensibilization, reduction of the feeling of life to its lowest point, sleep. Eternal rest. The feeling of power through the practice of mutual commiseration and comforting. Compensation for individual impotence with a feeling of communal power—organization, the work the herd does on itself. Good works, routine work, mechanization of the impulses, blindly raging industriousness. And especially the orgiastic release of feelings, feelings of anger, fear, voluptuousness, revenge, hope, triumph, despair, cruelty, and above all aggression, which interprets suffering as feelings of shame, fear, and punishment, and drives the machinery of self-torment, guilt-consciousness. All this functions to make the sick sicker, it locks the contaminated soul in a prison of self-contempt and reactive aggression. It gives an all-encompassing and unitary direction to the sick will, makes it into a longing for will-lessness.

With this means the multitudes will become ever more impotent and sterile; the constantly accumulating energies of rancor, which have to be detonated so that they not disintegrate the species, will be directed to willing willessness, death, in the species man. This is the expedient life invented so as to make sure that the future does not, cannot, come from this stock; even though ever more reproductive, they are the "last men." The way life does so is that it thus makes sure that *nothing* will issue from them.[25] They want nothing, will nothingness. For "we may not even suppose that the instinct of life contemplates or intends any sort of cure."[26]

But this mask of shepherd and healer, that is, of master of culture and master of nature—what else is it but the advance representation of *historian* and *scientist*, fixed as the highest ideals, the most valued life-types of *our* culture? The priest put himself forth as creator of institutions and values, founder of the only meaning suffering life was offered so far,[27] elaborator of the most thoroughly-thought-through system of interpretation, a closed system of will which in fact has no match and no rival.[28] But for us the historian, who by suspending value-commitment and transforming all cultural feats into facts rejects and combats none of them and appropriates all of them, is the true master of culture. As the natural scientist, elaborator of the "genuine philosophy of reality," is for us the true healer, the accomplished Socratic man, true corrector of nature. Objective scholarship, observation, and experiment are not only cognitive methods; they determine a form of life. Scientists, "the conscientious in spirit," those hard, severe, abstinent, heroic spirits insistent on intellectual cleanliness at any price, who constitute the honor of our age, in whom intellectual conscience is incarnate,[29] represent an ideal form of life, a form of life determined by ideals.

When we ask about the determinative force of this life and consult its own representation of its telos, we find it represents itself as directed toward elaborating a true representation of the universe of nature and of culture. For Nietzsche this representation is decisively characterized neither by the scrupulosity of its observation nor by its mathematical expression but rather by its refusal to admit any values.[30] What defines the modern objective representation of the universe is that in it nothing is defined by worth; it is a representation even divested of color, tone, melody, of the "secondary qualities"—of all that could give sensuality pleasure.

And man is himself represented according to these same methods; there is a will to reduce man to "pure passive, automatic, reflexive, molecular processes"[31] which is intrinsic to science. "Has not man's determination to belittle himself developed apace precisely since Copernicus? Alas, his belief that he was unique and irreplaceable in the hierarchy of being has been shattered for good; he has become an animal, quite literally and without reservations; he who, according to his earlier belief, had been almost God ('child of God,' 'God's own image')."[32]

The construction of a value-free objective representation of the universe is seen to require "the affects grown cool, the tempo of life slowed down, dialectics in place of instinct, seriousness imprinted on faces and gestures."[33] It is in his intellect, in his intellectual cleanliness at any price, that asceticism takes root in the scientific man. Whereas the intimate, intense and full knowledge, the seeing that alone is seeing *something*, is ardent and libidinal—"the *more* affects we allow to speak about one thing, the *more* eyes, different eyes, we use to observe one thing, the more complete will our 'concept' of this thing, our 'objectivity,' be"[34]—the objective reason set up in science is produced by a castration.[35]

But for Nietzsche this will to castrate is primary and constitutive; it is not to be explained by the end for which it would be the means. It is its own end; like every cruelty, it is immediately pleasure. The immediate conversion of life's own pain into pleasure is the strange production which now reveals the driving and not only the directing forces to the Nietzschean discernment. Far from the needs and the happiness of life determining the form of the scientific will, the scientific will is the sublimated form of asceticism. It is realized in the production of a representation of the universe stripped of all volition of its own and of every value susceptible of exciting the dreams and intoxications of life, a lunar universe immaculately perceived, which the ardor of life cannot embrace, which life cannot even inhabit. This immaculate perception of ascetic science Nietzsche contrasts with, and takes to be derivative of, lecherous on, the solar conception of the Zarathustran gay science, all innocence and creative longing, that which rises by its own force over the world and to which the depths themselves rise of their desire, the oceanic desire with a thousand breasts, craving to be kissed and sucked by the thirst of the sun, to become air and height and a footpath of light, and itself light.[36]

In this defining value-freeness of his representation of the universe, the scientist represents himself in unconditional, honest—Schopenhauerian—atheism.[37]

But this is a mask. Science never creates values but requires a value-creating power in the service of which it could believe in itself.[38] The scientist believes in truth and does so in such a way that he makes of his life the sacrificial animal of his faith. It is for him no objection that in order to elaborate and sustain such a representation of reality, one has to extinguish the Apollonian and Dionysian compulsions of life, the very power or the vitality of life. "*All* science . . . has at present the object of dissuading man from his former respect for himself. . . . One might even say that its own pride, its own austere form of stoical ataraxy, consists in sustaining this hard-won self-contempt for man as his ultimate and most serious claim to self-respect. . . ."[39] This belief, which requires its human sacrifice, Nietzsche consequently identifies as religious. "It is still a *metaphysical faith* upon which our faith in science rests—that even we seekers after knowledge today, we godless anti-metaphysicians still take our fire, too, from the flame lit by a faith that is thousands of years old, that Christian faith which was also the faith of Plato, that truth is divine, that God is truth. . . ."[40]

The *atheist* is the one that reveres nothing; he will appear on Zarathustra's mountain as the ugliest man, the one whose refusal to esteem anything is also the inability to enhance, to exalt himself, the one in whom the ultimate scientific claim to self-respect, the pride in sustaining its hard-won self-contempt, has become a pride in great misfortune, great ugliness, great failure, which repels all belittling pity. This ugliness is also the motivation of the active nihilist; the God of pity was murdered out of an extreme limit of shame that can no longer endure a witness. Thus the atheist is not the figure of the deliverance from shame, the highest Zarathustran hope and longing, but the figure of its extreme exasperation and consequence. The atheist is produced not as the enemy of the ascetic ideal but its strictest, most spiritual formulation, not its remnant but its kernel.[41]

Is the atheist in his honest unconditionality, "esoteric through and through, with all external additions abolished,"[42] without masks as he is without a higher witness? In fact atheism clothes itself in the garb of veracity. This guise is the terminal form of Christian morality, which, through its confessional rigor, sacramentalized an ever more strict demand for truthfulness. But this final development of Christian morality produced the collapse of Christian dogma. As the figure of the most extreme abjection, the atheist is the end-product or after-image of science; as the extreme figure of the exigency for truthfulness, he is the last zealot of Christian morality, heir of Europe's longest and bravest self-overcoming. In him the progression of the degeneration in the driving forces of life is no longer covered by a progression in the fabrication of ideal forms. Old forms of life are brought back from the back wings of culture to function again as masks; the seriousness of the progressive self-overcoming of representations becomes comedy.

The atheist for whom everything is permitted as the strictest and most spiritual formulation of Christian morality! Is the atheist then the comedian of ideals whom Nietzsche announces as the only kind of real enemy of the will to nothingness, which until this day has alone been able to offer meaning to life suffering over the meaninglessness of its suffering? Or does not rather the atheist, who negates all ideals out of his honest unconditionality, find himself one who no longer can know why he lives and why he believes in truth? Is he not one who can no longer live without raising this question, the one in whom life becomes for the first time for itself through and through questionable? Schopenhauer, Nietzsche wrote, the first admitted and inexorable atheist among philosophers, was the first to formulate existence as this question mark for itself. In the rigorous integrity of his thought, unconditional and honest atheism is the presupposition for a question which is the final triumph of the European conscience; it is an event after which this question was so certainly to be expected that "an astronomer of the soul could have calculated the very day and hour for it"—the question *"Has existence any meaning at all?"*[43] The atheist is the prefigurement of this question—this calamity and this terror.[44]

The atheist question summons the *active nihilist*—"uncanniest of all guests, that now stands at the door of European culture." In the light of his lantern the God who is dead is shown to be the God that was death. Can nihilist action be anything else but the will's ill will against itself and against the cosmic becoming in which nothing abides? Shall it not issue in European culture not imperial and dominating but vindictive, the unbridled will to debase life and to wrathfully wreak vengeance on all transience?

The genealogy of ideal types goes countercurrent to the phenomenology of the ideal forms of spirit. There is indeed a logic governing the succession of ideal forms in cultural history, but these forms do not represent ever more synthesized and ever truer exhibitions of the ruling finalities of the spirit. Each figure is indeed an advance representation of the directing force of a form of life but one functioning to dissimulate, rather than to reveal, that life. Nietzsche does not view the saintly form of life as a means pursued in order to obtain salvation and bliss beyond this life, and he does not view the scientific form of life as a means adopted in order to obtain the greatest happiness for the greatest number on the planet in this life—nor does he regard these as harsh means elaborated by the cunning of reason for the establishment of the rigorous truth. He regards each of these as the masquerade a powerful compulsion of life has created in order to cover over its own deep need to discharge its excesses, a need which it could not integrally affirm. Nietzsche has uncovered the format and the quality of that driving force; he has felt its ascetic, self-negating movement, he has detected the will's ill will against itself and the unreconciliation of life to its own transience that are paraded in the pageantry of ideals. It is then false to imagine that Nietzsche has nothing to advance but the ancient ideal of classicism and the Renaissance, constructed by synthetic integration of these different ideal types—Socrates who would practice music, Caesar with the soul of Jesus, philosopher-king and philosopher-physician, philosopher-artist. For the child yet to be conceived, the utterly integral and sacred Yes, is not to be fabricated by putting together these diverse forms of negativity.

And yet these ideal ends are not just so many false starts and deadened ends;

there is an obscure relationship between the succession of these moribund figures and the child to come. "It will be immediately obvious that such a self-contradiction as the ascetic appears to represent, 'life *against* life,' is physiologically considered and not merely psychologically, a simple absurdity. It can only be *apparent. . . .* [*T*]*he ascetic ideal springs from the protective instinct of a degenerating life* which tries by all means to sustain itself and to fight for its existence; it indicates a partial physiological obstruction and exhaustion against which the deepest instincts of life, which have remained intact, continually struggle with new expedients and devices. . . . [T]his ascetic priest, this apparent enemy of life, this *denier*—precisely he is among the greatest *conserving* and yes-creating forces of life."[45]

"The No he says to life brings to light, as if by magic, an abundance of tender Yeses; even when he *wounds* himself, this master of destruction, of self-destruction—the very wound itself afterward compels him *to live*—"[46] The explanation sounds, in its "as if by magic," dialectical; yet dialectical exposition is teleological, and Nietzsche's genealogy, where what is to be born is a telos-less reiteration of the present of life, does not repeat dialectics. The final pages of his history explain how the struggle against death has been shown to be a struggle against disgust with life, against exhaustion—against the meaninglessness of suffering. A form of life produced by asceticism, by castration, is represented as ideal, as the advance fixation of the direction of life. In the succession of these ideal representations Nietzsche has seen a will to get away from all appearance, change, becoming, death, wishing, from longing itself; this will prolongs itself in the creation of an ideal objectivity. The inability to will progressively converts into a will for nothingness; the constitution of ideals is the means for this conversion. In them agonizes not a conserving will to life but a will to represent this species as unwillable and unviable. The will to be something, to be someone, to make sense, to assume a destiny—this will, whose successive figures decide the epochs of culture, is found by Nietzsche to cover over nothingness negating in the driving instincts of life. Yet at the limit of this conversion, when all the expedients and devices are exhausted, when the pain is most inward, most guilty, Nietzsche announces a second conversion, or rather the mutation that produces a higher species.

Of all the ideal types human culture has so far invented, Nietzsche finds that in not one has there been devised a way for man to affirm his own nature. It is as though the total man is impossible, as though an ideal was only able to be devised at the cost of some mortification, some deadening, a turning of some of life's forces against life. All the ideal forms of life are a work of cruelty; it is as though what nature is doing in human nature is vivisection, done with eyes closed and without insight, in order to realize a dream it has and that no man has, the dream of another species. Each ideal, devised to save the will by giving meaning to suffering, is a new form of affliction, a "deeper, more inward, more poisonous, more life-destructive suffering."[47] The most positive interpretation of pain—and of this pain—is to cast it as the travail of a pregnancy. All the highest types culture has conceived as forms in which life is in some way in agony, tearing at itself . . . to give birth one day to a higher form of life, one which would be unrestrictedly affirmative, a child that "is innocence and forgetting, a new beginning, a game, a self-propelled wheel, a first movement, a sacred Yes."[48]

The child to come is not conceived by the cultural travail of producing representations of ideals; it is a child of nature. Of nature in our nature—of the Apollonian, visionary, and Dionysian compulsions in our nature. Compulsions, that is, to energize all our movements in a nonteleological dance. And to excite this dance with the Apollonian consecration.

This Apollonian drive is something essentially different from the production of ideals in ethical culture. In the representations of ideal types the species man is affirmed; from artist masked as sage to scientist masked as servant of truth at any cost man has idealized his serviceability, his subordination to the species. In the final image of culture, that of the integral nihilist, the most purely species man is represented, waiting his orders from anywhere and nowhere. The Nietzschean cause is not on the level of the direction to be given to the human species—the goal to be yoked on the species man.[49] The Nietzschean operation will not consist in afflicting man with a representation of himself as seat of responsibility and creative of order. The subject as substrate of acts and states, the ego as identity to which acts of cognitive syntheses are to be ascribed as to their cause or origin, Nietzsche declares a grammatical fiction. The will to responsibility which sustains it is itself induced by an essentially penal, vindictive will to accuse. The figure of master in Nietzsche then cannot be conceived in terms of a subject of responsibility as cause, source, origin, substrate, or identifying identity. The sovereign structure does not lie in any figure of being—subsistent identity—that could be represented in consciousness. It is not a question of fixing the human essence—that is, fixing a determination of the form in consciousness which would be the direction, sense, essence, end, *ens*. If the Nietzschean science is not a science of what man is but of what he can become, its task is not one of representation—that is, fixing the representation of the directing force in consciousness.

The operation that produces the mutation into the overman must affect the quality of the driving forces of life. This mutation does not consist in their preservation, integration, or hierarchization. It would consist in their unrestricted affirmation. Affirmation of forces which are not teleological and intentional but impulsive, pure intensifications of power which seek to discharge themselves. Affirmation of forces that are not compossible, do not form a coherence, an essential integrity, but a chaos. The operation to be performed on human nature is not to be conceived as a finalization of that nature upon an ideal but rather as a naturalization of our nature, an integration of our nature into nature.

2. The Imperative Force of Pure Nature

Nietzsche's work is essentially marked by the conviction that nature is—now—about to be discovered. The negative condition for this discovery is a reduction of the moral and aesthetic structure of our interpretation of nature, through the complete critique of the concept of causality, efficient and final. The critique of the concept of causality will have to be extended to pain, which will no longer be interpretable as the effect of designatable acts, of the essentially guilty attachment to the terrestrial, the transitory—to what passes away because it deserves to pass away.[50] The universe is not a penal apparatus. The critique of the concept of teleology forces us to concede that the universe "is neither perfect nor beautiful, nor noble, nor does it wish to become any of these things . . ."[51] But also the concepts of law, purpose, order, arrangement, form, beauty, wisdom, and the models of organism or machine in which they fit, are to be reduced; with them nature has been idealized—divinized. For us the discovery of nature will have to proceed through demoralization, de-aestheticization, de-deification.

Positively, nature is disclosed in the modern physics of force, its essence in the most scientific thought—the concept of eternal return. The conception of infinite force, a force that would bear against nothing, is self-contradictory; a universe of forces, however immense, is finite. Only the time in which modern science situates the universe is infinite. The universe is observably in a state of becoming. But if ever it has a goal, if it could reach an equilibrium, that state would have already been reached—since it has already had an infinite time to reach it. Consequently, no such goal is possible. The universe, having played out all its cards, having gone through all its possible combinations, can only recommence.

This doctrine, already known, already woven into the structure of all modern scientific knowledge, is yet to arrive into our lives. Another doctrine—that of being, of the logic of being—has proven necessary in order that this species survive. With a logic of identity and non-contradiction and an ontology of being, goals, final states, ends, were conceivable, and intentional life, action, was possible. The doctrine of eternal return, formulating the dissolution of all forms of identity and essentiality, declares the fundamental logico-ontological axioms to be errors.

"Duration 'in vain,' without end or aim is the most paralyzing idea. . . . Let us think this thought in its most terrible form: existence as it is, without meaning or aim, yet recurring inevitably without any finale of nothingness, '*the eternal recurrence*.' "[52] If Zarathustra is the teacher of the doctrine of eternal return, he is not the teacher of its truth; all modern learning is that, and in fact the coming formulation of this doctrine out of the development of modern science will be but its return—for this newest doctrine is also the oldest doctrine there is, found already taught wherever the first doctrines of ancient mankind were recorded. Zarathustra's mission is rather to teach how to live with this doctrine, how to bear this "heaviest burden," how to conceive not a new conceptual system but a new form of life, a new nature, capable of enduring truth.

On Zarathustra's mountain the old soothsayer formulates the ancient understanding of the doctrine as condemnation of all action. "All is empty, all is the same, all has been!" "Anybody coming in this height . . . would come in vain; caves he would find, and caves behind caves, hiding-places for those addicted to hiding, but no mines of happiness or treasure rooms or new gold veins of happiness. . . . But all is the same, nothing is worth while, no seeking avails, nor are there any blessed isles any more."[53] This paralyzing contemplation has its reflection in Zarathustra's own dark side; his shadow sees the repudiation of teleology as evacuation of reality and growing desert. "O eternal everywhere, O eternal nowhere, O eternal—in vain!"[54] Faced with the modern scientific representation of the universe, Kant saw the quandary of practical philosophy in the question of how free action can be possible in a universe shown to be universally and necessarily determined. But Kant assumed that what we see in sensuous objects and concepts can still lure the will. For Nietzsche the coming supreme formulation of the science of nature will make the very idea of the will first imagining goals derisory.

The thought of eternal return could only come to crush every life in which any hope, any expectation, any unrequited demand put on reality and on time yet subsisted. Only a life already favorably disposed to itself, utterly fulfilled, already sealed in its own unrestricted self-affirmation, could bear the weight of this thought, could even come to "crave for nothing more ardently than this last eternal confirmation and seal."[55] A sovereign nature is required in order to be able to endure the truth of universal nature. And an art, a sovereign art, will be required in order to be able to conform oneself with the truth.

But one need not do so. Nietzsche regards the logic of identity and non-contradiction and the metaphysics of beings, forms, or identities, which corresponds to it, as a systematic simplification and falsification operated on appearances. The result is what is called "truth"; it is rather value—anthropological value. For this simplification and falsification is what has enabled the species man to survive. There is an art, then, which is mendacious and which is shown to have been required in order that the species man prevail. Believing in entities, this man believes in ends; he lives in a world of finalities, labor, progress. But this form of life is subject existence; its impulses await from the outside—the simplified, falsified version of the outside—their complements and their sense.

The sovereign life is nowise under an imperative to survive. Nor does it act out of empirical ambition, Machiavellian quest for power, out of a fortuitous excess of solitary pride. Its action is no longer questing, demanding, intentional, desire and labor out of want. Yet the noble act is not arbitrary creation: it is necessary with a singular necessity: necessary for the singular life that makes it necessary for itself.[56] The sovereign life is under an imperative of sovereignty. Its own nature, its own nobility, is for it its law. In a nature utterly without ordinances, it is ordered imperatively by its own nature. In a universe where its existence, and the existence of each of its states and moments, is a fortuitous event among fortuitous events, it finds itself bound to *this* singular sequence.

This does not mean that it discovers itself to be the transcendental seat of order, which is actualized in ordering nature by laws. For the sovereign one is he that endures the doctrine of eternal return—that is, the knowledge that there are no legislators and no obedience but that what is necessary and fated is that each force of nature issue all its own consequences.[57] On the other hand, for Nietzsche the sovereign life is not in a transcendental sphere; what makes it sovereign is the ability to bear the weight of pure nature. The vision of all nature not surveyed from without but imaged in the form of the obsessive phantasm of eternal recurrence functions to bind one to one's own nature, a nature self-sufficient and sovereign.

For it is only when one adheres to each of one's acts and states—in their utter fortuity—with an unrestricted will, with all the will that one is, making them necessary for oneself and making oneself necessary, that one will be able to regard the nature in which they are entangled, ensnared, enamored as necessary for oneself.[58] Then the internal ordinance, which imposes necessity on each of one's states, setting it up as sovereign and perfect, is not a synthetic organization, by which the universal is affirmed in the particular, but an unrestricted and absolute affirmation of the singular. The form of this affirmation is affective, not predicative. It is a movement that adheres to the singular moment and doubles it up only in order to invest it immediately with the force of this doubling. It is joy vibrating unrestrictedly upon the singular moment. The Dionysian compulsion—production in life of an excess force which intensifies rather than extends the configurations of life—is the potentiality for this joy and this ordinance.

3. The Metaphysical Consolation of Tragedy and the Historical Sense

Such a life—such a joy—has once existed. In an age prior to historical, theoretical culture, in ritual, tragic culture. Nietzsche studied it in the presocratic, Dionysian age of Greek antiquity. His exposition is built on a radical opposition between art and science, between the theatrical, tragic culture, and the theoretical, optimist, Socratic, scientific culture which supplanted it, which was set up in order to suppress it. What is specific to Nietzsche is the line of cleavage he draws, not on the basis of the quality (or quantity) of forms which are the products of culture but on the basis of the *quality of force* out of which they issue. Of the active or reactive feeling—exultation or resentment—which a culture forms in all its systems of cognition, its political and moral institutions, its production and artwork.

The tragic age constituted a complete culture, comprising cosmology, explicative representation, ethics, social organization, production, and ritual. Its supreme form was the tragic theater. Niezsche's poetics, unlike that of Artistotle, seeks to understand tragic theater from the point of view of the actor rather than that of the spectator. In its original form it was theater without spectators, ritual and not representation of reality or of idealities. It aimed not at theological, political, or psychological pedagogy, but at an experience of transfiguration.

An actor's pleasure and power are that of creating a presence where each word and nonsensical utterance, each tonality of voice and each breath, each configuration and contingency of his physical appearance takes on significance, where the succession of movements takes on the necessity of fate, the shape of a destiny. Identities, personages, destinies issue out of the dissolution of the civic and utilitarian personality brought about in the lubricious excesses and out of the visionary, Apollonian compulsion excited by the rhythmic and melodic frenzy. The actor projects himself ecstatically wholly into these appearances. With artist pleasure, pleasure of creation! He is not saddened when these phantasms are led to their sublime deaths on the brink of dawn, for he feels himself undiminished by their deaths, knowing himself capable of producing them anew, feeling a force of life capable of producing and destroying innumerable forms of life. Such joy is the "metaphysical consolation" the tragic ritual produces—consolation for our grief, finally for our mortality. For here the sense of the end of a life-form, of a destiny, is not wretchedness and desolation, for the exultation centers the sentiment in the fund of life-force that is undiminished by that end. Only in living in that subterranean level is it possible to overcome the misery of sensing every life-form, every form of being, destined to be destroyed by the tide of universal Becoming.

And this joy is true! This theatrical exhilaration, this most superficial pleasure, that of the most superficial man, who is himself nobody, who represents everybody and anybody, in fact communicates with the ontological pleasure of the universe, whose force continually creates forms of being, and is contented, exhausted in that creation, but does not will any of them to survive—I believe the old Teutonic saying, Nietzsche in his adolescence wrote, all the gods must die.[59] The Dionysian ritual is a sacred experience, enlightenment, for the joy it imparts has also the ontological value of insight into the ultimate will of the eternal ontological process.

The tragic ritual has disappeared, the whole tragic culture has long since come to an end, supplanted by the historical, scientific, optimist, Socratic culture set up in order to suppress it. When, after two thousand five hundred years, out of this rational culture itself the doctrine of eternal return emerges, Nietzsche's task, the Zarathustran mission, is to find, now, in the midst of rational culture itself, the form of that ancient joy that might still be possible.

Theoretical culture is optimist, progressive, historical, technical: It is inhabited by the will to *correct reality*. It sets out not only to transform nature through knowledge for the service of human comfort and security but first to transform human nature through knowledge—Socrates' teaching that all evil, and hence all misfortune, is due to ignorance. But this optimism arises, in the Nietzschean explanation, not out of the results of theoretical practice (it will only be in modern times that theory will know how to massively transform external nature, and it never was true that human evil, and human misfortune, could be traced back to conscious ignorance as to its cause) but out of the immediate beatitude inherent in theory itself. The force of the theoretical attitude is its immediate joy; for it every event—portentous or inconsequential, humanly affecting or remote, an ultimate principle, final end or pure transition—is the occasion of immediate theoretical satisfaction. Nietzsche depicts Socrates as the discoverer of the theoretical gratification (happiness *is* knowledge) and depicts this gratification as strong enough to blur out all biological and political unsatisfactions. The energy released in the theoretical appropriation of the means, the intermediaries (which are without end) will prove to be stronger than the energy reserved for the attainment of biological and species ends.

On the one hand, the theoretical culture offers consolation—for our pain, finally for our mortality—in its claim to be able to correct reality through dialectical cognition. Through dialectics Socrates is able to overcome the fear of death, whence his uncanny power. On the other hand, Socrates knows the theoretical experience, knows that for the theoretical soul any event whatever is the immediate source of perfect gratification. There is a deep relationship between these two: There is something like an experience of immortality in the perfect gratification of the theoretical soul open to all the universe of being and perfectly gratified by every fortuitous event.

The later Nietzschean vision of theoretical culture as essentially vindictive, issued out of rancor, wreaking vengeance against all that is temporal, degrading and devaluing in image beforehand, in worth, all that is terrestrial, seems to be in violent contradiction with this conception. The theoretical practice shall be described as desert that grows without end and without ends, sustained by a metaphysics which judges that all that is earth, time, generation and corruption, passion, affection, corporeality, particularity, is of no value. "All that passes away deserves to pass away" is the formula of this metaphysics, of Platonism which not only instituted the axis of distinction between fact/ideal, time/eternity, space/unlimited, earth/ideality, sensation/concept, sense/intellect, body/soul, but instituted this conceptual system as a discrimination of value—metaphysics is fundamentally moral. Love is punished by the death of what it loves. But then the terrestrial sphere in its entirety is set up as a penal apparatus: All things terrestrial pass away, because they deserve to pass away, because they are without value, and every love of the terrestrial is always punished.

Nietzsche identifies the praxis that issues out of this metaphysico-moral conception as not simply dominating or exploiting but vindictive. The specifically Western practice, the scientific technology intrinsically metaphysico-moral, is not an operation to subjugate nature to sovereign human nature; it proceeds with a representation of all things which has first divested them of value, it can only transform them into realizations of this valuelessness.

The analyses of Socratism in *The Birth of Tragedy* did not contain this final interpretation of theoretical culture as intrinsically moral, penal, and vindictive. Yet Christianity is said to be only a "Platonism for the people," and the corpse of the willfully Crucified is, along with that of Socrates, but the embodied demonstration of the Platonic teaching "All things that pass away deserve to pass away." The Socratic theoretical happiness gratified by each event was not gratified by the singularity but by the universal idea or form in each event, not by the ephemeral gleam in it but by the recognition of something that does not pass with it, not by the sensuous lure in each terrestrial movement but by the recognition of the inconsistency of that lure. This happiness was at each moment a transcending of the attachment to the terrestrial, which attachment is the body. The Socratic happiness demanded at each moment, and willfully brought about at the last moment, the death of the body. But this non-reconciliation with time and with all things transitory was already resentment.

Nietzsche's judgment is not only that the theoretical practice issued out of metaphysical, moral thought is essentially vindictive, a devaluation and a devastation of the earth, but also that this culture is not a culture of man. For Nietzsche the problem of the possibility of a culture today is not that of whether the lessons of the creative epochs of culture can be recalled today. It is whether the forces of the creative ages of culture could recur today, whether the very feelings, the very dreams, from which the great cultural forms that stand issued as monuments of the festive moments of humanity, could recur in the late-born, civilized, rationalized life of today, that is, in the philistine life alone produced by our saturated, satisfied civilization.

The relationship to culture—the "historical sense"—has then for Nietzsche a structure essentially different from that in Hegel's dialectics. For Hegel culture is maintained in a comprehension that retains the meaning of the deeds that have come to pass and that are past, retains them not by simple accumulation but by comprehensive integration. Historical comprehension is systematic and dialectical, engendering the new forms of spirituality out of the integration of divergent and contradictory forms. For Nietzsche the monuments of spirituality are to be traced not to a dialectical fecundity of meaning but to forces that are not bound to meaning, not teleological—forces in a region beneath consciousness and the sphere of meanings. They are Apollonian and Dionysian compulsions, visionary or oneirotic forces, non-teleological, dance, movements. For Nietzsche to believe in the return of time in the present, the re-presentation of the past in the present, is to believe that all the possibilities, all the powers, that were once possible in humanity are still valid, in force in each individual and at each moment of history.[60] The historical sense is a moment that wants eternity, an eternity in depth and not in prolongation, that wills eternity by willing itself in all its depth, feeling itself living a life that has already been lived thousands of years ago, feeling there recur within itself all the possibilities of life that had ever been known and felt and guessed at and lived through. Feeling in the exorbitance of its feeling the possibility of dreaming once more as once they dreamt those white marble dreams of the Acropolis, those voluptuous dreams of Konarak, the possibility of dancing once more as once men knew how to dance in the Dionysian nights of antiquity, the possibility of dancing as the Shiva Nataraj dances on the ice-covered Himalayan summits, his four arms blessing and cursing, beating the drum of creation and lighting the fires of destruction.

The "historical sense"—"something altogether new and strange in history," the distinctive virtue and disease of the present age—is to produce the "most comprehensive soul." The historical sense is the highest form of our spirit; it is our participationist ritual, our orgy and our form of ecstasy. It is our means for enduring pure nature. This power is not that of the most comprehending soul, that which retains meaning from the deeds and misdeeds of history, from "the oldest, the newest, losses, hopes, conquests, and victories of humanity"; it is that of the most comprehensive soul, that in which the very griefs and the hopes, the loves and the woundings, the feeling, the very forces, recur.[61] This return is not brought about by an active memory which reproduces their meaning but by an active forgetting, which makes possible the resurgence of affects. That is, not of brute "sensations," sense data, data for sense, nor of pleasure and pain—but of laughter and tears, blessing and cursing—which are the active and powerful forms of receptivity.[62]

This field of resurgence and accumulation of affects, charged with all the strong feelings of history, Nietzsche calls humanity. It is the possibility that in the individual not the abstract form of humanity but all the affects, all the intensive forces, of all individuals recur.

The Nietzschean absolute spirit is not contemplative and stabilized in its integral articulation. It is produced not by an assembling of the meanings of all human experiences in a coherence but by the accumulation of all the feelings and forces of human prostrations and triumphs, a compacting of their contradictions. What is thus produced is a "godlike feeling," which is not blissful but ecstatic and explosive, which has in the tensions accumulated and produced in itself by virtue of these contradictions a constant source of excess energies. The action of the most godlike state of life is not a labor of negativity, an appropriative and reappropriative enterprise, whose exteriorizations are destined for reinteriorization at the end of history. The most divine form of life is equated with nature, with the sun, hub of nature, under whose compulsion Zarathustra's orbit turns. The explosive ecstasy of the most godlike feeling, "the happiness of a god full of power and love, full of tears and laughter," is "a happiness that, like the sun in the evening, continually bestows its inexhaustible riches, pouring them into the sea, feeling richest, as the sun does, only when even the poorest fisherman rows with golden oars!"[63]

4. The Comprehensive Artistry

The first characteristic of the nobles, the very meaning of the word, is truthful. The nobles are those who are capable of living by the truth. Their vital structure is such that they can affirm all that is and becomes—not only their own ideas and ideals, but all things that are and that become and that become nothing, honey and lees, drunken midnight, tombs and tomb-tears' comfort, gilded evening glow, woe, hell, hatred, disgrace, the cripple, world—"this world, oh, you know it!"[64] The condition for the possibility of such a most comprehensive soul, "which can run and stray and roam farthest within itself . . . in which all things have their sweep and countersweep and ebb and flood"[65] is not the most inordinate dialectical cleverness, which could, like divine reason, abominable spider, weave all things together in rational connections, finding or inventing a goal and purpose for each thing within the whole. "A *little* reason, to be sure, a seed of wisdom scattered from star to star—this leaven is mixed in with all things: for folly's sake, wisdom is mixed in with all things."[66] But "Gods are shrouded by their beauty; thus you—O heaven above me, pure and deep! You abyss of light!—thus you conceal your stars!"[67] "I," says Zarathustra, "have become one who blesses and says Yes; and I fought long for that and was a fighter that I might one day get my hands free to bless. But this is my blessing: to stand over every single thing as its own heaven, as its round roof, its azure bell, and eternal security; and blessed is he who blesses thus. . . . Verily, it is a blessing and not a blasphemy when I teach: 'Over all things stand the heaven Accident, the heaven Innocence, the heaven Chance, the heaven Prankishness,' . . . O heaven over me, pure and high! That is what your purity is to me now, that there is no eternal spider or spider web of reason; that you are to be a dance floor for divine accidents, that you are to be a divine table for divine dice and dice players."[68]

Zarathustra teaches a new way to "carry together into One what is fragment and riddle and dreadful accident."[69] The way of metaphysics, the way of comprehension, is to make the elements, unknowns, contingencies of the universe into one by composing into a totality, a system, their meanings. The way to affirm what is is to affirm its meaning. Metaphysical comprehension is the enterprise of exhibiting the universal meaning of the particulars, the system composed by all the fragments, the finality and necessity of all the events, the affirmation composed by all the negations, rendings and death. "Death . . . is of all things the most dreadful, and to hold fast what is dead requires the greatest strength," Hegel declared. "But the life of Spirit is not the life that shrinks from death, and keeps itself untouched by devastation, but rather the life that endures it and maintains itself in it. . . . [S]pirit is this power only by looking the negative in the face, and tarrying with it. This tarrying with the negative is the magical power that converts it into being."[70]

Nietzsche for his part does not believe in this magical power of the dialectical mind, to convert the pain, transience, and death of all things in the universe into something affirmative. His genealogy shows this magical conversion into meaning and ideality to have been in truth the systematic devaluation of transience and of all transitory things, the will's ill will against time and against all that passes away. Nietzsche does not come to teach a more clever way still to contrive meaning for all things and thus affirm them. He is seeking a mind that can affirm unconditionally, that can love, the fragmentary, the ephemeral, the transitory. This affirmation will consist not in subordinating them, through meaning, through significance, to one another and to the whole but in affirming the worth of what has no significance, in affirming as an end unto itself what does not serve another. What Nietzsche has found is an affirming of all things through affirming their value.[71] Value and meaning are no longer identical. To apprehend the value of something is not to grasp its referentiality. Value is no longer utilitarian or teleological; to affirm value absolutely is not to affirm that something is an end relatively, in view of something else, or in view of man; it is to affirm that it is an end unto itself, and not for us. "For all things have been baptized in the well of eternity and are beyond good and evil; and good and evil themselves are but intervening shadows and damp depressions and drifting clouds."[72]

Artist-metaphysics, then; it is an aesthetic and not a dialectical mind that Nietzsche finds can alone open to all things, can affirm all things. The distinction is made in Hegel. The Hegelian, metaphysical, understanding demands that all that is negative—the ugly, the transitory, the moribund—be magically converted into being, and this magic, Hegel declares, the aesthetic mind cannot perform. "Lacking strength, Beauty hates the Understanding for asking of her what it cannot do."[73] Hegel takes art—classical art—to be metaphysical; it seeks the same thing as the metaphysical understanding. The essential of the art lay in the composition, where the brute contingencies of the human anatomy come to incarnate spirituality, the colors found on the skin to visibilize character, the shapes given by chance in nature to form a significant event—where each fortuity of color, of density, of brute opaqueness, becomes expressive.

But in the dark splendor of the Dionysian rituals Nietzsche discovered another, preclassical, art. There art is participation in Dionysian force—excitant to life. The dissolution of utilitarian forms in non-signifying, musical sound and non-teleological, dance movement releases an excess force, which captures the cosmic rhythms and the cosmic pleasure. And the release of a representational power not conformed to reality, the Apollonian effulgence, works to isolate an ephemeral fragment, a phosphorescent surface, and to consecrate it with unrestricted worth the enchanted eye gives. Here art is sealing the sensuous fragment, the moment, with the worth of infinity.

For us the category of collage gives a post-classical idea of an artwork. The first thing it says is that it represents nothing and means nothing. It no longer constitutes significance as it composes materials; it sets forth, without blending or glazing, the merely found, haphazard and disproportionate forms, indecisive and murky colors, materials already in an advanced state of decay, noises, reverberations without consistency or pattern. Here the contingent, the insignificant, the ephemeral, the broken, the haphazard, is not composed but just set forth, affirmed. Salvaged, framed, protected by glass and the dehumidified temperature-constant air of museums, exhibited in public places. The artistry does not consist in giving it meaning, but in something else—giving it worth. When Breton called marvelous the chance encounter of an umbrella and a flatiron on an operating table, what delighted him was not the hitherto unnoticed relationship the encounter exhibited but the chance of the encounter between the unrelated things itself. The given non-sense no longer given sense but valued, for itself.

This would be the sort of artistry worked by the most noble soul—the most truthful.

Such a soul would itself have to be affirmative through and through. For Nietzsche connects the inability to comprehend and comprise the universe and rancor, the will's ill will against transience. The soul vast as the universe would have to be able to affirm itself absolutely, affirm all that is fragment, riddle and dreadful accident in itself, affirm all its impulsive nature, all that arises and dies away, discharges, in itself. It would have to not regret or feel remorse or despise any will in itself or anything it has ever willed, not feel discontent with any present will nor long for any will to come. Such a mind is no longer a portentous power of negativity but wholly self-affirmation. "This ultimate, most joyous, most wantonly extravagant Yes to life represents not only the highest insight but also the deepest."[74]

5. The Inner Circle

The soul affirms all of itself not by a grasping of its universal form in which each of its moments would be comprised in advance but in an unrestricted attachment to the now of its presence. This attachment by which it holds on to itself wholly, holds itself together, is not cognitive but affective: It is joy.

The law of the circle, the eternal return, is its ownmost thought, a thought that arises out of its own nature, the emblem of its own structure, of its joy. For the perfect joy wills eternity, the deep, deep eternity, eternity in depth and not in prolongation, eternal recurrence and not eternal endurance.

Joy wills infinitely this moment, just as it is, a moment, already passing, wills its passing—to the point of willing its return and passage innumerable times. Joy is a will for the now such that the now is not viewed as compensation for the moment past, a will that has no ill will against the past, that wills it still, without remorse or regret, wills still all it has ever willed. Joy is a will that has no ill will against the future, that wills it already, without anticipation or apprehensiveness, wills already all it can ever will, including its own dying. Each will past recurs already in the will of the present moment, and each will to come, in coming, returns, for it is willed already. "Have you ever said Yes to a single Joy?

O my friends, then you said Yes too to *all* woe. All things are entangled, ensnared, enamored; if ever you wanted one thing twice, if ever you said, 'You please me, happiness! Abide, moment!' then you wanted *all* back. All anew, all eternally, all entangled, ensnared, enamored—oh, then you *loved* the world. . . . All joy wants the eternity of all things, wants honey, wants lees, wants drunken midnight, wants tombs, wants tomb-tears' comfort, wants gilden evening glow. *What* does joy not want? It is thirstier, more cordial, hungrier, more terrible, more secret than all woe; it wants *itself,* it bites into itself, the ring's will strives in it; it wants love, it wants hatred, it is overrich, gives, throws away, begs that one might take it, thanks the taker, it would like to be hated; so rich is joy that it thirsts for woe, for hell, for hatred, for disgrace, for the cripple, for *world*—this world, oh, you know it!"[75]

Dionysian joy is exultant, expansive force and a power that holds itself together, a force by which a life holds itself together. This possession or appropriation of itself, by which it is a self, a singular individual, must not be conceived as a view upon the whole circle of its metamorphoses, an integral or integrating grasp of the diversity of moments through their common meaning, destiny or law. Joy knows itself inscribed on the infinite cycles of Becoming, knows its infinite repercussion on all the cycles of the universe, but does not view this circle or comprehend it, in the sense that diverse events of physical nature are comprehended through their common formula, or in the sense that the moments of a life are comprehended through the understanding that understands the destiny they realize. The Dionysian soul knows that it will die, that it has already lived innumerable lives and died innumerable deaths, and each time its whole identity has died.[76] Its destiny is the succession of identities which are engendered and brought to their conclusion, not by a force subsisting in itself, a depth ego, but by the entire force of the universe. The sole form in which all these identities, these personages, these destinies are held together is the recognition of the form "I have lived this moment already, innumerable times!" This recognition does not base itself on resemblances, it is not a recognizing suddenly something in this life that I have seen before, elsewhere—and which is therefore not *the same,* but similar. The recognition of eternal return could not have that form; for it recognizes that it is the same life, it recognizes identity. This recognition is not an induction from cases at all, from moments compared; it arises directly from within, out of the joy itself. There is in the most powerful joy the power to know the universal truth.

The thought of eternal return is the most extensive, exterior doctrine, and it is the most inward, insular and incommunicable truth, truth disclosed within, the law of the most singular will. It is a cosmic, ontological law, formulating for all that is what it means for it to be, to be in becoming. It formulates the meaning of being otherwise than does metaphysical history, which fixes being as a depth, a ground, through opposition to becoming, appearance, thought, and the ought. It is also the most scientific law, law of modern science which does not explain the sensory flux by the forms but explains the forms themselves. It formulates the essence of a universe of forces, where every force is forceful only in a field of forces and where the concept of infinite force, or force bounded but by nothingness, is impossible. It is the doctrine of the most ancient, cosmological, form of philosophy. But it is also the most modern form of philosophical doctrine, a truth in the first person singular, the law of all nature which Zarathustra discovers by withdrawing into his own nature. Even more indeclinable than the Cogito of Descartes, it is the truth of the Zarathustran will only. Not only indeclinable but selective; not only incomprehendable, unwillable, unendurable by the life that could put up with itself only by putting itself to use, confounding, paralyzing every life that is not utterly singularized, all herd life, humanity as such. Not only, like the Cartesian Cogito, valid only for me and as long as I think it, it has a validity incumbent on this sort of mind; the Zarathustran mind must believe it. The others—the human mind as such—cannot believe it and are constituted as human, all too human, by not believing it.

The thought of eternal return is not Zarathustra's ownmost thought because his intellect is the transcendental agency that constitutes it; like all philosophers' thoughts, it is not a thought fabricated by the spontaneity of subjectivity but one that strikes the subjective life from above and below, that weighs on it as the heaviest burden, that crushes it or transforms it, that sickens it with the terminal disease or heals it unto the great health. This thought befalls the singular life and functions imperatively.

It binds the life upon which it falls to each of its moments. Each of life's fragments, riddles, accidents, in their singularity, becomes imperative; their very fragmentary, incomprehendable, and contingent succession and series is necessary. Here the unconditional imperative seals the singular one in his singularity, in the singularity of each of his fragmentary, enigmatic, and contingent moments.[77] The concept of eternal return makes one's own singularity imperative. One is bound to one's own life.

The image of all nature in eternal return is the locus where the imperative is pronounced. More exactly, the phantasm. For, despite all of Nietzsche's efforts to formulate eternal return as an empirical law, it is given first as an image—an advance view of all nature, impossible to empirical observation. But it is not an objective image; it is not produced by the spontaneity of an imagination obedient to an understanding master of itself. Rather it is by being afflicted with this image that the master first becomes master. Eternal return is not comprehended, but willed, willed in a will that is unrestrictedly will, will for nothing, willing itself, joyous effulgence. One is not free not to think it. It afflicts the soul without distance. Imperative image.

6. The Most Powerful Moment

How reconcile the will to power and the doctrine of eternal return? The will to ever more force, to the accumulation of force[78] and the love of the world just as it is, the shouting *da capo!*[79] The overcoming of the human all too human, and the nauseated Zarathustran realization that the little man returns—the little man in oneself. . . ? That eternal return comes to say it is this very life, as you have lived it, each deed in the same series and sequence, that you will have to live again, and innumerable times—and the transformation that this very doctrine will effect, just by falling upon a moment of life? Does not this teaching itself, effacing everywhere all teleology, yoke every state and power of man to the goal of overman? The only resolution to these antinomies must consist in a strict formulation of the act that would still be power, after the revelation of the eternal return.

Such action is not to be conceived as labor, as a movement of negativity, arising out of lack or want in the agent and out of a negative appraisal of what is and becomes, and an affirming of an ideal beyond the real. "Art and nothing but art! . . . Art as the *redemption of the man of knowledge*—of those who see the terrifying and questionable character of existence, who want to see it, the men of tragic knowledge. Art as the *redemption of the man of action*—of those who not only see the terrifying and questionable character of existence but live it, want to live it, the tragic-warlike man, the hero. Art as the *redemption of the sufferer*— as the way to states in which suffering is willed, transfigured, deified, where suffering is a form of great delight."[80]

But how is the work of art to be conceived? As Apollonian artistry, which Nietzsche understands as a fragmenting, an individuating, an isolating of the contingent and enigmatic moment of the world and giving it the worth of eternity. The artistry does not consist in creation of being or of value out of nothingness or out of subjectivity, but in putting in perspective, simplifying and making cohesive, the work of "grand style."[81] This act declares each time: Rather than trying to see the universal, look only at this color, this contour, what is captured within this frame! Look long, look again, save this vision for generations to come! The light which the Apollonian artistry pours upon the phenomenal fragment, the surface, is the light of this infinite free time, this infinite free space. The formula for eternal return—to give the moment the worth of eternity—is first the formula for the Apollonian artistry.

And the work of art is to be conceived as Dionysian artistry—joining non-teleologically in the movement of the universe, with movements such that each step is an absolute in itself, a value in itself. " 'O Zarathustra,' the animals said, 'to those who think as we do, all things themselves are dancing. They come, offer their hands, they laugh, and part—and return! . . . The center is everywhere. Bent is the path of eternity.' "[82]

The sovereign action on the world has to be conceived as consecration— putting the azure bell of blessing over each thing. It is not to be conceived as transformation—into material and equipment subservient to human wants. It is not to be conceived as humanization or spiritualization of nature. It is not to be conceived as appropriation. Not even as that appropriation, the Heideggerian *Ereignis*, by which the terrestrial, the celestial, the divinities and the mortals, each comes into its own—contract identity, structure, essence, being. It is not even to be conceived as the Heideggerian care, force added so that what grows of itself may flourish and what does not grow of itself may rise. It is to be conceived as expropriation and ecstasy, natural artistry, that of the sun which as it sinks to the earth squanders its gold on the seas and feels happiest when even the poorest fisherman, the one that can repay nothing, rows with golden oars.[83]

And what of the overcoming that occurs in the soul of the one who has the force to bear the weight of the teaching of eternal return? This must likewise be conceived as an Apollonian and Dionysian work, artistry that works on the most precious clay and oil, flesh and blood. Sovereignty does not consist in subjugating universal nature for one's own needs; it is to exist without want in oneself, already superabundant and blissful from the pure fact, the pure chance, of being alive. It is not realized in seeking recognition from a consciousness exterior to oneself—for the Nietzschean master knows his own mastery from within, in the inner feeling of his superabundant force. It does not consist in an appropriation of all one's moments and phases, in an action of self-appropriation which would counteract the passage of time, negate one's own temporality. It does not consist in being present to oneself, re-presenting what passes of oneself, and articulating in advance the presentation of oneself—the appropriation and self-possession worked by consciousness. When Zarathustra learns, from within and from without, of his mission to be the teacher of eternal return, he withdraws into himself, not in an act of self-consciousness, but in an act of self-consecration.[84] The inner enhancement, exaltation of force by force, has to be conceived as an Apollonian consecration of each fragment, riddle, and dreadful accident within oneself, stamping each with the worth of infinity.[85] And it consists in moving with non-teleological, dance movements, where each step is its own goal and fulfillment, Dionysian art, which also knows the deep eternity and the deep joy, that of creating and destroying innumerable moments, fragmentary identities,[86] contingent destinies, singular enigmas.

7. The Experiment of Living with Truth

Nietzsche—but already the first Eleatic and Asian philosophers—regards the logical axioms of identity, non-contradiction, and excluded middle and the ontological principles of ultimate and subsistent beings, identities, presence, upon which propositional truth is rendered possible, to be simplifications, falsifications. These are basic errors, which have made it possible for the species to survive—and which have made men into species beings, herd animals. The logic of identity and non-contradiction and the metaphysics of substance and abiding presence posited to ground it and the sciences built on that logic and that metaphysics have only anthropological significance. They constitute the falsification, the artifice—the art—that made species man possible. These species-preserving errors have been incorporated: Our sense organs sense as the same what is only similar and as enduring what is incessant becoming, as fixed forms what is the recurrence of an incessant passage of force. That this evidence of the senses is mendacity and artifice was recognized at the beginning of history, but the Eleatics themselves were able only to misconstrue their own reality in terms of these same errors in order to denounce them in external reality. For long generations the species order was not able to tolerate any divergence from the species-preserving errors. The truth could not be said; language itself incorporates the "genius of the species." Even all the terms to formulate the speaker's own reality are common terms—herd signals—formulating lacks, wants, needs, negativities, which signal the speaker to himself and to the others as dependent, as servile.[87]

But now, after many millennia in which evil, anti-social, corrosive, doubting, aggressive instincts have learned how to subsist and thrive, many generations have learned to exist in this battle. It has been learned that conflicting and warring theorems can be drawn from the same set of fundamental incorporated errors and that one can survive with either set of alternative theorems. The time has come when it has become possible to ask whether it would not be possible to survive with the truth. Whether the truth can bear incorporation.

Yet art alone can make truth endurable. The truth of pure nature was possible only in a culture that invented the participationist transfigurations of Dionysian art, an art worked on the artist himself. If, for our age, the historical sense is the means which produces the "most comprehensive soul," that which can embrace the truth of nature, the oldest and newest truth which returns this time out of the supreme elaborations of logico-metaphysical science itself, this is so because the historical sense is conceived by Nietzsche as participationist ritual and our form of Orphic enlightenment.

But Nietzsche is the first philosopher to have put into question the supreme value of truth.[88] Beyond the conformity of the soul with the way things are and become, beyond the love of and unrestricted affirmation of this world, it is the gratuity and excess of art that is sovereign, that affirms itself, and in the very excess of its affirmation confers value—its own worth—upon the universe.

Nietzsche's published texts are concerned not with the reasons there can be to judge the thought of eternal return true but with the effect of this thought on the thinker that thinks it. Yet it has its effect only on condition that one believes it to be true.

The law of eternal return is not an empirical generalization; there cannot be any evidence for it. For there cannot be any trace—not even in the mind of the witness—to confirm that an event which is occurring now has occurred once before; the accumulation of traces would itself make this universe not the same as the one that assembled itself the last time.

As a scientific doctrine, it would then have the status of a cosmological law. But is it true that a representation of the universe such that the nodes of force are finite in number, while the temporal dimension is infinite, can only represent the combinations possible as infinite? Even a machine with only three elements set in motion can produce an infinite number of combinations and would not reproduce the original position.[89]

It is one's joy that one believes and must believe.

Eternal return is the thought that is conceived by the most joyous state, which is the most veridical state, the state that wills and affirms every "It was," that "is deeper yet than all agony," that "is thirstier, more cordial, hungrier, more terrible, more secret than all woe."[90] The Dionysian joy is capable of embracing all things, entangled, ensnared, enamored, because it holds together in a ring, in a round dance, all its own fragments, enigmas, accidents, because it contains and crowds into a single feeling all the oldest, the newest, losses, hopes, conquests, and victories of humanity. The thought of eternal return arises out of the abysses of that joy; it is the thought with which the soul opens itself in depth to the compulsions of nature in its nature, with which it opens itself for the return of all the dreams and intoxications of history. Is it then a thought, itself beyond truth and falsity, which first makes the veridical soul possible? Is the doctrine of eternal return a postulate of practical reason that makes sovereignty intelligible to itself? Or, if in Nietzsche the sovereign individual is not an end unto himself and for himself but an issue through which the power of life pursues its expenditure without recompense, is the belief in eternal return an artifice through which nature pursues its own resplendence? Is it posited as the condition for the possibility for what is and what was to be affirmed?

Or is it a phantasm engendered by a sovereign will to lies? Is it not, like the representation of an ideal in ascetic history, a beautifying pretext and a self-delusion not validated by what it makes possible, but rather by what it makes impossible: the human all too human?

Is not the phantasm of eternal return the lie that makes the soul veridical? The *vitiosus circulus deus* . . .

IV

THE WORK OF THE MASTERS

1. Theory as Idealization

Theory, as Husserl explains it, is not simply an operation of recording the real or of representing it in a form that would deliver it over to technological manipulation. Theory idealizes its objects. Its viewing incorporates into the transitory given something of an abiding, ideal existence. Idealization in general is conceived by Husserl as infinitization. The theoretical viewing sees an absolute, an infinity, in the given. The infinitization of the field of cognition makes possible and requires the idealization of goals and the idealization of practice. Goals are subjected to norms that claim unconditional validity; practice is given a practical field whose horizons are infinite.

Theory then is not separated from practice as a pure recording of reality from an action that would transform it and which would be adventitiously added to theory. In reality theory itself enhances the world. Is not this indeed our conviction with regard to every form of theory? Nietzsche says that even in the measure that the world is found to be mathematizable, discovered to be ordered, dependable, it acquires more worth for us. "Splendid discoveries: everything is not unforeseeable (incalculable), indeterminate! There are laws that beyond the measure of the individual remain true! Another result *could* have obtained! The individual no longer an eternal singularity, nor venerable. But as the most complex fact of the world, the *supreme* CHANCE."[1]

Theoretical observation, in Husserl's explanation, effects two operations on the data. On the one hand, the given is *identified*. It is taken as an adumbration *(Abschattung)* of an identity term; another given can be taken as an *Abschattung* of the same identity term. An identity is recognized in a sensuous diversity. The identity recognized in the given is not necessarily a simple; it may be a nucleus of traits that belong together in such a way that if one of them occurs, they all recur. If this structure could recur the same but once, it could recur at any time, anywhere; its identity is not dependent on a place and a time. Recurrable at any time, anywhere, it transcends the space-time determinateness of the real; it is ideal. Recurrability an infinitum defines the ideality of the ideal. A dimension of infinity thus enters into the constitution of every object identified by theoretical cognition. The idea that expresses the identity of the given is not the simple product of an abstraction, which would disengage the form in the given, for example, from the content or the material which it informs. The form simply isolated by abstractive perception is not given as recurring the same. That it be taken as recurring the same, identical in the perception of another moment, from another point of view, is the result of an idealization. This idealization is the ideation that constitutes the theoretical idea out of the abstracted form. Ideation incorporates infinity into the objectified givens of the natural world.

In addition, theoretical observation situates the identified object on infinite space-time dimensions. Greek mathematics constructed the idea of infinite space and time; post-Galilean science situates nature in mathematical space and time. Theoretical space is infinite space; theoretical time is an infinite order of succession. Situated on infinite dimensions of space, each datum is taken as an *Abschattung* visible from one of an infinite number of alternative viewpoints. And each datum present is recorded on the infinite number of moments of time which can be retained by, or retain, its moment. A theoretical object is invested with this infinite system of *Abschattungen*. Whereas natural experience lives in a finite sphere, theoretical experience gives itself a universe of objects each of whose identities is recurrable ad infinitum, each of whose sensuous aspects is recorded on all the points and all the moments of an infinite field of space-time.

Infinity also enters into the representation of the given. The perceptual judgments which represent the given are meant as true, with theoretical truth. Reality is theoretically represented in representations that are everywhere and at every moment verifiable, valid for all real and possible witnesses. The validity of a judgment is situated on a dimension of infinite verifiability. A proposition is proposed to a theoretical intersubjectivity in principle infinite.

In thus idealizing the universe, the theorizing subject idealizes itself. It idealizes its inner time-format. And it idealizes its own identity.

The infinite space in which nature is situated presupposes infinite time, that of the number of the moments of a synthetic viewing for which each expanse of space could exist. This infinite time the subject finds in itself or produces in itself by its way of grasping, of identifying, its moment of presence. For Husserl argues that the subject which grasps the moment of its presence, identifies the moment, necessarily situates it in a succession of equally identifiable moments which is without end as it is without a beginning.

The separation of matter and form, making possible the identification of the form of the present, its constitution as a unit, is the result of an idealization. For although Husserl does not recognize this, his own concept of the form of the now—as the boundaries the clarity and distinctness of the content delineate against the already passing and still coming temporal contents—admits of these boundaries' being dilated or contracted by the content. Then the identification of a form of time that recurs the same was in fact produced by an imaginative equalization of moments whose form has first been abstracted from their content. What Husserl takes as an intuition of the internal form of consciousness in fact constitutes that form through an idealization.

Thus Husserl's transcendental reflection reveals how theoretical consciousness idealizes—infinitizes—its internal, temporal form. Husserl's genetic analysis shows how theoretical subjectivity also idealizes its own identity.

Theoretical consciousness sets up its representations of its objects as true, by supplying for each judgment of perception a reason—and a reason for every reason. This practice is responsible for the form of science. For a science is not simply an accumulation of representations taken as verified by judgments of perception; it has the form of an explanatory system. Ideally each fact is verifiable by all observers and deducible from a universal law. The scientific form of science is thus produced by a theoretical practice committed to answering to every contestation and to supplying for the phenomena that present themselves to consciousness a reason, which theoretical consciousness draws out of itself.

Such a theoretical practice presupposes a consciousness that can maintain its identity. More exactly, consciousness maintains its own identity in assembling all the facts of the world that constitute the contents of its phases, its moments, into a systematic body of truth.

Theoretical consciousness determines the truth of phenomena; it situates them in the field of the infinite series of real and possible witnesses. It does so by undertaking to answer for what it represents as given, to give a reason for its presence, a reason that would be valid for anyone. Answering for what is given to it and answering to all coming and possible contestations, the theoretical subjectivity makes itself equivalent to any of the infinite series of real and possible subjects.

Answering in each moment for all its moments, for the infinite series of moments it projects, theoretical subjectivity maintains its identity. It maintains in each moment the true reason, the valid reason for each of its past and future states. Existing in this perfect self-possession, impervious to all alienation because accepting in advance every contestation, theoretical subjectivity maintains itself always. This perfect, ideal, presence is the highest form of being; it is the absolute being to which mundane reality is relative.

Husserl presents this idealization of nature and this self-idealization as the telos that the Western form of cognition and the Western praxis pursued always. His phenomenology is set up to promote this intrinsic telos of Western history by bringing it to final clarity, through an intentional and genetic analysis of that history. If this Western idealism is today in a state of crisis, this is due, Husserl declares, to a great weariness and to a loss of faith in itself.[2] But this weariness and loss of faith he attributes to an obnubilation of the sense of the perfect, ideal form of subjectivity Western theory and practice engenders and requires— and, indeed, of all sense of subjectivity. The historical reason for the loss of the sense of subjectivity he locates in the naturalization of subjectivity in scientism.

Phenomenology, conceived by Husserl as the rigorous science of subjectivity, combats this naturalist aberration, responsible for the crisis of reason in the West.

In Husserl the idealization of the universe is at bottom the way by which the subject assumes a responsibility for itself without restriction, promotes itself to abiding and ideal identity, recuperates itself in the very passage of its time, stands security for itself, and stands absolutely, attains the highest form of ideal presence. The idealization of nature is the way by which the subject idealizes itself. Scientific, rational, civilization does not consist in conquering alien nature so as to serve the needs of man positing himself sovereign. The transformation which is essential in this civilization is not the technological and industrial exploitation but the idealization of nature, which is already worked by all theory. The idealization of nature is not at all a representation of nature relativized in function of the wants or needs of natural humanity. Rather, through the idealization of nature the natural man is transformed into a higher form of subjectivity, rendered absolutely self-responsible, the highest, ideal form of existence. This idealized subjectivity is the hidden telos which the Western rational project has pursued from the beginning.

For Nietzsche it is the reverse: Nietzsche posits a life which is sovereign from the start, which has been endowed with superabundant, excess force by nature before any ordering or praxis it may undertake. There is a Nietzschean denunciation of idealization, of that which is a devaluation of the real, positing an ideal order above or beyond it. But there is also a Nietzschean idealization, a theory seeing an absolute, an infinity, in the real. This idealization of the real is not conceived as the means by which the subject idealizes itself. The subjectivity that idealizes is one that is driven to squander its forces upon the world by reason of the very excess of force its sovereign life ceaselessly engenders within itself. Its infinitization of the world is not the means for it to attain to sovereign existence; it is rather the byproduct of its compulsion to discharge its sovereign plenitude, to die.

For Nietzsche Western spirituality is not only at a moment of crisis because the understanding of the sovereignty of subjectivity contained in the fundamental project of theoretical culture has been obscured and forgotten; Nietzsche means to contest the very sensibility and the idealizing operation of the subjectivity which, according to Husserl, is the subject of Western theoretical life. Its sensibility is now shown to be weak and untruthful; its theoretical idealization formulates the false ontology of Being.

Husserl conceived sensibility as intuition, the immediate presence of given being. Sensibility is passive or receptive consciousness, in which the empty gropings of intentionality terminate in the resolution of data in the clarity and distinctness of their presence. The active factor in perception, which recognizes something the same in the various *Abschattungen*, which constitutes the object as the identity pole of all these *Abschattungen*, is but the grasping at once of a structure that forms in the passage of the sensuous data, a synthetic grasping as one what is spread across time and space. The identification, the apprehension, of the identity-pole is but the way that the data spread across time and space can be taken in.

For Nietzsche intuitive immediacy, this form of resolution of what is given, is a derivative phase; there is a prior form of sensibility. The prior and the derivative are distinguished as strong and weak. The intuitive sensibility which can receive the clearly and distinctly composed sensuous diversity synoptically, with equity, with justice, comes when the turmoil of sensation dies down. It is a terminal stage of sensation.

There is a sensibility that apprehends in the given not an identity but the chaos, the flux, the passage. A sensibility that apprehends that what is given are not things, identities, beings, but flows, differentiations, streams of becoming. This sensibility does not coalesce into a unified ray of identifying intentionality; it turns multiple impulses upon the given. The sensibility in act is not to be conceived as a synergic apprehension of a single form; the more impulses, and different impulses, the more affects, turned upon something, the more "objective" it is.[3] The strong grasp of the sensuous phenomenon is effected by a chaos of conflicting impulses.

Sensation means not only sense impression, impression of a meaning, but also sensuousness, susceptibility. The sensuous impulses turned on the datum are affected by it, affective. But the original susceptibility is not conceived by Nietzsche as pleasure and pain consequent upon impressions. It is the weak who are only pleased, contented with what is given; their most positive state is contentment, "wretched contentment." They are only pained by what is, debilitated.

All that is does something, is a force, is will to power, and the sensibility itself is real, a force, exists in the discharge. In the confrontation with the phenomenal it must be conceived as active and not only reactive. Sensibility does not exist only because something is given, passively received; it itself gives.

The original, and strong, mode of sensibility is laughter, weeping, blessing, cursing.[4] These are not conceived by Nietzsche as subsequent to intuition, which would give the datum, the being, "just as it is, just as it shows itself to be."[5] They are sensibility itself, the strong modes of confronting what gives itself in its force, its weight, or its worth. They confront not data given in the quiescence and resolution of their self-sufficient plenitude, which can only be acknowledged in the immediacy of intuition, but data in their contingency, groundlessness, absurdity, brute obtrusion, in laughter and weeping, data in their luster and their malignancy, in blessing and cursing. It is in the sense of the absurd, the contingent, that which is not the simple correlate of our concepts, and in the sense of the terrible, the irreducibly inhuman, that which is not the simple respondent of human wishes, that the exterior impinges upon the strong, vital sensibility. The positive state of sensibility of the strong is not merely pleasure but exultation, the exultation that rises over what is given to enhance it, it is blessing. It does not merely suffer the intrusion of the baleful; it conjures it off, it curses. What the sensibility reviles is diminished—that is shown by vindictive sensibility writ large, the Platonic-Christian sensibility, which has really made the world bad.[6]

Already from the period of *The Birth of Tragedy*, Nietzsche came to believe that the comic and tragic sentiments are deeper far than the rationalized sensibility which gathers only sense data, data for meaning for its own deductions, and which takes the given as already human, already formed by our mathematics, by, as he puts it, our multiplication tables and our logical axioms.

The sensibility of the philosophical, Socratic age of Western culture is a sensibility already regulated according to the logical axioms of identity, excluded middle, and non-contradiction, perceiving identities, things, enduring beings. Nietzsche depicts this sensibility as corresponding to a terminal phase of contact with the streams of sensuous becoming; the moment of integration, of a synoptic hold on the object he takes to be a pact, an armistice due not to justice, to a just view of the thing, but to endopsychic exhaustion. The sensation is stabilized into an identity, a thing, a being, by a weak, simplifying, falsifying perception. This weak perception prevailed not because of its truth but because of its anthropomorphic value: it was the sensibility that was needed in order that the species survive. But the sensibility that senses under the imperative of survival is the sensibility of the weak, the degenerate, the last men. The sensibility of the first ones, of the true men, the men who are true and truthful, is not ruled by the imperative of survival. It is only when the imperative of survival has not yet fallen in place that the sensibility is strong enough to confront the given in its contingency and illogicality, in its inhumanity. Such is the comic and tragic sensibility, the sensibility that laughs and weeps on contact with the forces of the world.

Nietzsche conceives of artistry as "approbation, benediction, divinization,"[7] as consecration. The isolating, the distinguishing, the making distinct, and the intensification, the illumination of things that artistry effects, gives something to the things. Gives something of the artist subjectivity, not its judgments, but its force and its consecration. But Nietzsche also conceived of all perception as artistry;[8] perception is not passive recording, it is enhancement, consecration, or execration, imprecation.

Nietzsche thus opposes weak and strong sensibility, anthropogenic and anthropo-transcending, rationalized and tragic-comic sensibility; this opposition is also cast as an opposition between the moral and the aesthetic perception. In the moral perception weakness relativizes and degrades. Nietzsche traces back the utilitarian, the teleological perception, to this moral origin. To him neither the Husserlian *Lebenswelt* organized teleologically nor the Heideggerian world of *Zeuge* would be primary. The vision of the perceptual field as a field of means is the vision exercised by an agent seen as a complex of needs; but this sentiment of life as the vectors of need is itself second and degenerate. The utilitarian-teleological perception is originally fixed by the affects of pleasure and pain. It is a perception that questions the world with the question Why do I suffer?[9] The moral vision of the world as a penal apparatus, with the external antagonistic will that it implies as its metaphysical prolongation and postulate, answers to a perception that questions thus.

There is then in Nietzsche a project of lifting this moral-metaphysical sediment, of recovering a demetaphysicized vision, a naturalized vision of nature.[10] Such a vision is innocent and blessing. It extracts nature from the spider-web of a transcendental will; it strips the field of becoming of purpose, which relativizes and degrades each phenomenal form. It sees through the rational network cast over all things, which subjects each force to reckoning and hence to utility and measure. It rediscovers in all things the non-teleological movement which takes each phase of itself as its end and its perfection: "O Zarathustra, to those who think as we do, all things themselves are dancing."

"I have become one who blesses and says Yes; and I fought long for that and was a fighter that I might one day get my hands free to bless. But this is my blessing: to stand over every single thing as its own heaven, as its round roof, its azure bell, and eternal security; and blessed is he who blesses thus."[11] The blessing perception consists in putting each thing in a dimension of height and of depth, which is the luminous sphere of the open heavens. It is a making each thing luminously visible by putting over it the heaven of an abyss of light and baptizing it in the well of eternity such that it is seen beyond good and evil.

Situating the events of the universe on a dimension of infinite time is the essential operation of the Nietzschean theory, the Nietzschean gay science. Not the eidetic identity, but the very differentiation, the becoming, of the phenomena are taken to recur ad infinitum.

What does situating the phenomena in an infinite and cyclic time effect? It *maintains* the phenomena. In both senses: On the one hand, it affirms their utterly and irredeemably transitory nature, their becoming without being. But these passing phenomena are integrally maintained by the cyclic nature of infinite time, endowed with imperishable, ideal presence. The real, in its very contingency and transience, is idealized.

Each phenomenon thus acquires a definitive inscription in being, an infinite import. Not only because its incidence is multiplied to infinity. In addition it is itself one of the causes of the eternal return of all things. While rejecting, with Humean reasons, the causality which would make all phenomena in principle rationally calculable, Zarathustra does nonetheless affirm that all things are "entangled, ensnared, enamored," such that each thing entails the succession of things and eventually its own return.[12] "Entangled"—they do not form a coexistence that is logically ordered but are involved in one another in a disorder. "Ensnared"—they are caught up, trapped in one another; there are no extramundane or extraphenomenal entities, no idealities which would be unaffected by phenomenal transience. "Enamored"—they are affected with one another, bound to one another with bonds of love. For if Nietzsche identifies phenomena as forces, he also conceives of all forces, and not only the force of striving man, as will to power and as affect.[13] The Zarathustran love which binds him to the world so securely like a ship that need be tied to the shore with but a thread spun by a spider[14] is not a sublime or spiritual force; it has to be understood as an index of the *naturalization* which Zarathustra has effected in himself. To become natural, to abandon all supralapsarian metaphysical fantasies, is for Zarathustra equivalent to attachment to the world, and Zarathustra discovers in himself the same attachment with which each mundane event is attached to the others, and thus he composes a world. The cyclic movement of infinite time is nothing else than the movement of entities which are fluxes of becoming entangled, ensnared, enamored of one another.

Knowing all things in the infinite dimension of their time is the art and artistry of theoretical cognition. An artist selects a momentarily blended color, a brief arrangement of forms, and his work consists in isolating it, framing it, saying, in effect, that this is to be conserved for unnumbered eyes to come, this is worth contemplating for hours, for centuries to come. The projection of the infinity of the time of eternal return works just this artistry on every mundane phenomenon. The idealizing thought that isolates a phenomenon by circumscribing the brief boundaries of its transitory flux and stamping it with the worth and weight of eternity illuminates the phenomena with the Apollonian light.

On the other hand, the vision of eternal return maintains each phenomenon in its becoming, without directing it by an aim toward a final state. It maintains each phenomenon in a movement that does not move as steps in view of an end; each of its phases is itself an end in itself, or valued in itself. "O Zarathustra, to those who think as we do, all things themselves are dancing . . ." The thought that thinks that is not an immobile intuition but a movement that follows or joins with the movements of the phenomena it thinks, itself capturing their kind of non-teleological, dance movement. This theory is itself a Dionysian movement.

This artistry is, however, the supreme cognition. For if projecting a dimension of infinite cyclic time is the idealization which theory works, this artist operation yields an acknowledgement of the irreducible flux in each thing and in all things. Whereas, we have seen, the Husserlian way of projecting a dimension of infinite space-time posits an order of ideal identities whose "unreality" means that they are definitively beings and not becomings. The thesis of the irreducible and universal becoming is an ontological thesis. The cosmological hypothesis of a time of eternal return is the means to reach this ontological thesis.

In addition, acknowledging, affirming, becoming is not only acknowledging transition but acknowledging movement from being to nothingness, acknowledging negativity, suffering, decline, death. As in Hegel, in Nietzsche the existential problem of affirming the transience of each moment of one's life and of affirming one's final mortality is reflected as a theoretical problem of affirming negativity. But whereas in Hegel the process negated is rediscovered in an affirmative form, in Nietzsche the process turning into nothingness is to be rediscovered in the same form.

We have seen that Husserl located also an idealization in the theoretical representation of reality; what is represented is represented as true with theoretical truth, subjected to unrestricted verification, true for every real and possible theoretical consciousness. Nietzsche for his part idealizes the representation of the world not by exposing it to the infinity of all possible affirmers but rather by turning to it the infinity of one's own affirmation. The affirmation of the theoretical consciousness that posits the representation is not confirmed by the open number of affirmations whose magnitude proportionately diminishes the possibility of negation. Rather the representation of the world in consciousness is affirmed without negation, with an utterly affirmative and self-affirmative act of thought, affirming it unrestrictedly. The dimension of infinite time upon which it is inscribed is not a time composed by an infinite intersubjectivity; it is the singular subject, the Zarathustran soul that finds the infinite structure of time within itself.

In Nietzsche the idealization of nature is not a means for the natural subjectivity to idealize itself. Rather, there is a kind of life, that of "the most comprehensive soul," "in which all things have their sweep and countersweep and ebb and flood,"[15] which has in itself resources for every engendering excess power, whose existence is a superabundance and an excess by nature. The infinitization, the idealization it works on nature is the byproduct of its own need to discharge the excesses of its power.

This subject is produced by nature; the Third Essay of *The Genealogy of Morals* set out to show that each of the ideal types with which natural man idealized his existence in the successive epochs of culture are in fact figures of an ever more integral will to self-negation.

The mind, Aristotle said, is by its nature open to all things. But it does not automatically open to the universe; this openness is the work of force, a force which must energize the mind from within. In order to be able to affirm all that is and becomes—honey, lees, drunken midnight, tombs, tomb-tears' comfort, cripple, world—"this world, O you know it!"—the mind has to be able to affirm each of its own states which are affected by each absurdity and each terror, each contingency and each chance, each birth and each death in the world. It must be able to affirm itself absolutely, in that exultant return of force upon itself by which Dionysian life incessantly intensifies itself. Such a mind is one that affirms, that wills unrestrictedly, its actual pulse of force confronting the forces of the world, that wills still all it has ever willed, to the point of willing its incessant return, that wills already all it can ever will, so that all that is to come, when it comes, returns. This will for its own unending return is the inner form of the most comprehensive soul, that "in which all things have their sweep and countersweep and ebb and flood." This will that is utterly without regret, remorse, demand or anticipation, is also the inner diagram of joy.

This Nietzschean "most comprehensive soul" is opposed to the most comprehending mind of Western classicism and of Husserl. For Husserl that which can promote each thing to its truth must be the mind that synthetically embraces all points of view for which it exists in the infinite expanse of space and time. The theoretical mind is synthesizing. To this Nietzsche opposes a mind that can affirm each stream of becoming without negating or subordinating it—affirm not only the entities but the transitions and the eclipses, not only the forms but the fluxes, not only the constancies and invariants but the divergencies and the aberrations, not only the things but the nothing. This mind is structured not as a synthesis but as a synopsis or a collage, it only "compresses into one soul all the hopes, victories, despairs, deaths";[16] it is a field of laughing, weeping, blessing, cursing forces in conflict and in chaos. It is only its own subjective force and not the force of reason or order that keeps all that together. The tensions, conflicts, contradictions with which the forces in combat within it affect one another generate the excess force that it discharges in the idealization of the world.

Idealization and Truth

The idealization of nature involved in theory is not a relativization of nature, a subordination of nature to the human subjectivity. It is on the contrary an absolutization of nature, incorporating into it a dimension of infinity. What is at stake is the unrestricted affirmation of what is and becomes. It is pursued in obedience to the mind's ontological destination.

1. A Nietzschean judgment on the Husserlian mode of idealization would be, first, that the Husserlian account of the operations theory effects on nature is not verified in the contemporary forms of science.

What is decisive, what is cognitive, in perception, according to the Husserlian conception, is the idealizing identification of identities. This theory of perception already commits the Husserlian account of theory to an ontology of entities, of forms, of beings. The Nietzschean judgment would be that modern science is a science of forces and not of forms, that its formulas delineate a relational and not substantive ontology of nature.

But in addition the major Nietzschean accusation would be that the Husserlian kind of idealization is in reality a devaluation, a nihilism. Such an accusation seems paradoxical; is not Husserlian philosophy through and through teleological, a philosophy that finds everywhere goals, final states in the life of consciousness as in the projects of cultures? For Husserl intuitive fulfillment is primary; the empty intentionalities of discursive operations are possible only because a given intuitive plenitude has adumbrated variants and possibilities within itself. All presence functions as a telos for consciousness; all theoretical consciousness is teleological, aims at presence, arises out of presence.

That is incontestably true. But to Nietzsche the Husserlian perception is a positing of abiding identity and a non-recognition of the flux. The infinite field of space-time in which the theory situates the perceptum functions to make ideally possible the definitive fixing of its invariant form, its *eidos*. To Nietzsche every valuation of being functions as a devaluation of becoming, time, life. It would seem that life is gratified by being supplied a universe of plenary being, graspable entities, comprehendable identities, and indeed being made itself, through self-consciousness, an abiding identity, apodictically graspable, indefinitely self-reproducible, aiming at total self-responsibility. Nietzsche, however, puts life not in abiding identity but in force, self-expropriation, gratuitous discharge.

For Nietzsche a universe radically non-teleological, universe of eternal return without any final states, alone admits the worth of life, the first example of a gratuitous becoming. A universe where each of the processes is of infinite weight and worth, reverberated across all the infinite cycles of becoming, and where none of them exists only relative to a human need is a universe in which a sovereign life can reign.

2. But can the Nietzschean idealization really be formulated theoretically? Can the gay science be scientific? Nietzsche gave it only literary form; the clearest statement of the intellectual operations he envisaged is found in *Thus Spoke Zarathustra*. *The Birth of Tragedy* in fact opposed theoretical culture to theatrical culture, the dialectical representation of nature to the dramatic representation that arises in the participationist rites of Orphism. The ontological ultimacy of becoming and the cosmological law of eternal return and the most powerful experience of the subject, as a participant in the "joy of the universe" which consists not in the maintenance of certain forms but in the gratuitous creation and destruction of forms—these were not theoretical themes but an articulation of the idealization of nature and of human nature realized in the images and rituals of Dionysian theater. Nietzsche has presented theoretical, rational, scientific, optimist, Socratic culture as supplanting, indeed as contrived in order to repress the theatrical, ritual, tragic culture. Yet the conflict dramatized in that first book was paradoxically foreseen to end by a return of the tragic vision at the limits of the development of scientific culture. This idea was expressed in one of the last fragments collected in *The Will to Power,* "Let me show you my world . . ."[17] The ancient science was a science of forms, modern science is a science of forces; Nietzsche translated this as an ontological conversion from an ontology of Being to an ontology of Becoming. Modern science depicts the universal field of forces in a dimension of infinite time. Then, Nietzsche reasons, if nature ever had a goal, it would already have been reached (since it has already had an infinite time to reach it); if nature ever aimed at a final state, it would long have been attained, and all movement stopped. Becoming then is the ultimate format of nature. Then the mathematized

formulas of the scientific representation of nature—which record not intrinsic forms but relational patterns of events—would fix the idealized vision of nature, where each event is invested with an infinite import—not a human value but a natural value, an infinite density of being. In addition, the modern representation of the events which compose nature not in terms of eidetic identities but in terms of multiple endoatomic processes would correspond not to an immediately intuitive sensory receptivity but to the differential, forceful sensibility which Nietzsche formulated as laughter, weeping, blessing, cursing.

3. But is the form of eternal return really the time of the modern scientific representation of the universe? Does the infinite dimension of time which science postulates really require the recurrence of all events in a universe of forces of finite extent? Georg Simmel[18] had already proposed a model where three entities would turn forever without ever reproducing the initial position. It would be enough to set three wheels of the same size on a common axle and set them in motion rotating at speeds of n, 2n, and $\frac{n}{\pi}$. This cosmic model is constructed with wheels, fixed entities, and considers their combinations; one could object that the Nietzschean universe is constructed not with entities but with processes. Arthur Danto[19] has argued that any process moves through infinitely divisible states of magnitude between 0 and n; hence even a finite number of events could show an infinite number of states through the infinite axis of time. The argument forces us to admit the possibility of an infinite number of states of finite processes; the infinity of time does not necessitate the recurrence of the same events.

Does this kind of argument refute the thesis of the eternal return of all things? It has been argued, by Heidegger and others, that the Nietzschean doctrine can be neither refuted nor confirmed by empirical methods. The universality and ultimacy of Becoming is not an empirical but an ontological thesis; the infinity of time has not empirical but transcendental grounds; the law of the structure of time not an empirical generalization but a cosmological law.

What is distinctive in Husserl's theory of time is not only the infinite form of time but its subjective origin. The cosmic time in which the events of nature are represented is a time constituted; the constitutive process is a temporalizing which Husserl equates with the inner form—or formative process—of transcendental subjectivity. Husserl seeks the ultimate explanation for the infinity of time in the power of transcendental subjectivity to reproduce without loss or diminution the form of the present. The constituted dimension of infinite time is traced back to indefinite repeatability as a power of constitutive subjectivity. The time dimensions that the idealizing theoretical work extends about the givens of nature are a priori and of subjective origin.

The Nietzschean position is not completely worked out, and there are conflicting texts. Certainly there are pages—particularly in the unpublished notes—where Nietzsche subscribes completely to a Kantian conception of the subjective and a priori character of space and time. But in the most mature, and published, work, the decisive texts of *Zarathustra* present a different view. We have seen how the definition of time as a recurrability ad infinitum of an identical form, the moment, and the consequent Husserlian reduction to the constitutive sphere of transcendental subjectivity are dependent on the isolation of the form of time from the content. In Nietzsche the concept of the cyclic return of all temporal things involves a consideration of temporal content as well as form.

In the Husserlian conception the form of the present can be said to be the cause of the form of the future, and thus of the infinite extent of time. In the Nietzschean conception the present can be said to be one of the causes of the return of the present only when not only its form but also its content is considered. It is the content of the present that entails the content of the future—all things are entangled, ensnared, enamored. This material entailment finally requires the return of the present, when all the material events possible in nature have been exhausted. "Behold, we know what you teach," the animals say to Zarathustra. "You would say, 'I myself belong to the causes of the eternal recurrence.' "[20]

Thus it would seem that the Nietzschean doctrine of the structure of infinite time is indeed a cosmological law; it belongs to what Husserl named the pure or a priori ontology of nature. The Simmel-Danto arguments then tend to show that this law is not part of the ontology of nature articulated in our natural sciences. That it is not "the most scientific idea."

There is certainly a sense in which the law of eternal return is first a law of the structure of subjectivity—of the most powerful, Zarathustran form of subjectivity. It is the structure of the Zarathustran will, utterly without resentment or regret, in which all its past wills recur, utterly without demands or expectations, in which all it can will it wills already, such that the will to come shall be a will that returns. And yet this is not to say that the structure of time is constituted in the sphere of transcendental subjectivity, as in Husserl, and thus eludes the cosmological refutations of Simmel and Danto. For the pattern of time in the inner nature of the Zarathustran soul is in fact the rhythm of all nature. And it is just this that reveals to us the most distinctive structures of Nietzschean philosophy. The theorist discovers the widest, most all-encompassing law, the law of all nature, not by the most extensive eternal observation, but by the most intensive inner scrutiny: Zarathustra discovers the law of all nature in uncovering the law of his own most singular nature.

This paradox or this circle is not an objection, but the expression of the quite extraordinary way in which the idealization involved in theory is equated with truth. The idealization of nature, the incorporation of a dimension of infinity in the transitory phenomenal events of nature, is indeed the work of, the gift given by, the theorizing subject. But this subject is itself idealized, made a movement of self-transcendence ad infinitum, by nature.

2. The Will and its Law

Nietzsche's philosophy thus represents a fundamental contestation of what Husserl has shown to be the ideal character of the theorizing subject of the Western rational tradition, which pursues its own idealization in the idealization of nature. His philosophy also represents a fundamental contestation of the ideal type of the rational agent, such as is formulated in the Kantian practical philosophy. The contestation is both on the level of the will which the practical philosophy seeks to activate, and on the level of the law which is to order the will.

Kant works with an opposition between the sensuous will and the rational will, an opposition conceived in terms of passivity and activity. The rational will, activated by representations of principle, which are valid and in force in all circumstances, is activated always, wills always, is the ideal state of will. The sensuous will, that activated by representations or sensuous particulars, is activated from the outside; it is dependent, servile, reactive. And it is activated by the promise of pleasure the representations of sensuous particulars contain; it is thus activated contingently. Kant devalues the sensuous will, alleging its contingency and its dependency, its servility. The rational will is a will motivated from within, by its own representational faculty, and motivating itself always.

But Nietzsche has distinguished a strong and a weak, a sovereign and a servile mode of sensibility. The weak form of sensibility, that which is receptive, is conceived as a degradation of a strong form, which is prior. Life *degenerates* into a succession of reactions and adaptations; of itself it is a force, and engendering of excess force. Sentient life is not simply the sum of the vectors of stabilization and adaptation in a material mass; it is a force that intensifies itself of itself, with representations not of reality but of unreality—Dionysian-Apollonian force.

In the sensuous encounter with the world the sensibility is not merely passive; it is a force and encounters the phenomena forcefully—weeping, laughing, blessing, cursing. These modes of sensibility are not passive states; they are discharges of force. In addition they are not servile, dependent states, contingent upon the data impinging on the sensibility. In his reflection on Greek sensibility, Nietzsche first saw that whether the fortuity, unrationality, unlogicality, the materiality, the absurdity, of the sensuous universe overwhelms the sensibility and makes it willless or whether they are acknowledged in spasms of laughter depends on the weakness or force of the sensible life itself. The ancient Greeks could perceive the comedy of the chaotic world and the nobility of its terrible course, not because they had some superior way of understanding it but because their very sensibility was intrinsically stronger. Modern sensibility is given to pessimistic philosophies, such that the bare fact of suffering seems to it to be an indictment of existence itself, not because modern life knows more pain and deeper pain than ancient mankind; to the contrary, modern civilization, servile and philistine, is above all the civilization devoted to comfort. But modern sensibility has become weaker and weaker, to the point that the pure thought of pain is enough to induce despair, formulated in the pessimistic philosophies that today gain wide currency.[21]

Both Kant and Nietzsche are concerned with formulating the conditions for a state in which the will wills itself indefectably, wills itself always. Both conceive this as a matter of bracketing the will upon the universe. But Kant conceives this universalized will formally, whereas Nietzsche conceives it materially. For Kant the rational will is one activated by law, valid universally and necessarily. This law is a priori, found incumbent upon the mind itself. But it is also the law according to which the sense data are ordered into a universe, by the universal and necessary forms of objectivity. Hence the will activated by law is activated by the universal and necessary form of the universe. The mind that can thus be bracketed upon the universal and necessary forms of objectivity is the most comprehending mind, that which has detached itself from sensuous particulars to become formalizing.

Nietzsche conceived and required rather a "most comprehensive soul," that "which can run and stray and roam farthest within itself; the most necessary soul, which out of sheer joy plunges itself into chance; the soul which, having being, dives into becoming; the soul which *has*, but *wants* to want and will; the soul which flees itself and catches up with itself in the widest circle; the wisest soul, which folly exhorts most sweetly; the soul which loves itself most, in which all things have their sweep and countersweep and ebb and flood."[22] The most comprehensive soul is a soul bracketed upon the universe in its materiality: not the form of the universe, the framework of laws that govern its events and shape its objects, but the chaos of lawless events and chance objects themselves. Not only those that abide but those that die and those that destroy. ". . . [O]ne has to consider the denied aspects of existence not only as *necessary* but as desirable; and not only as desirable with respect to aspects hitherto approved (for example, as their complements or first conditions), but for themselves, as more powerful, more fecund, more *true* aspects of existence, in which its will expresses itself most clearly."[23] The "most comprehensive soul" must be able to affirm each event and not turn away from every decay, pain, or death. And it must be able to affirm each becoming and not cease to will when the phenomenon which it affirms is extinguished. It must not die with the death of the form it affirms and attaches itself to. For that to be possible, it is not required that it detach itself from the whole sphere of genesis and corruption in order to elevate itself to the deathless forms, the framework of laws ever in force. Rather it must attach itself to the cosmic force, never augmented nor subtracted, which sustains all the forms and which is not diminished when they are deformed and dissipated, which creates ever new forms equally destined to pass and to vanish. This kind of total and universal affirmation Nietzsche calls love of the world.

Such a "most comprehensive soul" must affirm in itself not only the faculty of engendering representations of the permanent and the abiding but every pulse and impulse, every moment of sensibility which confronted a momentary and passing phenomenon and itself passed. It must be attached to itself in all the succession of its states; it must affirm each will which passed and each will to come; it must contain and maintain all the chaos of its own reality. The totality of sensuous impulses, of sensuous wills must be maintained, not in their integral assemblage, but in their very conflict and chaos. The supplement of soul that maintains each of the sensuous wills in this most comprehensive state is not a rational overview which integrates and organizes them; it is a force of affirmation that returns to them, a love and a consecration that the soul itself puts on them, and which intensifies them.

The transformation of the soul into its most comprehensive state is thus for Nietzsche an affective, not a formalizing, transformation: It is not the positioning of the soul in a formalizing intuition of law, but unconditional affirmation, and love. Love as an attachment to the material world issues out of joy, the inner exultation of a soul that feels the gratuitous expansion of force within.

That the soul is—or is destined to become—somehow everything, this Aristotelian thought defines classicism, for which spiritualization is universalization. The spirit is the very power in the individual speaker to render his words valid for everyone, making him the seat of a logos which is universal. It is the power to make his utterances not merely expressive of particular impressions and particular sensations but true, that is, conveying a presence of evidence that transcends every point of view, that is no longer bound to a here and a now. It is the power to transcend the particularity of sense impressions toward the generality of concepts. It is also the power to suspend the attachment to the personally useful and the immediately pleasing which arouses sensuous appetites, in order to judge what is valid always, what is normative and good in itself. The spirit is the inner strength to systematically detach one's initiatives from sensuous lures, which feed one's own appetitive core and attach it to the here and the now, for one finds one has the power to activate one's will with rational representations of principle that one's understanding can formulate. The sovereignty of the spiritual agent consists in being able to deliberately act in such a way that the maxims according to which one regulates one's own moves could function as enacting universal rules. In responding to the here and the now, he decides for everywhere and for always. He would as a mind be the locus where universally valid meaning is elaborated; he would as an agency be the seat in which the legislation that governs the universe is promulgated. In his understanding the classical man recognizes the universe as such to be the proper object of his mind; in his action he deliberately makes himself a citizen of the universe, agency through which a law valid universally is formulated and obeyed. He embraces the laws that regulate the universe in each of his initiatives, embracing the form of the universe in each of his acts.

Against this classical ideal, Nietzschean thought opposes first a negative version of the universal agent. To exist and to act with laws universal and necessary, laws valid for everyone, is for Nietzsche to not have a law of one's own, a destiny of one's own. It is to regulate one's life with a law in force in any other. But this defines for Nietzsche the species individual, the herd individual. The individual makes himself but a medium, of himself indistinguishable from any other individual, upon which the patterns of action valid anywhere, at any time, are impressed. Such an existence makes itself equivalent to and interchangeable with others: This is its universality. But this existence does not affirm itself. The power of existence in it affirms the other, the anonymous form. It does not value itself, has no value for itself. It affirms the other, values the other. In addition, this existence *serves*. Each one makes himself equivalent to and interchangeable with any other; each can replace another at his tasks. No one has tasks of his own. This existence is useful, is servile.

This negative critique of the universal agent, telos of classicism and last man, has its positive counterpart in a new concept of the universal mind. The truly universal mind is the Zarathustran most comprehensive soul, conceived as a singular hold on the universe and not as transcending particularity toward the universal. Unlike the master consciousness in Hegel, its universality does not come to it from without, from being a particular recognized by all, affirmed by all. It is rather a natural power which embraces all nature, all its sensuous particulars, all its fortuitous events. The universal mind of classicism is denounced not in the name of the particularity of the individual but in the name of a sovereign individual more universal still. This sovereign individual is the most comprehensive soul, embracing the universe in its own singular destiny. What singularizes this individual is not the particularity, that is, the limitation, the finiteness, of a perspective but the singularity of its intrinsic law.

The artist is the example upon which Nietzsche has conceived his concept of the imperative that rules in the individual, singularizing him. An artist is convinced not only that the inner consummation of his own existence is a process in which worth is engendered, in which obligation takes hold, but that this value is valid beyond it, is an ordinance for which he is invested as its executor. The world must hear the music Beethoven's sensibility alone could engender; this music was necessary. No obligation is more binding than the imperative to maintain all his forces at the point at which a singular compulsion drives the artist to do what he alone can do. No transgression could be more calamitous than that deviation of the gaze, by which the paths and patterns of another would be taken to legislate for him.

The effect of the law must be to bind the sensuous will. "What makes the nobility of a being is that the passion that affects him is a singularity, without him knowing it; it is the usage of a rare and singular criterion, almost a folly; the sensation of heat in things which remain cold for all the others; the intuition of values for which one has not yet invented any scales; the holocaust offered on the altars of an unknown god; bravado without aspiration for honors; the modesty which abounds in resources and enriches men and things."[24]

The singular law does not constitute an atomic individual, and it must not be conceived as a solitary task. It does not fix some abiding trait or even some enduring line of behavior. It belongs to the nature of the idea of a singular law that it cannot be grasped in a common concept or expressed in a proposition constructed out of universal terms. For Kant too law is not comprehended, represented in a synthetic a priori proposition; it is first obeyed. It does not owe its legality to its being representable. Comprehending the law is forming universally valid and necessary representations for the will, in conformity with law. So in Nietzsche knowing a singular destiny is being obedient to an inward imperative to be master, is becoming what you are.

Its obedience is disobedience to the herd imperative: It is a law that requires one act beyond good and evil. But it is not simple singularity that is incumbent; the imperative mastery is not only singularity but power, an inner structure such that there pours forth an incessant excess of power. This power is known inwardly in joy. "What must I do in order to be happy? That I know not; be happy, and do what you will."[25] Happiness is not a telos which the action of suffering will can attain through action. But everything done out of happiness, out of sovereign power, such that it knows no demands to put on the world or on its gods, will be a blessing put on things.

The law binds one to one's own life, to the singular succession of fortuities, contingencies, chances of one's own history. It strips each moment of the justice of any claim regret and resentment formulate over the emptiness of moments past; it strips the moment of claims the anticipation and expectation make for moments to come. It gives unreserved weight, worth, to the moment.

What has this effect is the cosmic law of eternal return. The law of all nature has as its effect a law binding one's nature to its own existence.

It is not really the singularity of one's own law that is thus given a representation; the law is represented in a cosmic representation of all that is and becomes. The apophantic image of all that is has an imperative effect on the will.

This also has the confounding result that the image of nature forming on cycles of infinite time will have the imperative effect desired only if it is taken as true.

But does the sovereign effect Nietzsche seeks really require the projection of all that is and becomes on a time of eternal return? The doctrine of the eternal return is the Nietzschean way to affirm each event infinitely, to idealize it, to invest it with unrestricted worth. Behind this ontological valuation is the ancient idea that the distance from nothingness to being is infinite, that each event in its becoming realizes an infinite leap. This infinite weight, this infinite ontological import, is translated by thought into an infinite time of existence. The ontological density of each finite and finishing event is understood by seeing it sustained by the infinity of all nature, which in both the Husserlian and the Nietzschean theory is projected on infinite dimensions of time. The transcription of this ontological infinity, this infinity of being or of worth, into chronological eternity is a representation, an image of what Nietzsche must affirm, rather than its exact equivalent. The well of eternity that one falls into in falling into a moment is this infinity, deep, deep eternity.

This ultimate ontological-axiological intention in Nietzsche separates his implication of infinity in the moment from that of Husserl. In Husserl it is the *identification* of the moment, the positing of its form in its fully determinate boundaries, and its recognition that leads one to see that what bounds this moment so decisively and positively on either side can only be other moments of the same form. It is true that when Nietzsche formulates the infinity in time as the eternal return of the same, he paradoxically fixes the moment in its identity, whereas he has denied identity of the temporal contents.

But there is another intuition of time in Nietzsche, where the moment is conceived as vast, as equivalent to eternity. Where eternity is not the linear extension of its recurrence, but depth, "deep, deep eternity," "the well of eternity."

> "Still! Did not the world become perfect just now? . . .
>
> "O happiness, how little is sufficient for happiness! Thus I spoke once and seemed clever to myself. But it was a blasphemy: *that* I have learned now. Clever fools speak better. Precisely the least, the softest, lightest, a lizard's rustling, a breath, a breeze, a moment's glance—it is *little* that makes the *best* happiness. Still!
>
> "What happened to me? Listen! Did time perhaps fly away? Did I not fall? Did I not fall—listen!—into the well of eternity?"[26]

Here the immense love for the least, the softest, the lightest is equivalent to the experience of eternity. This immensity in the moment, this depth, is the inscription of the momentary content on infinite reverberations. But the moment does not implicate an infinity of moments or its own infinite repetition; it is itself equivalent to eternity. "Behold the sun still stood straight over his head." The swoon into the depths of the moment, which closes off all remembrance of the moments past and all expectancy of moments to come, erects the moment with the worth, the immensity of eternity.

Nietzsche's thought arises in contestation of the idealization that theoretical thought works on nature. It breaks radically with the kind of synthesizing, conceptual thought that is at work in metaphysical understanding. It requires a differentiating, utterly a posteriori kind of thought. It requires a theory of language that is not built on the opposition between the diversity of sensuous signs and the ideal identity of meanings signified. It adumbrates, without inaugurating, contemporary theories of language, which do not, however, really build along the directions Nietzsche indicated.

The Nietzschean thought is also a contestation of the law that makes mastery imperative. The Nietzschen image of mastery requires a wholly new concept of law, which neither the scientific concept of a law of nature, discovered as a determinism in the agent, nor the political concept of positive law in its essential publicness enables us to understand. The post-Christian era, in which divine law is no longer heard, is also a post-political and post-positivist era. The concept of law that makes mastery imperative has to be derived out of the destiny that rules artists.

Can the law that makes mastery imperative be rigorously formulated? Can it be separated from the cosmological thesis of the eternal return of all things?

For Nietzsche the concept of sovereignty is bound up with a sense of the infinite ontological density of the transitory moments, and of one's own transitory moments; it can only be formulated when projected on the dimension of infinite time. Sovereignty is immortality. The infinite ontological density of its own moments gets expressed as a law of its own singular destiny, which is utterly inward. Sovereignty is ruled by an imperative which is in no way received from the outside. A death that would be definitive, an "It was" that could not be made a "Thus I will it!"[27] would shatter the sovereignty of the master life.

Heidegger's philosophy represents the effort to conceive just such a *mortal sovereignty*. Levinas's practical philosophy represents the effort to conceive its law as located entirely outside, a radically heteronomous agent.

Part II
THE SUBJECTION

And the light that shines above the
heavenly vault, the support of all creation,
the support of the universe, in the supreme and
highest realms, is none other than the
light that dwells in the human body. Its actual
manifestation is the warmth that is felt when
the flesh is touched.

—Upanishads

V

DEATHBOUND THOUGHT

That the human spirit is mortal, deathbound, that death does not befall our existence by accident or as a catastrophe, but that our existence, of its own nature, projects itself, with all its forces, unto its death—this conviction is at the core of Heidegger's thought. Death is the law—the imperative—of our existence. And that death is not intrinsically unthinkable, the irremediable refutation of the significance and worth our existence stakes out, but that the deathbound propulsion of our existence is the spirit itself is what makes our movements comprehending and our existence exultant, ecstatic—the understanding that understands that is authentic thought; Heidegger's philosophy of existence is intended to formulate it. Death is the law—the ordinance of our existence. This deathbound thought breaks radically with the metaphysical as well as with the scientific forms of thought. But that our life establish with death a relationship of freedom—would that not be the highest stakes of modern Western thought?

1. The General Form of the World

The question What is our existence? is already misleading in its form; it asks for a quiddity. Against the metaphysics which, answering this question, conceives our existence as something subsistent in itself, a substance, Heidegger sets out to formulate it relationally, such that the relationship with death and the relationship with the world enter into its definition. In us existence is movement into the world—and projection into death.

The world comes to exist for us first through our functional, practical movements. Our moves, self-launching, self-steering, make things exist for us, taking them from the first as manipulatable, serviceable, resistant, or useful. With such moves we make contact with reality, and there is already a comprehension in them. For in reaching out for things our practical moves grasp things with their contexts, in their fields, are comprehending. And discern sequences of like things, are recognizing. The world first takes form as a field of manipulanda, gear.

This primary understanding comprehends the general form of things and of the world. Something utilizable is useful not just for an instant nor forever but for a time, being used up as it is being used. And it is useful not just for a single use of the hand but for a certain range of manipulations. In utilizing it I contract one of a range of equivalent and interchangeable figures of movement. I sit on this chair as another weary body for which it was made, I operate the punch press as a punch press operator, I look at the green of the grass and the light of the sky as eyes of flesh look at green and at light. I enact existence as a series of moves equivalent to and interchangeable with any variant within the range of moves this utilizable thing, and equivalent things, call for, tropisms being enacted elsewhere, before and after me. My existence takes form as one variant on a pattern picked up from others, passed on to others, read off from the things, whose endurance and the persistence of whose exigencies induce these successive operations. I take my place before these things by displacing others, changing places with them. In day to day existence, where each day, with its equipment and its demands, takes the place of an equivalent day, where the day provided me is equivalent to that provided anyone else.

One need not contrive one's own understanding; to function one need but take things as equivalent things were taken, take up in turn the comprehension of things already formulated in the talk at large in the world. Occupied then with a field of gear that was known in advance to be there, equivalent to that known by others, equivalent to that known yesterday, one does each day what there is to be done, as it is easier to do, and there is a specific feeling of contentment made of this assurance and this ease.

Thus the pulse of existence in me takes form in its mundane anonymity, its *Uneigentlichkeit*, a wave on a stream of existence where nothing begins, nothing ends. Only the material cleared away or rearranged by these movements has its finality, day's work of a city or of a social order that has to get done. The pulse of existence itself is inessential, without essence. Without a structure of its own, that would posit and maintain itself. Without unity, without identity of its own. Without an action of its own. Here existence itself is not an achievement, an accomplishment. It is without telos, without end. It leads nowhere. Its time passes by, day by day, an *und so weiter*. It passes, without having importance, neither for itself nor for others—especially not for itself. Senseless, insignificant, without meaning of its own, the anonymous force of existence is something incomprehensible, unintelligible; it is at best observable and calculable.

And anonymous everyday existence is senseless, unintelligible, to such an extent that it is only relative to an existence that is on its own, is *eigen*, that one can formulate the least concept about it—and that always in a negative and privative way.[1] Either one conceives it, negatively and privatively, as *in*authentic, or else one conceives it, by a thought completely astray, with the substantive or functional categories worked out for intramundane entities, as part of the system of subsistent things or as a sort of self-moving mechanism.

2. The Essence, and the Essential Time

The theoretical question What is our existence? then requires us to seek a species of existence that is essential, that has contracted an essence of its own. The existence that is authentic, *eigentlich,* is on its own, is *eigen,* relates not simply to its properties or faculties but to its existence as its own, appropriates being as its own. It has its own being. It is an identity for itself and unto itself by appropriating all its being, identifying itself, and not merely by reproducing some identifiable, that is, recognizable, general pattern. It has a structure, determination, and an internal unity, by which it holds together of itself. Here existence contracts essence. It exists in the striving to become *what* it is, it exists oriented toward its own being as toward its telos, its assigned destiny. And this structure that holds together of itself is graspable, this essence is comprehensible, has sense, is qua ex-istence, qua teleological striving, signifyingness itself.

We must even ask, of existence, not what? but who?, for the task of theoretical inquiry is henceforth no longer to understand the essence of man in each man, but to understand the essence in, of, each man, the *Dasein* each time mine. Our singularity does not amount simply to some individuating differences on the ground of our common human essence. Precisely our singularity is the essential. The task will be to understand this essentially singular essence, the existence that essentially exists in the first person singular. Each authentic existence, contracting being as its own, has its own essence, its own sense, its own destiny, its own intrinsic intelligibility.

This theoretical question pursues, in its own register, an existential quest for essence—for structure, for meaning, for finality—that belongs to the inmost will, the conscience of life. The will for essence characterizes life precisely as Dasein—as the place where the meaning of Being is manifested, the place where Being's own striving for essence is effected. It is only in a Dasein that is authentic, that appropriates Being as its own, that Being itself comes into its own. It is only in the *Eigentlichkeit* of Dasein that the *Ereignis* of Being is effected, Logos or assembling of things—which are themselves to be conceived not as assemblages of *Eigenshaften,* properties, but as assemblers of *Geeignetheiten,* modes of appropriateness.[2]

But the singular essence of an existence is engendered in the assembling not of its parts or its faculties but of its times. For, according to the modern analysis, time is the internal order or structure of the soul; time is its *principium individuationis.* An existence that is on its own has a time of its own. Its moves are inscribed not in the public line of nows endlessly succeeding one another—time of recurrence, everydayness—but in a trajectory of time that originates by birth to project itself to its death.

Heidegger then sets out to show that an existence comes to contract an essence and to be on its own by dropping out of the interminable public and natural, universal and objective, time, by projecting itself to its death, by closing in on itself, over the nullity of its past, the nothingness of its future, in guilt and anxiety. *Eigentlichkeit* is this production of a time that is one's own.

At the same time it is the *Ereignis*—the coming into their own—of times, of a future that is veritably future, *Zu-künft*, and not an absent present represented in advance, of a past that has definitively and irrevocably come to pass and is not but a present replaced by, and represented by, the actual present. For what characterizes the time of inauthenticity is not only that it is an infinite succession of nows, but that the times—the past, the present, the future—are equivalent and interchangeable—and indeed it is because none of them has an essence of its own that they are equivalent and succeed one another interminably. Authentic existence in its presence answers for what has come to pass in itself, takes hold of what is to come to it. Only in authenticity, when existence contracts an essence of its own, is future veritably to come, past veritably come to pass, and present veritably presenting. When it contracts its own essence our existence becomes veritably temporal.

3. The Essential Mortality

The invitation to anonymity comes from being, from the very structure of mundane things. An existence is wrenched from its natural absorption in the world and posited for itself not, as in Descartes, by the critical dissolution of the apparently solid things in which methodic doubt insinuates a suspicion of inconsistency and not by an imaginative annihilation of the world, as in Husserl, but by the anticipated annihilation of the world about me, the anticipation of dying, which is what is being rehearsed in anxiety. Anxiety senses emptiness, void, opening up in the interstices of being. It begins, Heidegger says, in the sense of insignificance;[3] the signifyingness of things, the ways they lead to one another, begin being readable either way, end up where they began, sink into a universal equivalence. Anxiety arises in the midst of the everyday absorption with things, and out of it. The recurrence of the problems and tasks the things compose, ever equivalent and interchangeable, and the equivalence of one's operations on them with equivalent and ever recurrent operations on things elsewhere makes the everyday things lose the force of their presence and tasks lose their urgency. The time of everydayness provokes the insignificance of the world it presents and induces anxiety. Existence finds itself drifting and feels the emptiness.

I get a sense that my life is threatened obscurely and imminently with nothingness, that death will single me out and put an end to me, one day, but that the operations, the tropisms, my life consisted in will go on, will be taken up by others, equivalent to and interchangeable with me. It is then that I get a feeling of a pulse, a heat of life in me, that is singular and alone feels itself, and in its feeling clings to itself, and that is to be snuffed out one day and never be repeated. The sense of void imminent makes my life pulsate for me with anxiety, that is, more palpably, more keenly, more ardently: It separates the individual line of the pulse of life in me from the anonymous and everywhere recurrent patterns of behavior that I have thus far used my life force to repeat.

And yet it is not the nothingness that delimits that individuates, for of itself the confrontation with nothingness which has no front lines in anxiety is dissolute and disintegrating and the anticipation of death is already a dying. The apprehension of the existence whose scope and span are measured by nothingness, by death, must be a life's own work, a work that is positive and internal. For Heidegger this comprehension, this making my being exist for-me, this appropriation, is not the work of consciousness, always self-conscious, but of conscience. In spite of the order of the chapters in his book, for Heidegger the sense of conscience precedes and engenders the sense of mortality. The positive, positing apprehension of the being I have to be, singular nexus of potentialities destined for a singular set of tasks, engenders the anxiety that catches sight of the nothingness that bounds the uttermost confines of that being that is to be my own. Anxiety is anxiety of conscience.

4. The Sense of What Is to Come

Both the sense of conscience and the sense of mortality are anticipatory; the voice of conscience simultaneously articulates and calls me unto the being I have to become, and anxiety apprehends the non-being that is to come to me. The anxious conscience anticipates—that is, does not merely represent but projects me into—the full expanse of what is possible for me, anticipates the uttermost limits of the possible, unto the possibility of impossibility, of irreversible and definitive impotence. Once one has anticipated one's death one has anticipated what is possible, all that is possible. One has understood the possible as such. For Heidegger the sense of the possible and the sense of mortality are the same thing. And they are the veritable sense of the future, which is thus originally protended not by representation but by guilt and anxiety.

But why does Heidegger identify the veritable sense of the future with the sense of the possible? And why is the pure essence of the possible given in the sense of death, in the anticipation of impossibility?

One might assert that we know nothing of death and that the syllogism that tries to proceed from the empirical fact of the death of all men so far to my own death cannot claim essential certainty. But anxiety *knows*. What anxiety knows of death is that it is imminent—the last instant may be the next instant—and that it is, for me, impotence in existence. Anxiety is the premonition not of something deleterious whose approach could be surveyed, situated somewhere in the succession of moments, but of the pure menace of an instant that would be the last instant—instant, punctual cut in time utterly without duration, utterly ungraspable. Instant of impotence. The sense of mortality then is the sense of the vertical dimension of imminence, the sense that the present, the actual, is menaced by what we absolutely could not get our hands on, by the utterly elusive, the ungraspable, the incomprehensible. Because it is nothing.

The possible is what is situated in this region of imminence. It is not what is represented by a thought that has grasped the coherence of the actual and elaborates variations on it. The real possible weighs on us. And approaches, of itself, produces itself, is parturition in being.[4] And is certain, certainly there. Only then is it really possible, is there a real possible. Pure imminence, that weighs, on anxiety, that threatens of itself—death is possible, is the pure essence of the possible, opens the dimension of the possible as such.

Heidegger has identified the original and veritable sense of the future with the sense of the possible. To have a sense of the future is not to represent, in advance, in the present, an absent, still remote, present. It is to have a sense of the possible, of the really possible, that is, not what we represent, present, to ourselves, by prolonging the lines of the actual but what comes of itself. For the future—the *zukünftig*—is what comes to us, not what we produce. It is not that we have a sense of our death in the future; we have a sense of the future in our sense of death, in that dimension of imminence upon which our mortal anxiety opens.

The possible is not what stabilizes before our intuition like a representation. The possible is what proposes itself to, and answers to, a capacity, a power. We let the possible be possible for us, then, when we open ourselves to it, when we take it up, when we cast ourselves into it. We let the future be future for us, we let the *Zukünft* come to us, we let death gain power over us, when we allow it to possibilize our own being, to render our being but possible for us.[5] To appropriate death is to let it be possible, to let it affect me, let it come to me, let it gain power over me, let it make my being possible.

The imminence of death singles me out; the impossible with which death menaces is only my impotence. Death approaches to extinguish an existence destined for me to exist, but the tropisms, the operations my life enacted day after day will go on, will be taken up by others equivalent to and interchangeable with me. The menace of death affects a pulse of existence that lets itself be formed, be taken up into those tropisms, but that involved potentialities of its own. It is the force of those potentialities that anxiety is anxious about, that are disengaged by the death that closes in on them, making my force of existence something only possible. Anxiety anticipates, projects itself across, my whole future, all its possibility, unto the confines of the impossible; it disengages what possibilities are but for me from those that are for anyone. Opening my whole being to the threat of total and definitive impotence, I take over in advance, I project myself into, my whole future, with all I am, I apprehend the whole range of the potentialities for being that are my own.

My own being henceforth is but a possible being, but a possible being that calls upon me, that speaks to me as the voice of conscience. A possible being that activates me, that makes me exist ecstatically as a propulsion toward it, that is, as an ex-istence.

To my own potentialities for existence there would correspond, in the world, equally singular possibilities.[6] We are to believe that the world is rich enough for that, that it harbors a set of tasks destined singularly for me alone, for this singular node of potentialities that has arisen in its midst. Opened to my death, I open to all that in the world lets me be, gives me the possibility to be me, all that gives place for me to be. I am then not just thrown into a world where it is possible to operate as anyone operates; I am sent forth into a world for destined tasks, singular and finite.

5. The Past One Has

The imminence of impossibility makes the being I have to be but possible, and makes the existence I exist a potentiality for being that possible, and possibly impossible, being. And it makes that which has come to pass in me, the being that has come to birth in me, the determination of that potentiality. Such is the authentic past, the past that is my own, the being that has come to pass in me. For Heidegger if there is a past, if the past is, it is that being that has been, that has come to pass, that has come to be—*das Gewesen*—the irrevocable, the definitive; it is not the being that has passed away—*das Vergangen*—that has come to be nothingness.[7] I have a past, take possession of it, by answering for it. The irrevocable and definitive being that has come to pass in me renders definite, finite, the capacity for non-being I am, the potentiality for being I am. At once.

For I discover each time that each assignation kept with someone I was given to be means a death sentence for someone else I was also destined to be. In setting out to live a potentiality destined for me I put to death something in me; in taking up existing I convert potential being into nothingness. My power to exist some of my potentialities for being is an impotence to exist all my potentialities for being. The sense that my being in projecting itself into existence is responsible for nothingness is its guilt with regard to its own being.[8]

This situation expresses the fact that power is not power all the way through and with regard to itself, does not engender itself but finds itself generated, finds itself born.[9] The being given a being to have, being committed to its potentiality, is the impotence of power. It is the failing, the guilt of having been born.

Then the nothingness that anxious existence knows when it knows itself to be but potential is not only outside of it or ahead of it, its absolute other, an exterior threat. The very power of existing is responsible for, produces, its impotence and nothingness. In taking up a potentiality for being existence projects itself, with its own force, unto a terminal nothingness, and already at each moment consigns to nothingness potentiality for being that is its own. In projecting myself, anxiously, into the nothingness ahead of me I come back, guiltily, to the nothingness my existing produces of itself in coming to birth as a determinate power.[10] The anxiety that discloses my future overtakes, and is overtaken by, the guilt that reveals my birth. It is in the death sentence I seal for the someone I was destined to be that I understand the meaning of the final assignation to which the someone I have chosen to be is destined. The sense of mortality is given in conscience, alsways bad conscience.

6. The Ecstatic Present

Anxiety *knows*. Anxiety comprehends existence—that is, discloses what is possible for existence—and overtakes and takes over existence as a whole, holds existence together as a whole. It is the movement by which a destiny is sealed, a time of one's own contracted.

For in the shudder of anxiety the times of my existence disconnect from universal and objective time, close in on themselves, my future no longer opening upon the *und so weiter* of the anonymous future, the day to day, my past no longer passing away into the universal innocence of the bygone.

My future and my past become mine, are possessed, held in presence, in the contraction of the anxious present. My future is no longer a present still absent, still remote, but a possible that affects me already, imminent, weighing on the present; my past is no longer a present passed away, bygone, but a being that has come to pass, come to be in me, definitive and irrevocable.

Anxiety knows what has come to pass in me is now but possible, but a possible that has come to be, determinate, irrevocable: a potential. As a determinate potential, it calls upon me; it is what I have to be. Anxiety circumscribes this potential being with the darkness of nothingness. The very extendedness of existence is stretched out[11] by this assembling of past and future by which what has come to pass becomes potential and what is still to come is irrevocable and definitive.[12] In this circuit—this pregnant past, this irrevocable future—existence contracts structure and destiny: essence. This structure contracting in the present gives definitiveness to each deed, de- cisiveness. With each deed something is decided, the comedy, tragedy, or farce of my existence. The authentic life breaks with the irresoluteness of a life inscribed in unending time, where nothing is ever decided. Each deed is not only an upsurge of determinate potential but fatal. One lives in, and dies from, each act.

The moment of destiny—destination and fatality—is the moment in which the whole of one's life is lived. The will to essence, to authenticity, is this will to have, to possess, at each moment, all one's time, to exist, in the moment, with all one's time. It is the will to give to the present, to one's presence in the world, the richest possible content, to pour into it one's whole past, one's whole future.

The time of a destiny is lived in a moment when the pulse of existence anticipates its whole future, retains its whole past, is wholly present, utterly there. Such an existence has given determination to all its potentialities and has made everything definitive in it a potential. It no longer requires an infinite time for its accomplishment; its accomplishment in the now is better than the eternal adjournment of its expiration.

To exist authentically, in the first person singular, is to know that high noon instant in which one recognizes that one is where one was destined to be, that one was born to be here, that everything that has come to pass in one was to bring one here, a presence that is accomplished in itself, such that one is free to die forthwith. Existence assembled to that point, ecstatic to that extent, still at its birth, already wholly at death, discharging all its forces in a decisive, fatal gesture which determines and terminates itself.

The essential existence is wholly potential, wholly power. It is the most powerful form of life. But it is so because it is first potentiality for not being, potentiality for impotence. Power in its essence has then to be understood as a discharge, as a projection all the way unto its end, unto impotency. To be able to give a term to, to determine, a force is the condition for force to be power, and not outburst and dissipation. To be able to die is still a power; we not only perish, we can die, Heidegger says.[13] If we die it is because our existence projects itself, of its own forces, to its end, unto the impossible. The project with which existence effects its potential—or makes its being-there a potential—casts it unto being, unto the world—but this movement is possible because the world surrounds it as the future, as the clearing of the possible, which is possibly impossible. Each step into the openness of the world is at the same time attracted by the void. Each move of power delivers itself of itself.

The most negative experience, exposure to nothingness itself, is utterly positive in its effect: it posits being, the being I am, wholly potential coming to itself, wholly power. The anticipation in the projection of one's forces, in one's power, proceeds unto one's own death, sets its free, lets it extend its sway over one, lets it come, lets it be future, and renders one free for it. It is the death to come that makes my own being possible. To deliver oneself over to one's death is to liberate oneself, is to set free the sphere of potential-being, of power, that is one's own.

Anxiety, at the extreme limit of passivity, of prostration, anticipating already the projection into final and definitive impotence, converts into extreme activity, no longer undergoing the passing of time but enacting the trajectory of its own time, enacting the projection of the being that has come to pass in me to the nothingness that is to come for me.

7. The Certainty of Conscience

When our existence becomes essential, comes into its own, contracts its own time, it becomes Dasein: the place—or, better, the time, the moment—where Being is revealed. To seek now such a moment is not the same as to seek absolute spirit, or consciousness, immediately self-conscious, which, as the self-evident place of all evidence, could function as the metaphysical foundation for objective and universal truth. For Heidegger the appropriation of my own being, the setting up of the sphere of ownness, the *eigen*, the *Eigentlichkeit*, never will be a matter of grasping the *sum* of the *cogito*:[14] of apprehending, conceiving, my being, representing it or maintaining it present, positing it as something assured. Authentic understanding is not grounded in the "I am!", the self-confirming affirmation of being in consciousness, apodictically self-conscious, but in the anxiety of conscience that discovers that to be Dasein is to be the place of death, *Platzhalter, lieu-tenant*, of nothingness.[15]

For in Heidegger it is my death, in its pure possibility, that is the first intelligible, as it is the first certitude. The anticipation that apprehends all my being is assured not of my being but of my non-being; it is the death in the depths of me it apprehends in an immediate, ineluctable fashion. Anxiety is this very indubitability.

No induction from the demise of all men so far—that rigor mortis I can observe in the stillness of being—leads rigorously to the certainty of my death; no deduction from laws ever in force enables me to conclude to the certainty of my coming reduction to definitive impotence. It is the certainty of my imminent death, which is the way the certainty of non-being comes to me, that makes doubt about the present beings, and consequently the quest for empirical certainty, first possible. The appropriation of my being does not then come into possession of an assured substance or foundation from which to proceed to the ascertainment of beings in the world and of the world; it is not my being nor my non-being, not my substance but my ex-istence or my possibility, that is certain, and it is this certainty that first makes possible doubt about the beings of the world about me. It also makes it first possible for me to understand them. The imminence of death, opening the possible as such, first gives me the power of understanding those nodes of instrumental possibilities which the things of the world are.[16] The deathbound understanding understands things in their reality: not substances inhering in themselves without affecting us, not matter formed by a demiurge transcending us or by a transcendental subjectivity in us, not clusters of sensations reflected in the passive mirror of a mind,[17] for which our own self-subsistent being would be the foundation, but an exhibition of forms to which we are ourselves exposed, sensible being to which we are sensitive and susceptible, receptive of their forms and thereby exposed to wounding, objects to which we are subject, vectors of resistance and force which can overpower us, beings existing really, in themselves, able to put an end to our being. Our death is in our hands, *zuhanden, vorhanden*. And we are certain of the things within reach, certain of the world delivered over to us, with the very certainty of our mortality.

8. The Everyday Equivocation

This understanding is not available in objective or anonymous talk about things. Such talk intersubjectively constituted aims at being true by prescinding from the narrowness and the illusions of a particular subjectivity. Yet it is itself always equivocal, means to equivocate, and expresses the mendacious intent of everyday existence. The talk that circulates—and that equivocates—can be stabilized, held fixed and its truth ascertained, only by a subject existing on its own, in its own time, a subject assured of its own mortality.

Talk—*das Gerede*, the said, constituted speech—circulates anonymously; it circulates because it is anonymous, because doing what there is to be done one says what there is to be said. But the very constitution of statements, then, the recasting of utterances in the first person singular into utterances in the anonymous form that can circulate freely, is for Heidegger a degradation.[18] Statements empty of their meaning when they circulate, already when they are recast in such a way that they can circulate—and they now function to cover up, a sediment of signs forming over the public world.

For Husserl's phenomenology to recover the meaning or revealing power of constituted talk is to reenact the moment of its constitution in the utterance of a speaking subject. To understand constituted statements one must reactivate the evidence for which their linguistic formulation is the signs. This evidence is the presence of the things themselves, intuitive evidence in a subjectivity which if real is always singular, says "I." For Husserl every "it is said that . . ." becomes true in the moment that "*I* see."

For Heidegger too if the meaning, and the truth, of constituted discourse is to be uncovered, it has to be converted into speech in the first person singular. It has to be appropriated by an essentially reticent authentic existence which assumes responsibility for the utterance—reissues it as its own and answers for it. This answerability is the essential for Heidegger; it establishes and maintains univocity. It is not the reference to evidence, to intuition, that converts constituted talk into utterances in the first person singular, for sight, intuition, can form anonymously.

Anonymous evidence and the anonymous talk that expresses it is of itself essentially equivocal. The equivocation consists not in articulating two divergent meanings but in concealing with the very discursive operation upon structures that discloses them. A voice that takes up and passes on what there is to be said inscribes in its turn the recurrent forms of things and the general form of a world over the singularity of its own situation. This is the only way that the evidence of the singular, the ephemeral, the fleeting, and the unrecurrent can be blurred and the circumspect gaze be glanced off from the matrix of all singularity, death, in each case only mine.[19]

Speech loses its univocity when an existence loses sight of the direction in which it is headed. Utterances that represent *what there is to be said* are the expression of equivocal existence which makes itself equivalent to any other existence in the time-format of recurrence, everydayness. The double-en-tendre by which only what there is to be said gets put forth as what I have to say, the equivocation by which only the everyday gets seen, is not explained by some weakness, some congenital myopia of finite man, but is explained entirely as aversion to the time that projects itself univocally, irreversibly, into its death, evasiveness in the face of one's own time.

Talk means nothing. *C'est parler pour rien dire.* Talk means to articulate nothingness, to fill time, to share, or generalize, the singularity of a lifetime, to pass over in silence the mortality of a lifetime. And talk means—signifies—that nothingness, its meaning becoming empty in the measure that it is constituted. If talk empties of its meaning in the measure that it circulates, that is because it was first constituted in such a way that it can circulate in order to not say something, in order to pass over in silence the singularity of one's situation and the summons of death pronounced by its form.[20]

The prudence of the practical talk of the everyday world propagates in empty equivocation, as in the underworld scenes in Shakespeare where the anti-language of sorcerers mocks the questions of men of action. Everyday talk equivocates as it circulates, conceals as it reveals, empties of its meaning and means this emptiness. The everyday world slips into insignificance in the measure that its sense is articulated. Whence the finally derisory character of everyday existence. One gives oneself a sense of emptiness in the midst of the very solidity of things in place, in the midst of the assurances of tasks and exigencies recognized by everyone.

The day-to-day agitation represents an enormous expenditure not simply to supply for the natural needs of finite and incomplete beings and to satisfy the caprices and fantasies of imaginative beings but to shore up the emptiness, to fill time.

For in all the forms of acting, feeling, looking, and speaking Heidegger's existential analysis uncovers an underlying time motivation—a will to form one's existence according to a certain form of time. Whereas Husserl's inten-tional analysis was the identification of the objects of conscious acts, the existential analysis is the exhibition of the time-format of states of life—and the identifying of that time-format as their very objective. The will to exist in the time of recurrence is opposed to the will to exist in a time of one's own as the will to dissimulate is opposed to the will to truth. But it is from the beings that the invitation to the mendacious anonymity comes. The will to dissimulate adjusts itself to beings; the will to truth is produced as the impossible adjustment to nothingness.

The distinction between authentic and inauthentic speech is thus nowise the same as the classical distinction between the subjective and the objective, which is based on, and required by, the ontological assumption that being for its part is in itself definite, distinct, and phosphorescent in the clarity of its ostentation. If we did not succeed in constituting a representation adequate to this being, the real, this was taken to be due to the proper nature of our subjectivity—to the opaqueness of sensuous intuition and confused sentiments, to the blind passions, the weighted discursive moves. Due, finally, to the receptive character, the weakness, the finitude of our being. There would be ways to compensate for this finitude; we must supply ourselves with method, apparatus to control our observations, rules to fix the mind on the straight line of right thinking. Intersubjective concord would compensate for the perspective finitude of subjectivity. The suspicion that being itself is *fragwürdig*, that being itself *is* in a questionable mode,[21] does not arise; being is taken to be in itself wholly positive, to be position or auto-affirmation. If it does not achieve its high noon truth in the space of our subjectivity, it is our being that would have to be indicted.

For Heidegger the flight from finitude is an evasiveness in the face of the end, a fear of dying. It is not our finitude as such that leads us astray but the fleeting, fugitive character of our gaze passing from one thing to the next, whose apparent curiosity is but anxious evasiveness. Our gaze makes itself anonymous from the first and concerns itself with the day to day, with a time that recurs without end. It structures itself anonymously or intersubjectively; one sees what anyone can see, one says what there is to be said. The movement of everyday existence is an erring,[22] an existence intent on lying to itself. It is to articulate the world in day-to-day time that the essentially equivocating universal or intersubjective talk is constituted.

But this invitation to anonymity comes from being itself, from the general format of the world.

9. The Science of the Singular

No one can know my anxiety, foreboding of a death that shall not pass me by, for which I am inescapably destined by what makes existence my own. The dying of which anxiety is the premonition can be shared with no one, allows of no generalization. The others, in passing away, immobilize into cadavers which subsist, in a world which subsists; I shall know their demise in that silence I feel in my soul when I find myself continuing to address my private thoughts to that other from whom my distress recognizes henceforth no response shall come. But there is nothing in common between that silence and that immobilization in the plenitude of a world intact, exposed to my observation, and the menace whose approach is unlocatable and which weighs inwardly on my heart like a personal condemnation, the instantaneous engulfment of the world about me in total and definitive void.

That the dying I anticipate for myself in the vertigo of anxiety is not, is never, understood in the talk that circulates is not surprising; the speech that is no longer the anguished cry of the moribund one but a statement about our common predicament is always dissembling. Here inauthenticity is always erring and equivocation—mendacity. The general concept of death, the concept of death in general, is an essentially hypocritical concept.

Dying eludes comprehension, it is what we cannot take hold of, what on the contrary comes to take us—that is, to take me. For if dying is incomprehensible, that is not because it is invisible and intangible, inobservable, nothingness; it is because it is radically singular. Unconceptualizable, being ungeneralizable, it is not therefore unintelligible; as purely possible, the pure possible, it is the first intelligible, eminently understood in all understanding, which is always prehension of the possible. The understanding of the singular death makes understanding real, understanding of reality, for all real beings are in the singular.

What is intelligible is not first a singular being, the being that exists in the first person singular, but the singularity of nonbeing, the incomparable and solitary absoluteness of nothingness unrelentingly closing in on me. Nothingness cannot make sense, make itself sensed, except as a singular and unrepeatable catastrophe, in the univocity of my own destination for it. Its truth consists in this correspondence.

I do not get a sense of being singular, a being unto myself, from my sense of being active, a cause, a power in the world. For, we have seen, my first gearing into the world effaces me. In taking form, my existence generalizes, becomes anonymous. What disengages something singular—a pulse, a trouble, a question of existence beneath the tropisms of life in general that my functioning, practical life instantiates—is the singular fate that closes in on it, the singular and incomparable dying for which this existence is uniquely destined.

The singularity of an existence in the first person singular does not consist in the singularity of a nucleus of ego whose acts and states are comprehensible in categories but which itself would have to be conceived as a subsistent constant *sui generis*. It consists in a single and singular trajectory of time projected to its incomparable end.[23] This time, engendering and appropriating itself, irreversible and unrepeatable, disconnected from objective and universal time, is the form of the first person singular.

In disconnecting itself from recurrence, in casting itself, with all its own forces, into the void, existence goes nowhere else than into the world. The world is the order ordaining things, the cosmos that holds all things together, the possible that engenders all things, the space or clearing that opens to give place to things—and it is also emptiness of space, abyss, *Unheimlichkeit*, interminable zone of the uncanny in which we cannot fix our dwelling. It is the embrace of the world that makes our power, our existence, real, but this embrace is ineluctably fatal. The world is not a shelter from death; on the contrary death is everywhere in the world, is the world itself. The end, nothingness, is everywhere latent; in opening the door upon the landscape of the world I open it upon the abyss. In advancing down the pathways of the world I very certainly go to my death. It is with one and the same movement that our existence projects itself, fascinated, into the world and projects itself, anxiously, unto its death. The movement of existence is a groping. Heidegger means to define our existence in such a way that its attachment to the world and its destination to total impotence enter into its very definition.

The impotence of my death discloses to me my impotence with regard to my birth. Destined to death, delivered over to being: such is the specific nature of my passivity—the passivity of ecstatic ex-istence. Sensibility is this passivity of ecstatic existence. Exposed to being but, thereby, exposed to nothing. Mortality belongs to the essence of a sensible consciousness. Ecstatic existence, in delivering itself of its own being, is affected by the things and afflicted with itself. To be delivered over to beings is to be delivered over to death; it is to be subject to things—not only a subject in which their refracted attributes can inhere but subject to them, exposed to their forms and their qualities but also to their force and their aggression, mortified by them. It is an essentially mortal structure that is expressed in our taste for the colors, our ear for what is intoned across the fields of being, our appetite for the honey and the lees of the day.

If a mortal force of life can still assemble and steer itself, it is because it makes contact still with a ground, a density of being closed in itself, the supporting element of the terrestrial.[24] Precarious, fortuitous, the grain of substances takes form under the hand, the opaque still sustains the palpation of the gaze. And gives place for the pressure, the force of this life; here are possibilities still that are my own. Beneath the general and abstract outlines of the recurrent things, a mortal clairvoyance discerns the unrecurrent, the ephemeral, the fleeting; it discerns a field of chances, understands real beings, which are in the singular. The singular death imminent about me takes form in the singular constellation of possibilities, instrumentalities, chances, and snares which forms the singular landscape of the sensible world arrayed for me.

10. A Prophetic Sense of the Future

Apprehension of the possible, assured of the certain, the deathbound understanding is divinatory, a prophetic understanding of the future. It is the discernment, in the general form of the world's recurrent gear, of what is made but once for me; it is the discernment in the possibilities the world engenders of what possibilities are for me, the distinguishing from those that are for others. It is the discernment, in the general forms and potentialities of life, of potentialities that are for me alone to be.

The potentialities of existence are not indeterminate nor to be invented ex nihilo as one's existence projects itself out of the being it is into the future, the void before it. In the closure of authentic existence the potential is certain, is definitive and irrevocable; authentic understanding is understanding of destiny. It finds the potentialities for existence destined for oneself in the existences that have already come to pass, come to be.

That does not mean a science of human nature, having surveyed the lives of men past, could inventory a definite set of potentialities of a general form which every human existence has to live out and which I can know in advance that my life shall but repeat, with whatever individual variations the empirical state of affairs imposes. For what is possible for me is delineated not by the general and the recurrent, the everyday—but by the singular ones. In the singular trajectories of their existence they diagram other potentialities beyond those that subsist by recurrence—potentialities that are still but possible, potentialities for others.

In this way an existence accomplished, concluded in its extinction, concerns the lives to come. Not that the singular one, in the accomplishment and perfection of his singular potentialities, describes a form of existence that is henceforth to be reenacted, that is an invitation to anonymity. But that his existence, in living out and discharging all its own potentialities, delineates potentialities that are not for him to realize, potentialities that are for others.[25] —Just as thought can constitute a heritage in that it is only in the understanding of those who thought on their own that we find not our answers but our questions: that which makes a thought of our own possible. The real heritage of heroes is not what is accomplished and endures like an acquisition, it is a heritage of potentialities. Not only the works then but the very existence of the singular ones constitutes itself, deathbound, into a heritage.

This is the sense in which an existence of one's own can be a good. The good is defined by Heidegger as that which makes authentic existence possible.[26] What makes my own existence, an existence become my own, possible, are potentialities destined for me. Those who accomplish their own potentialities delineate what is possible; the effectuation of their own mortal itineraries destines potentialities for others. Authentic understanding is in this way an understanding of the goodness of existence.

11. The Poetry of Conscience

The mortal clairvoyance Heidegger names *Entschlossenheit*, this resolute hold on the possible, the singular, the future, is not really conscious. It is not effected in the sphere of consciousness, always self-conscious, an intuitive or immediate presence of the being I am to itself.

What makes authentic understanding possible is conscience, the sense of the being I have to be. Conscience, essentially anxious, has its own mortal certainty. It is nowise ineffable, refractory to speech; on the contrary, conscience takes form as speech and not as intuition. Conscience speaks—but not in the indicative mode, which designates the being that is. It speaks in the vocative mode, simultaneously articulating the being I am to be and calling me unto it.

What speaks, in the voice of conscience? My own being speaks to me. My own being is not, as for the phenomenology of consciousness, immediately before me as something I can intuit; it is ahead of me as a possibility. I do not see the being that is mine to appropriate, but I am called unto it, by the reticence of conscience speaking in the silences of the death that already harbors all my being in its possibly impossible possibility.

It is then not only the existence I enact that is discursive, says something, expresses something, makes sense, in its signifying, ecstatic, or teleological movement—and that tells one tale, in the univocity of its projection unto definitive and irreversible death. The existence ahead of me speaks already. It is to be conceived not in the optical element of a form still in germ nor in the dynamic element of a force still contained in its potentiality but in the auditory element of an articulation that calls forth. My own possible being is not only manifested to me in the voice of conscience; it is itself to be conceived as a voice.

That my own being speak is what seemed impossible to Nietzsche.[27] For is not the area of the speakable in a life, the zone of consciousness, the most superficial and the worst part, the zone dominated by herd instincts? Does not becoming conscious consist in subsuming whatever is singular under general terms, herd signals, determining the possible in terms of the actual and the future in terms of the past? Is not then what of our life we become conscious of what is useful for the herd, what is not our own?

But naming does not only mean coding, covering over the singularity of the singular.[28] The first uttering of names is not labeling but greeting and invocation. If my own being has a name, a name of its own, a proper name, it is the name by which I am invoked and not that by which I am classified.

My ownmost being speaks to me not in legislative pronouncements nor judicial decrees but in the vocative word that names the singular, that articulates the possible, with the oracular voice that calls up a future, that calls unto a destiny. For Heidegger the voice of conscience is not, as for Kant, a legislative dictum, and a singular life does not make sense by making itself a law for everyone. The voice of conscience is essential poetry, and it is a poetic composition that my own being speaks and makes sense.[29] When he hears the voice of his conscience

> Full of merit, yet poetically, man
> Dwells on this earth.

Authentic existence is the existence that appropriates being as its own. Its being is being itself; the voice that calls in conscience and that is my being speaking is the voice of being, is being as a voice. Being is no longer to be conceived in the optical element, as eidos, form, aspect, or Idea. And it is no longer to be conceived as energeia, force, substance, or subject. Being in beings, occulted by beings, is not what one sees but what one hearkens to. Being resounds in language, being is heard as language[30] —whose words do not depict or represent beings but name invoke, call upon and call forth.

12. Reduction of Infinite Time

The theoretical cognition that idealizes its objects situates them on an infinite dimension of time, a dimension of time conceived as the unending succession of moments of the same form. As did Husserl and Nietzsche, Heidegger traces back the origin of this constituted time-format to a structure of life that makes itself present, to the will of that life to maintain itself in presence. This will is not a fortuitous velleity of the substance of life; it is the power that constitutes life originally. For life, according to Husserl, has the unconditional power to produce and reproduce selfsame the form of the present. This power is the consciousness in life. Life, according to Nietzsche, is the power to affirm itself, to will itself; in its sovereign form it is the power to will itself just as it is. This will is the joy in life. And our existence, according to Heidegger, is the pure power to produce presence; to make being present in the form of a world. This power is Dasein.

The constitution of a time dimension for the world in the form of an unending succession of moments of the same form originates in a certain will of life. Husserl has identified this will as the will to maintain itself absolutely in presence, a self-idealizing will, which takes the fundamentally ethical form of a will for absolute self-responsibility. Neitzsche has identified this will as joy; the unrestricted affirmation, the love, of all temporal things takes the form of a will for their unending recurrence. This joy is the sovereign form of life, but every life contains this joy, for life is the production of an excess force affirming itself and needing to discharge itself in the affirmation of all that is beyond itself.

The will that forms time as an unending succession of moments of the same form Heidegger has identified as fear of anxiety, evasiveness in the face of the premonition of nothingness. The infinite expanse of time is, paradoxically, formed by a contraction of the focus of sight, which circumscribes the boundaries of what is present and can be apprehended—and takes this set of affairs as something that reproduces itself of itself. It is not then a formal but a material intuition; the recurrence of what is each day to be done gives one the assurance that the day reproduces itself, that time is the never-ending production of day after day.

This fear of anxiety[31] is the practical life.

Heidegger's hermeneutical phenomenology is from the first an effort to recover something concealed in what is immediately revealed: *The world as such* hides in the beings it exhibits. What takes form, first, in practical life, is the work to be done. The layout of the world, the context of references or the field of significance in which a work takes form, recedes from view. The inconspicuousness of the field is a condition for the possibility of the evidence of an objective. Erring, losing sight of the whole by centering in on a determinate objective, is always involved in the disclosure or truth that moves of our existence work out.[32] Understanding this reciprocal involvement of truth with erring, unconcealment with concealment, presence with remoteness, existence with death, finally nothingness with being, is a continual preoccupation in Heidegger's whole ontological effort. In *Being and Time* the analysis shows that erring in the everyday world is produced by the fear of anxiety.

It is not that our finite gaze fails to penetrate to the distances to see the world as such; it is that one shrinks back from the open clearing of the world because one senses the nothingness and the death of which it is made. Our existence, from the first open to the universe, myopically attaches itself to what is within reach. This strange adhesion to the everyday, the close at hand, the entities that shut off the horizons of the world, in a being whose very essence is transcendence, a being destined for the world, has to be explained. It is explained by finitude—not the natural finitude of a being whose range of movement is de facto limited but the finitude of a power of transcendence that will come to an end, will die, and senses that already.

One then clings to what is at hand, feeling the abyss. Existence makes itself representation, a holding on to presence, a reinstating of what is presented. Everyday existence is attachment to what is at hand, addiction to the manipulanda presented, absorption in what is within reach.

Heidegger says that the existential analytic has to be begun now, at this late date in the history of Western thought, because our kind of being has always been interpreted after the model of intramundane entities.[33] This is not a simple category mistake or oversight; it is essentially motivated by aversion to our mortal and transitory existence, the inordinate attachment to and valuation of the stock of intramundane entities. This attachment is not a puzzling taking of means for the end, a losing sight of that "for the sake of" which means are means and works are done. It is not effective means, implements, that are taken as the primary form of being but the *Vorhanden*, that which is on hand, that which can be counted on to be there, the presented. What we want to see in our house is not the refrigeration but the rustproof and stainfree sleek block of the refrigerator. The art of Nathalie Sarraute[34] makes palpable the dread of the transitory, of the generated and corruptible, that governs bourgeois taste for brocades, leather gloves, crystal vases, oak chests of drawers, marble-floored bathrooms, solid-silver tableware. They exhibit the value that does not depreciate with time, are the mausoleums in which human effort is enshrined, pyramids in Hegel's sense, in which life is buried, harbored, and glorified.[35] Yet their very rarity bears witness also to their possible disappearance, and the human effort on them whose imprint they monumentalize silently induces despondent nostalgia for the bygone. If modern taste prefers the futuristic, the machine made, the insured and replaceable, it is because such things materialize about one the advancing power and the infinite repeatability of modern mechanized industry.

The compulsion to trivialize the spirit, the myopia that adheres to what is within reach, the distraction that ever moves on from what one has in one's hands but only to what is equivalent—this is explained by the dread of the open roads which open upon openness and emptiness, upon the world. That about which we are anxious, Heidegger says, is the world itself and being in the world. For the world is the openness as such, made of abyss and death.

Heidegger then derives theoretical life—with its privileging of the present-on-hand, the factually given, within the confines of forms that abide and are ceaselessly reiterated in the flux of material, and its privileging of disinterested, dispassionate viewing, observation, and representation—from the practical life.[36] Theoretical life does not break with, but is a more emphatic form of, the will to presence, the affirmation of beings and the aversion to nothingness, that characterizes practical existence.[37] The dimension of the ideally infinitely repeatable which enters into the constitution of the objects of theory is derived from the recurrence that practical existence wills in adjusting to the general format of the world and the reproduceable forms of implements.[38] The idea of infinity is not a pure creation of the theoretical attitude, invented ex nihilo; it is derived from the day-to-day format of practical time. Answerability, which Husserl set forth as the supreme form of Western subjectivity to be achieved through theoretical reason and theoretical praxis, would derive existentially from a will to reckon and account for time, from the essentially calculative reason that seeks to ensure the day-to-day world.

Husserl credited classical Greece with the institution of the theoretical attitude and the constitution of the idea of infinity. Heidegger derives theoretical existence and the idea of infinite time existentially from praxis and its day-to-day format, but he then locates in Greek antiquity the origin of praxis and of the instrumental structure of the world. The Greek world is not only the source from which the existential analytic draws the concepts of praxis and pragmata, which the existential analytic only had to work out to discover the essence of the primary form of existence and of the world.[39] In fact not only the words but the "thing itself" were formed by the Greeks; "primitive" man did not confront a world which could be described with the concepts of *Vorhandenen* and *Zuhandenen*, and "primitive" man does not live a practical existence.[40] The analysis then of the everyday world in *Being and Time* is not the analysis of the "natural world" which the treatise calls for; it is an analysis of the form of the world and the basic form of our existence in what later Heideggerian texts will call one "ontological epoch."[41]

Theory—Greek, rational, logico-metaphysical theory—articulated in advance the form of the world and of its intramundane entities; technology effectively transforms the world into the image and likeness of the theoretical or metaphysical representation of the world. The industrial era and now the atomic age represent the decisive moments when the theoretical prepossession of the world takes possession of extrahuman and finally unlimited power.[42] The most modern form of praxis, technology, transforms the world into a pure fund or stock of energy units, indefinitely transformable into the equivalent in an infinite space-time field. For Heidegger the essential Nietzschean vision, that of the universe in eternal recurrence, corresponds to, and is produced by, this final form of the Western ontological epoch.[43]

Thus beneath the infinite horizons in which Husserl sees the idealizing praxis of Western culture and beneath the eternal cycles in which Nietzsche sees the dreams and dances of artistic creation, Heidegger sees the day-after-day eternity of practical existence. A practical existence whose concern with mundane entities is made of its anxiety in the face of death.

13. The Practical Authenticity

The fear of anxiety and the everyday practical life it elaborates can be reversed. One can appropriate, make one's own, the dying that appropriates one's existence, makes one's existence one's own. The passive synthesis of time, the passive passing of time toward its end, can be converted into an active synthesis of time, a powerful and empowering enactment of time, a projecting of one's own existence, of its own forces, into its end. One can deliver oneself, of one's own force, into one's dying.

This free and resolute making one's own existence deathbound, this "being able to die," is not simply the action that deliberately contrives the means at hand which bring about one's empirical demise. For "as soon as we are born we are able to die."[44] One's own dying is living out one's life, the living that consists in assembling all one's potential and delivering it over to its release and its discharge. Dying on one's own consists in committting all one's potential for existing in the complex of possibilities the world offers at the moment.

The conversion to authenticity which Heidegger names *Entschlossenheit*, resoluteness, is not to be understood in a voluntarist way, as Löwith has proposed.[45] The exercise of power which unlocks the possibilities of the situation and first reveals them is not a fiat of will. For Heidegger if our existence is all potential for being, this does not mean that it is a quantum of force first accumulated and then applied to implements. The existential analytic teaches that to speak thus is to still apply substantive categories to power whose essence, whose way of being, is precisely ex-istence. Power is assembled in organizing and manipulating the possibilities which mundane things are. Possibilities which are, however, revealed in the power applied to them.

But our being first becomes potential in being centered upon the nothingness. This does not mean that, isolated from the world, it assembles itself. Our being becomes ecstatic, ex-ists, aspired by the void. The void we flee in fear of anxiety first affects us, weighs on us, afflicts us of itself. It belongs to the essence of death that it comes, of itself. Death is inapprehendable, ungraspable; if we are able to die and not merely perish like beasts, this does not mean that we have power over death, can take it up, appropriate it. It means that we appropriate our own being by delivering it over to the death that approaches and whose power to take us is absolute and certain.

This certainty cannot be doubted, it can only be evaded. The existence that resolves to evade it no longer comes to grips with its possibility, with the possibility and the eventuality of utter impossibility. It knows all that is possible, the possible as such. It stands forth in the uncanniness, the *Unheimlichkeit*,[46] of the world as that in which we cannot fix our dwelling.

And in this stand that upon which it stands, the closure and materiality of the terrestrial, is held in its possibilities. Contingent, ready to give way at any moment, unsure substantiality or material determinations of possibility, instrumentalities delineate the form of a world. A nothingness visible only to me, circumscribing me alone, takes form in them. What gives their substantial contours their depth of possibility is this pure possibility, this possibility of impossibility, made for me. What reveals the world not as substances or forms before me but as possibilities, instrumentalities, for me is the abyss opening for me alone over which they are suspended.

Taking hold then of these singular possibilities my existence becomes revealing, reveals a singular configuration of possibilities, instrumentalities, a world. The determination of the entities of the world is not a merely mental or contemplative operation. "One knows the hammer by hammering." Authentic understanding is praxis.

This kind of praxis deserves to be called poetic[47] already because it has the character not of a manipulation of material determined by a model possessed in advance, a manipulation that would then be essentially repetitive, day-to-day labor or technological operation—but of a "projective" leap upon singular possibilities. It deserves to be called poetic also in that it is not production of being ex nihilo but composition. The composition does not exist without the composer. The composer puts himself into the composition—he enters it as one of its components.

The inaugural teaching of the fundamental ontology of *Being and Time* was that man's essence has to be conceived not substantively but relationally; man is, in his ex-istence, a transporting of what has come to pass in him to what is possible for him. In him existing is the continual engendering of possibilities and the continual projecting itself into those possibilities. Existing is this transport, this relating. Relating itself continually to its own non-being or possibility, it relates itself to non-being or possibility universally—to death or to the world.

But Heidegger went on to conceive all the constituents of the world relationally. The four causes of classical metaphysics[48] have to be understood not as
subsistent entities but as modes of relatedness. Thus the matter of things is
disclosed not in itself but in the instrument, as "the whereof" it is made or
drawn. It is determinate not in resistance simply but in that which "sustains,
collects, calms."[49] With these terms a late Heideggerian text determines not
only the sensuous element but the materiality of the world, not negatively, as
resistance, or opacity, or unintelligibility, or the unformed, but positively, as
ground, support, *the terrestrial*. The terrestrial is the reliability in implements,
that which supports and holds our movements in the world, because it holds
together of itself, is closed in itself.

Similarly the form of things is not disclosed in itself but in the implement, as
the "for which" it is oriented. The form of the hammer is not simply the
contour marking the limit where being ends and nothingness or something else
begins; it refers to the nails for which the hammer's solidity is directed and to
the force and elasticity of the hand and arm for which it is molded. The shape of
the jug determines the water or wine which it contains and which it also pours
forth. Far then from the form enclosing each entity in itself, it inserts it into
chains and fields of implements, into the world; it delineates the lines of force
of *a world*. For it is not blankness that can constitute the world as a clearing, and
not the dimensions of geometrical space either; it is the open roads, the
oriented paths of force of an instrumental field. In hammering one operates in a
field of nails, shingles, storms and sunshine, a world; in pouring forth the water
or the wine one operates in a field of rock strata and springs, melting snows and
rains, sun ripening grain and friends gathered for labor or for feasting—a world.

The material and the form of an implement are not selected willfully but in
function of *the purpose*, the telos, the final cause, of the instrument.[50] A specific
serviceability is the underlying essence of an implement; it is what supports the
assembling of a certain material and a certain form. The instrumentality is itself
relational; it is that by which the implement is useful for a user. An instrumental
entity is essentially for-someone. It exists not as a phenomenon, that is, an
appearance for a gazer or in the immediacy of intuition, but as *Zu-handen*,
manipulanda, existing for hands, for a user himself material, mundane, corporeal. And, by virtue of the abiding constancy of its materiality, existing for a
time; by virtue of the schematic character of its form, existing for a certain range
of manipulations. Existing, then, and useful, not for me in particular but for any
one of a series of users equivalent to and interchangeable with me. Existing
publicly, for anyone. And referring to me as a materialized support for my
movements in the openness of the world and in the openness of death—
referring to me in my mortality. It is *for mortals* that equipment is useful;
equipment refers, in its instrumental essence, to me in my mortality, refers me
to my mortality. The hammer is known in the hammering—in the hammering
shingles over a shelter for me exposed to the inclemencies of weather—but the
hammer also becomes a hammer by the hammering. The carpenter is an

essential constituent of the hammer, and the host makes the jug a jug. Without the host the jug cannot maintain itself; if it endures it may reappear in a home where there is no feasting as an ornament or an investment or in an anthropological museum as an exhibit.

An implement is a concretion of closure in being and openness in being, existing in itself and for other implements, a term and a means, a concretion of the terrestrial and the openness of dimensions of skies. Earth and skies come together in the materiality of the form of the implement.[51]

In *Being and Time* our own existence was the finality, the "for the sake of which" the entities take form. Their instrumental essence is relative to our existence. Finality would occur in being because our existence is such that its own being is set before it as its possibility and its task. Yet the possibility that lies before it lies in the world, is a being in the world. There is a goodness in things which is not an exterior plenary presence that could be appropriated; it draws our existence forth to the being that is its own to be. This *way of the good*, this drawing as it withdraws, this scintillation of the distances on the things at hand, is what Heidegger will in later texts identify as the divine. The builder is not an efficacious agent who, by assembling material and imposing form upon it, produces the home as his transitive product, for the essence of a home precedes and presides over the selection of material and of forms, and also precedes and presides over the determination of mortals as inhabitants of this earth rather than wayfarers in alien spaces.[52] It is the pouring forth, in offering to many, in superabundance, to drink to health and to feasting and to the morrow, to the goodness of days, that determines the shape and also the materials for the jug and that makes man a maker of jugs.

Authentic praxis then is composition. It is not production of being ex nihilo, and it is not the chinking in the interstices through which the nothingness seeps in with whatever is at hand, which characterizes everyday concerns. It is also not the transformation of the stock of material without end and without ends which characterizes technological industry. Things—*Dingen*—etymologically but also essentially are assemblers.[53] Things—bridges, homes, jugs, shoes—assemble the reliability of the terrestrial and the serviceability of the openness, assemble mortals and the divine, the goodness. In them the axes of the world are collected.

This composition is groundless, this work is a play.[54] It is not an effect of causes exterior to it nor is it necessitated by laws that prevail over it. For the essences of things are not fabricated by accumulation of factors subsisting outside of them, nor are they derived from laws prevailing universally and necessarily over the composition of the world. It is the essences of things that assemble the material, the forms, the workmen, and the goodness that enter into their composition. All the necessity and universality of the laws we can formulate derives from the things given and the world given. Even all the laws of physical and mathematical science derive their validity from the contingency and facticity of the given things and the given world.

Praxis as a projective leap upon singular possibilities and as composition is poetic praxis.

This authentic, authentifying praxis is contrasted with the anonymous utilitarian existence first by its temporal form. The existential analytic has revealed that the cause that drives anonymous utilitarian existence is not biological or human imperatives but the constitution of the day-to-day format of time, the unending succession of moments by which the fear of anxiety is conjured and mortality evaded. In the authentic, authentifying composition of things we are brought into our vulnerability, our mortality, into time enacted as a singular trajectory cast into its singular end.

Authentifying praxis is then contrasted with technological production. Commanded by a calculative mathematico-metaphysical logos which has lost the sense of the essence of things, technological production drives a transformation of the pure fund or stock of being without ends and without end. In the universe of technological production the biological or human needs or wants of men do not fix an end, for they are themselves a fund or stock of vital or psychic energy subject to technological transformation without end and without ends.

The authentifying praxis is conceived as *inhabitation* and contrasted with alienation. Against the metaphysical conception of human praxis, denounced by Nietzsche and Marx as alienation, Heidegger set out to understand being-in-the-world in the sense of inhabiting the world, being at home in the world (in the opening pages of Part I of *Being and Time*[55]), as *care*, and as thinking-dwelling-building, that is, dwelling as the hidden essence of understanding and of praxis.

The inner movement of authentifying praxis is conceived by Heidegger as appropriation—*Eigentlichkeit*. Expropriating appropriation. In the assembling of things and of the world, the terrestrial is set forth and the space, the skies, the open clearing of a world is set up. In their interplay each is brought to itself by being brought out of itself. It is in the clearing of a world that the terrestrial grounds, supports what is moved and what is at rest, and sustains what moves itself; it is on the ground of the terrestrial that skies open, the light illuminates, and there is an apparition. In entering into the composition of things man becomes potter, cultivator, builder, is delivered over to his own vulnerability, susceptibility, mortality, delivered over to what is his own, to his own being and his own death, which he shall surely find in the proximity of things and in the clearing of the world. And by scintillating over the surfaces of things and across the distances of the world, by drawing mortal men into the proximity of things, into the inhabitation of the world, by drawing as it withdraws, the divine, the goodness, is.

The *Eigentlichkeit*—the coming into his own—of man is but a moment in the *Ereignis*,[56] the coming into their own of things, world, the divine.

The authentifying praxis, this deathbound free and resolute building a home that is not a shelter on the earth in the world from death but a harbor for the earth and for the world and for the goodness as well as for oneself, this most powerful and most ecstatic form of existence, is for Heidegger not a creative outpouring of life's work upon what of itself has no value. It is not a transformation of the real into the image and likeness of the idealization which theory has already effected. Heidegger set out to show not only that there is understanding in praxis, that what discloses is not intuition or discursive operations with the categories of the mind but praxis, but also that truth is the work that praxis aims at and achieves. The thesis of the primacy of praxis means not that understanding is for the sake of praxis but that understanding is in praxis and that praxis is for the sake of understanding or, better, that truth works itself out and being comes to its epiphany. "Truth is that to which man aspires, that which he requires to reign in all he does or omits to do, in all he desires, all he gives freely, all he lives through and forms, all he suffers and all that makes him overcome." Man's existing utterly on his own, his most powerful and most ecstatic state, his authenticity, his supreme dignity is "to watch over the occultation and non-occultation of all things."[57]

VI

FACE TO FACE

1. Phenomenology of the Face

When a face faces, there is not only another visible and tangible surface turned to me. In facing, *the other* takes up a stand before me. The phenomenology of the face worked out by Emmanuel Levinas and the ethical metaphysics (or heterology) he has built on it are devoted to the elucidation of this alterity.

The other takes up a stand before me, faces, to speak. The distance marked by the face of another opens an interval in which things will be distinguished and clarified, in which the world itself will take form. For it is in speaking that the fragments of the visible, movable, apprehendable exterior I can discover by my own initiatives are inserted into a network that extends beyond the horizons of all my perceptions and that endures when they vanish from my eyes.

The distance marked by the alterity of the other is not an interval measured in the space of the world, for it is within it that the correlates of my sensibility become subsistent objects and the space of the world is opened. The other faces me from a distance of alterity other than that of all shapes that take form in visible, palpable, traversable distances.

One can, to be sure, observe the other, and one can question him, make him tell his name, explain what he has to say, reveal himself. One can take initiatives to reduce the strangeness of the stranger. But in his face the other is not other only by virtue of the gradient of difference in the similarities of attributes which one situated above us discerns and measures. The other reaffirms his otherness in questioning me, disturbing the order of my perspectives and of my reasons, contesting me.

This I know in the pain of veracity. The other presents himself before me, makes signs to me, speaks, but I interpret and I remain in command of my interpretation. Then, in the moment of sincerity, I say to the other what I have been saying about him, present to the other my representation of him. They do not coincide. Beyond all I have observed and understood of him, beyond all that I have comprised in my representation of him, the other presents himself. He presents his otherness in the assent he gives to my interpretation, in the contestation he makes of it, in the silence to which he returns.

The other faces in the difference between the landscapes of which he speaks and those I inhabit, in the surprise, suspense, skepticism with which he hears what I say, in the force, hesitation, the dead time, out-of-phase, with which his response affirms, develops, or refuses what I present. His otherness is not the sum-total of the differences which I can represent. Even when he assents to all with which I have identified him, his very assent, as his reticence, reveals an authority to confirm and to contest, to silence and to summons, by which he arises behind all that I have seen and said of him, apart.

The other stands apart from the forms one takes hold of; his face is the trace[1] left among the surfaces of beings of the passage of otherness. Alterity turns to me in this unendingly reiterated departure, this *infinition*.[2]

Speech is indicative, informative; the world becomes clear and distinct in its formulations. In the interval opened up by the alterity that faces, distance opens unendingly in which the sites and spans of the world's space will be charted with the empty gestures and the vanishing sounds of speech. Marked by signs common to all, the sensuous forms by which reality exists for-me come to subsist in the interval as objects, present for-anyone.

Speech has also vocative and imperative force. Facing me, the other greets me, singles me out, appeals to me, calls up an I out of the anonymity of sensuous life and practical operations. And contests me, questions me, makes demands on me, judges me, orders me. In calling upon me, the other comes in the poverty and nakedness of his face. In contesting me, he arises before me in height, in the uprightness of his face.

The other appeals to me with his eyes, in his word, in a movement of his face or a gesture of his hand. With a look or word of greeting the other faces, and every sign and sentence he addresses to me acknowledges me and calls for a response, is intended with the force of an appeal.

Facing me, the other looks at me, exposing to me the defenselessness of his eyes. His look does not lay hold of me but lays him open to me. In facing the other denudes himself. The nakedness of things, of bare walls and naked revolvers, derives from the nakedness of the other. The nakedness of the body and of the face derives from the nakedness of the eyes that look at me. Erotic nudity, which has an intent of its own, derives from the extreme nakedness of the face; only the one that faces can denude himself erotically. Exposing to me what is most naked, most vulnerable, the other in facing addresses me in destitution. He looks to me out of indigence and mortality, exposing wants to me.

In facing me, the other addresses me with his word, which is not an arm or an instrument, which I can resist without doing anything, by just doing whatever I was doing. Confiding his presence to a breath that hardly stirs the air, the other comes disarmed and disarming.

To be sure one can clothe one's words, as one can mask one's eyes—in contrived intonations, affected timbre, in the polite and polished forms which are the commonplaces and uniforms of authority. Words can indeed threaten, and the shapes of the world can loom threatening when they are designated by the menacing power of the words that announce them. Danger abides in the word, Heidegger says.[3] Yet in the threat of words one also hears what is more vulnerable than anything in the world, the passing of alterity. One hears it in the momentary timbre and the vanishing breath of the alien voice. To choose to approach only in his word is for the other to be there in the traces of an abandon and a disarming.

In facing me, the other signals to me with a gesture of his hand. Hands are prehensible organs, implements; with them one takes hold of being. They are also sense organs; when they make contact with the solid but refrain from taking hold, hands explore and perceive.[4] They are also organs for caressing— when they make contact and take hold of nothing, grasp and operate nothing, when they profane a secrecy without discovering anything, uncovering and denuding the enigma of the carnal. And when hands take hold and draw nothing to themselves, when they are turned to exteriority, taking form and deforming themselves, forming nothing, they speak. To speak is to approach empty-handed.

The face of another can address an appeal to me because it can make demands on me. The approach of the other is not simply the exposure of a nothingness. The other turns to me in the uprightness of his face. His approach summons me, calls up an I out of the anonymity of sensuous and utilitarian existence, because his presence orders me.

Facing me, the other contests me. He requires of me a response, makes demands on me. To respond to him, already to answer to his greeting, is to recognize his right to question me. What I say I address to the other for his judgment. I can, to be sure, debate what he says, set myself up as judge of my judge, question his right to question me, deny him rights over me. But these stratagems are possible because his approach puts me in question. The cunning which employs language and signs in order to produce effects on the other, the rhetoric, seduction, propaganda, human engineering, that there is in all speech, are possible as ruses, showing that the exactions and exigencies of the other put into question all I am. In the face of another, the question of truth is put on each proposition of which my discourse is made, each move and gesture of my exposed life.

Located beneath me in destitution, above me in uprightness, in the never meeting of these nonparallel lines, the other faces me in the distress and the unending demand of alterity.

2. Sign, Index, and Trace

The carnal materiality of the other weighs on one. This imperative force is not simply that of a model in intercorporeality or a law instantiated. One's stances and attitudes are to be sure ordered by the stances and attitudes of others. One's body is a sort of plastic substance which captures its diagrams of internal organization, its postures and the forms of its gestures from the inner axes of the bodies it perceives. To catch on to the sense of the positions and moves of another is to capture his diagrams of motility in the axes of one's own body; thus the infant misunderstands as aggression sexual behavior of adults he chances to perceive, until they become possibilities of his own body coordination. The other communicates not only the sense of his postures and gestures but also the sense of his scowls, murmurs, sighs, utterances, and coded words to me by ordering their reproduction in me, by ordering my body with his. But this indicative and informative ordering of the forms his voice and limbs diagram are directed by the imperative force with which he approaches when he faces. This imperative governs the way his perceptible shape exposes itself to me. In his flesh I see not only the anonymity and susceptibility of his want but the demanding insistence of his being.

Skin is not hide nor covering, camouflage, uniform, adornment. It is a surface of exposure, zone of susceptibility, of vulnerability, of pain and abuse.[5] In the skin inscribed with its own wrinkles, one does not read the signs of nothingness but the vulnerability of what is other. One's eyes touch it lightly, affected by the susceptibility of youth, the frailty of age, the organic dead-ends of birthmarks, the languor of eyes that close. The eyes and the hands that touch the face are afflicted with what they do not seek to heal, that is, to take charge of, approaching with the touch of a complacent compassion.

In this exposedness the other does not affect me as another substance that solidifies under my hold, that sustains and supports. His face is not the surface of another being. It is flesh of no identifiable color, that does not hold its shape. There is want of being in all flesh; what faces is not something whose identity I can grasp. The eyes that look at me are bared, denuded even of identity. The anonymity of fingers, legs, genitals is not that of implements utilizable by anyone but the unrepresentable importunity of a want, the inapprehendable movement of a contestation, the unmeasurable force of a question that badgers and disrupts.

When I face someone I address myself to an authority beyond the position sighted in the social and practical field, a nakedness behind the uniforms which give the other a social identity and a recognizable function, a signifying beyond the signs of the code which his moves, gestures, and words inscribe, an insistence behind the physiognomy and the emotional pantomime. I address the instance that appeals and that commands, beyond all that I can perceive, apprehend, comprehend. Alterity is incognito; there is no concept of this you. It is the a posteriori for which there were no a prioris.

The relationship between the alterity of the other and the face in which the other presents himself is not that of a whole to its part nor that of a substance to its property nor that of an essence to its phenomenon. Alterity is not the internal organization of the features of the face nor an ideality of which those features would be the signs nor the identity of a being of which this sensuous diversity would be the apparition. What faces is not revealed in this surface, is not fixed in the screen of appearances: It is what is wanting and what contests the order with which my environment appears to me. The other is the imperative that already binds me when I act to consolidate the flux of appearances into a landscape in which he is a figure; the forming of this phenomenon is solicited and ordered by his voice. His voice has already departed from the surface my gaze now arranges among the phenomena of the world.

The other presents himself by facing, by speaking. But the signs made by the forms of his moves do not manifest the other in the same way that they inform me about things. It is I who misinform myself if I interpret ignorantly the forms traced on the surfaces of beings, but the signs made on the face of another may deceive me by corresponding truly to the things they signify. Thus Freud told of the Jewish merchant who accosted his competitor with: "Liar! Why did you tell me you were going to Minsk, so that I would think you were going to Pinsk—and then you went to Minsk!" All that the said indicates and designates is but appearance, phenomena that equivocate; to be veridical they require the rectitude of the intention that issues them. They themselves function as indices of that intention—but indices that are also but phenomena that equivocate. They do not unequivocably reveal the quality of the intention present—they mark the fact that someone passed incognito through them.[6] They function as traces that reveal only by covering up the intention that puts them forth as signs that reveal but also deceive.

Levinas distinguishes the concept of *trace* from that of *indicative* and of *significant signs*. A criminal, he who acts for the sake of crime and not to inscribe the sign of his vengeance against or his power over the social order, acts to disrupt the order of social life or property. He wishes to quit the scene of the crime; his deed is not a sign made signifying his intention. The deed is perpetrated, and passed. It leaves traces. The traces are *indices* in Husserl's sense; they can indicate to the intention of the detective the identity of the deed and of its perpetrator. The criminal takes pains then to cover up his traces. But the intention to efface the traces of his act from the scene, to depart absolutely, itself leaves traces. The order has been disturbed irremediably. The traces left by the one that acts to cover up his traces are traces in this narrow or specific sense.[7] They are not signs or indices; the criminal meant to say nothing with them and to indicate nothing by them. They are traces, in the present, of the definitiveness and irrevocability, the irremediable passivity, of what only sought to pass completely out of the present. They mark the locus where order has been disturbed.

The forms given another's gestures, his physiognomy, and the stream of his voice are *signs* and signify the subsistent layout of the world; the pacing, hesitations, tempo, cadences, idiom are *indices* indicating the identity and states of mind of an alter ego. They signify and indicate because in the commanding nakedness of the eyes that address them to me, in the disarming vulnerability of the voice that summons me, in the empty-handed gestures that disturb my hold on things—in this insistence of carnal materiality—I detect the *traces* of an order contesting my comprehension and my apprehension, traces of the vocative and imperative force that addresses the signs and indices to me.

In Kant the other—the expressions, the acts that originate in his autonomy and not in forces of the external environment nor in the passionate forces of his sensuous nature—figures as a *type* of the law.[8] In the other the law becomes a *phenomenon*. The law that binds me is formulated in the expressions of the other. Yet I can recognize the words and deeds of the other as instantiating maxims which bind me also because I first know the law—know it within my own understanding, know it by my own understanding. In fact I do not *know* that the *deeds and words of the other I perceive* typify the law because I can never be sure that his behaviors are not in fact controlled by empirical factors unknown and unobservable by me.[9] If I take the image his deeds present me to typify the law that binds me as it does him, that is because I *must believe* that my, and his, sensuous nature can obey law. This belief and the typifying imagination this belief commands are the first thing required by the imperative that weighs on the mind—required as the means whereby the mind can bring about the obedience of one's whole nature to law.

Kant has borrowed the properties of the imperative—universality and necessity—from the logico-theoretical definition of law, that is, from the domain of pure speculative reason, which is itself elaborated in obedience to the imperative. But if the imperative is addressed specifically to *me*, then its ordinance is not to make me cease to be as such—make me subsist solely as a simple instance of universal or indeterminate subjectivity. The imperative that constitutes the subject subjectivity constitutes it in its singularity. Levinas sees the singular I arising inasmuch as it is singled out by the order addressed to it and to no one else; the subject is backed up to itself, exiled in itself by the exactions laid on it—and which are not to be left to another.

This already forces us to disengage ourselves from the Kantian reasoning that the imperative, qua exigency for the universal and the necessary, is seated in the pure understanding and that the type-image—here, the presence of the autonomous other—is derivative of a prior apprehension of the imperative in the understanding's own—affective—nature.

There are not then, Levinas reasons, two moments, the respect for law, the feeling of being afflicted by the imperative, in one's receptive nature, and the perception of the law as instantiated in the expression of the other. To perceive the autonomy or the alterity of the other is to find oneself afflicted with an imperative, is to be ordered by him. To "understand" the imperative is not to comprehend it, to represent it before one's understanding in a synthetic form or formulation; it is to perceive—more exactly, respect—the other. For Kant this respect is an interpretation of the gestures, words, and deeds of the other as instantiations of the universal and the necessary. But is it not rather a divining of a disturbance in the universal order my comprehension extends across the world, a perception of the other's words and gestures engraving traces of an appeal made to, and a contestation made of, my apprehension and my comprehension?

Heidegger also criticizes the Kantian specification of the properties of law and therefore also the Kantian locating of the incidence of law in the faculty of understanding. Formal universality and necessity are properties law exhibits—in one metaphysical epoch, which is our technologico-mathematico-metaphysical epoch. They are themselves not directly inscribed on the understanding but formalized from the objectified representation of nature produced by logico-mathematical calculative reason. The world, then, the law-governed empirical nature of Kant's first type, is not merely the instantiation or imaginative illustration of law; it is the original locus of manifestation of law. Heidegger reasons then that law—the ordaining order, Logos as Dikè, the sacred that draws as it withdraws and that supplies the measure, the axes of uprightness and destiny for us that dwell and build in the world—is a dimension of, or is dimensionality in, the world. It is that with which the world is extended, with which the world "worlds."[10] That is, opens according to axes of near and far, intimacy and openness, recollection and aspiration; axes of up and down, sublime and base; axes of birth and death, inauguration, triumph, and defeat, in which humans are called to their destiny.

Levinas speaks as little of the world as locus of inscription of the imperative as Heidegger does of the other. From Heidegger's world-historical perspective, the world that Levinas sees is positivist, the world of the modern metaphysico-technological epoch; Levinas would say it is the desacralized world of monotheism.[11] For him the world-order of paganism as well as the divinities of Hölderlin's post-Christian paganism, are immanent to world history, and function to make the world hospitable to human building, and to make humans build their dwelling in the world. They do not make it possible to judge the course of the world. For Levinas the imperative, transcendent to the world, otherwise than its being, rages against its dark, pours tears of non-reconciliation and non-forgiveness over the old that think of the dreams of their youth, over the martyrs whose ideals also are perishing, over the heros on the evening of battles that have won nothing and left the brave dead, over the beauty that is ravaged, the weak that are massacred, the sacrifices that profit the self-aggrandizing. Such an imperative is "otherwise than being." Its trace is perceived in the alterity of the other.

We are subjected to the imperative then not only in our faculty for the universal and the necessary, our formal understanding, but in all our particularity. It is because what is perceived perspectively by me is subjected to the exactions and contestations of the other that the field of the sensibility is, by the universalizing understanding, to be made a universe open to anyone. We are subjected to the imperative in our *sensibility* that is not only exposed to beings and to the nothingness in which the world of sensuous beings is contingently suspended but is also exposed to alterity.

3. The Sensibility

There is, Heidegger explained, a mortal taste to our contact with the sensible things about us. Our sensibility is not just a recording of their sense, their messages, meanings, or directions; it is also a susceptibility. In our sensibility we are sensitive first not to what makes contact with us but to the emptiness or void opening about us. The sense of finding oneself in the emptiness is a shrinking back; it is anxiety. Anxiety, the finding oneself adrift in the nothingness, with nothing to hold on to, nothing to support one, is an anticipation of dying. The "strong force" in our material composition that makes us concern ourselves with the sense, the messages, meaning, or direction of beings is that of our anxious shrinking back from the nothingness, from death. Our orientation to the open clearing in which things are discernible, the world, is in fact our exposedness to the nothingness of death. If our sensibility grasps for beings, apprehends the solid, the substantial, it does so out of this apprehensiveness in the midst of the void.

For Levinas the sensibly given things are not grasped in the empty spaces of nothingness—but *in the light, in the blue skies, distributed over the earth.* Before sensibility is perception of forms and substances, it is open upon the sensuous element. Earth, as the depth of support which maintains things in place and permits us to circulate about them and observe their sides; light and the field-color in which patterns become visible by diverging from it; the key or field tone which particular sounds diverge from and thus acquire pitch and density; the forest murmurs and rumble of the city our hearing is adjusted to so that it can then discern particular sound patterns—these are not things but not nothingness either; Levinas calls them the *elemental.*[12] They are plenitude without contours, depth without surfaces, qualities that are not properties of substances. They have intensity, and boundless extension, without horizons.

Sensibility finds itself not adrift in an abyss of imminent nothingness but steeped in the elemental plenum.

The relationship with the elemental is not that of intentionality which directs itself through the openness toward a term, the object—a lack aiming at a content. One finds oneself within the element, in the light, in air, in sound; with one's first move the support of the ground arises within one. One feels the plenitude of the content with a contentment; one enjoys light, enjoys support, enjoys color that buoys up one's gaze and does not block it. The sensibility first open to the sensuous elements moves in a movement of involution, steeped in what is there without distances, by incessant oncoming. The involution describes a spiral, that of the eddy of egoism in sensibility, enjoying the plenitude in which it is steeped, becoming substantial with the sustenance of the elements, enjoying its own plenitude—over and beyond existing enjoying existing. The appetite for the sensibility is not a negativity, a want, but is surfeited from the start by the superabundant bounty of the elements in which one is steeped. The eye is not moved by its invisibility but by the superabundance of all there is there to be seen.

Thus while Heidegger has conceived of the perception of things as apprehension of being on the ground of an apprehensiveness in the face of nothingness, Levinas conceives it as discernment and articulation, definition of the definite in the midst of the *apeiron*.

One is not sensitive to the sense of things, their messages, meanings or directions, without being subject to them, susceptible to being wounded and annihilated by them. The factor of order is not a priori and seated in the subject's own nature—for then sensibility would never be subjection to what it touches, susceptibility to being wounded and crushed by its forms. (In Kant and in Husserl, where all the ordering in sensibility is seated in the subject, the subject is in principle immortal.)[13] What orders the sensibility to the exterior must be itself exterior. For Heidegger this means that beneath our ex-istence as active movement into the world, reaching for beings, there is our having been cast into the nothingness in which they are found, our having been drawn by the death that comes, of itself, for us. For Levinas what opens the sensibility to the elements and to beings and to the world they compose is contact with alterity. Sensibility is not simply vulnerability, adhering to whatever it encounters drifting contingently in the nothingness; it is susceptibility to being appealed to and to being ordered. For Heidegger it is the abyss of nothingness that draws, the term that makes determinate our movements unto beings, the final destination that destines every intention. Yet death is precisely that whose oncoming cannot be sighted, that which cannot give a direction because it is everywhere and in each moment imminent. That which can appeal to and can order our sensibility is what can keep its distances, that whose approach is a withdrawal—alterity.

Sensibility means then susceptibility to being appealed to and ordered. Its movements are susceptible of being ordered by the moves of the other. Merleau-Ponty has written, "My eyes move over the things freely, yet the views taken are not random, the moves not desultory. Whence comes this pre-established concordance of my eye with the contours of the things, this inspired exegesis?"[14] For Levinas our moves can follow obediently the lines and directions of all exterior beings because for us to be sensitive is to be susceptible to being ordered by what is irremediably exterior to us, what is alterity itself—that of which the face of another is the trace.

Sensibility means subjection to what one makes contact with, susceptibility to being wounded by the forms of things, crushed by what is substantial. For Levinas, sensibility begins not in an insubstantial emptiness or a want that aims at beings but in a body immersed in the elemental, buoyed up and sustained by it, contented by the gratuitous abundance of its content. If such a being is, by its sensibility, open to the exterior, to the most remote distances, to the world, it is because from the first it is susceptible to being affected by an appeal made to it. Its enjoyment of the immediate, its contentment, is from the first susceptible to being emptied out by an appeal coming from the outside. Subtending the subjection to beings is this subjection to alterity.

This striking thesis can be elaborated in another way. What sensibility in me opens me upon is neither my own immanent content nor a private theater but "objective being," "the common world," being that is for-others. Husserl showed that the objective world rests on intersubjectivity. The purely laboratory concept of a sphere of my own [*die Eigenheitlichkeit*][15] is not yet the experience of reality; it is a purely phenomenal experience of the hyletic flux. Consciousness needs the others to maintain an object-identity in place, to supply the points of view which can maintain the facets of the objects absent from me. Views on an object only possible for it become realized with the reality of other viewers. The perception in me which issues in the disengagement of a sensible object thus presupposes a susceptibility to being coordinated with the perceiving of others.

For Heidegger the primary world of implements is a field of essentially anonymous possibilities, implicating an indefinite series of practical agents, variants of me as I of them. Everything in the world of implements is supplied by others, made for others—and usable by anyone. The most elementary grasp of an implement reveals a susceptibility to being oriented by the praxis of others.

In Husserl the emergence of an objective world presupposes a community of cognitive subjects not simply coordinated but bound by reciprocal contestation. Each one exposes all he perceives to the others, submits to all questions. In this sense an ethical intersubjectivity subtends the constitution of the objective world.

In the practicable world of implements that Heidegger describes, the solicitude for others that makes possible the concern for implements—that is, entities usable by others, made by others, supplied for others—is a movement to put oneself in the place of another, a susceptibility to being positioned by the moves of another. But this inauthentifying form of coexistence derives from and presupposes the authentifying form—that in which the situation of another is perceived as other, beset with tasks different from mine. The perception is practical and has the form of an intervention to give the other the time and the place for his own tasks. And this in turn supposes in me the susceptibility of being solicited and ordered by the praxis of the other.

Levinas's exposition of the essence of sensibility has gone further than Husserl's and Heidegger's in two directions. On the one hand, whereas both Husserl and Heidegger presuppose a subject not simply regulated heteronomously by the other, but appealed to and commanded by the other, their concept of the other remains that of an alter ego, variant of me, parallel to me. For Levinas the other is not other by difference from, and therefore in similitude with, me but other in appealing to me and in contesting me. The perception and understanding of his difference is preceded by the sensibility affected by his demand and his judgment. It is because he stands apart in addressing me and in contesting me that his differences from me are then revealed.

On the other hand, Levinas takes the impact of the other to affect the core of the sensibility that is oneself; even the sensuous enjoyment of the elements and the suffering that turns within oneself are subtended by the exposedness to alterity. The appeal and the command of the other subtend one's enjoyment of the solid earth, the open skies, the light, and the fields of tone. The movement of pleasure closes in upon itself, forms the discreteness of an instant, the horizons of the past and the future are opaque with the incessant oncoming of the element in the present. The movement by which sensibility is present is not, as for Heidegger, an ecstatic transport but an instant, insistence, closure. What opens the sensibility then is not its own inner movement of involution but the summons and the order that can command it from without.[16] It is this exposedness to alterity in the sensibility that exposes itself to sensuous being that makes the sensuous element from the start something that exists for anyone.

4. Responsibility

To recognize the other is to be ordered by another, to respond to a summons. It is not to identify him, to see what is the same in him, to comprehend in him what is the same as another, same as oneself.

The one that faces singles me out. His imperative singles me out without totalizing me, without divesting me of my particularity to make me a pure exemplar of the universal will. What commands is alterity—otherwise than universality and identity. The other that faces requires first that I answer in my own name, that I stand in the first person singular. Out of the anonymity of the seeing that goes on, the skin that feels, the breathing, the hands that extend and the fingers that wander over things, the I is singled out to answer with what no one can put forth in its place.

For the other to face me is to come disarmed and divested. He looks to me out of indigence and mortality, exposing wants to me. This appeals calls up the I to answer to it; the I that answers answers as riches of being answers to want and distress. The I arises in a sensibility that is sustained by air, light, colors, tones, the substance of the elements, that stands and propels itself toward distant things because it is supported by the density of a ground. The terrestrial element supports, a world sustains, the I. The I that arises knows its own being as a harbor from the mortality threatening the other.[17]

The I arises wholly in response to the other. It is with oneself that one is summoned to respond—not with one's accouterments or one's surplus only. One begins by consenting to talk, just to pass the time—talk is cheap—and little by little one finds one has given everything away. One answers with one's hands, to which all the contours of things offer their substance, with one's stand, whose uprightness draws the support from the inexhaustible reservoir of the earth. One answers with words, but the words are not empty words. And they do not simply function to signal to another what is already available indifferently to either of us. They make what was given to me available to another. Their abstractness lifts the profiles of things out of the perspective by which they are given to me and turns them to another.[18]

The more one has given the more one sees one owes. Responsibility hurts; one finds one must give of one's own share, not just of the surplus. One gives of one's own sustenance, "gives the bread from one's own mouth."[19] The responsibility of the parent for a child is not a rational calculation of the equitable distribution of exchanged products but the sacrifice of one's own time and the supplying of the best of that of which the child has want.

To answer to the other is thus to find oneself summoned out of the retreat one provides for onself to bear burdens that are not one's own. It is to find oneself put in another's place. To answer to another is to answer for another, to bear the burdens of the other, to answer for his wants and his failings. To be singular, some*one*, is to be singled out such that no one can answer in my place. The movement, the life, and also the breathfailing effort[20] of the I consists in this being backed up to oneself, thrown back upon one's own, and finding oneself wanting elsewhere.

Responsibility is not acknowledgment of authorship. It is not simply the way I give continuation and continuity to my life by answering for what began with me. Responsibility originates in finding oneself summoned to answer to the other for the wants and failings, the deeds and the misdeeds, and even the very responsibility of the other. It is to find oneself a hostage.[21]

In pursuit of my destiny I have enlisted the Sherpa youth on the expedition. It is for his physical prowess and his inmost loyalty to his own ideals that I have chosen him. To recognize him is to have taken on responsibility for him, to find myself commanded by his physical breakdown and his very irresponsibility. There is no question of the logic of material distribution of goods appropriated in common and distributed to each according to his position in the regulated field of the exchange of goods. To be responsible is to be commanded by his failings more imperiously than by the law of the governments of the kingdom of ends, to harbor the bandit and the outlaw; it is to be commanded more rigorously than by the economic laws of the structures of the social order, to hijack the oil company plane for the rescue; it is to be commanded more urgently than by divine law, to feed the shamanist boy with the eucharistic hosts from the altar. Responsibility is not measured in consciousness, in the comprehension that embraces the phases of my life, retaining them by making my existence the practice of answering in each moment for all the moves I have initiated. Responsibility is not at the beginning; I was not there when the world was made. I do not measure my responsibility by locating the causes, the moments of commencement, by recognizing that this youth is stricken with cholera now because no one has taught him the necessities of killing bacteria by boiling the water, by recognizing that he is blind now because those who have conquered Nepalese and world economy have ruled it in such a way that he was not able to acquire high-altitude goggles and no teacher was sent to his village to tell him of the perils of existence far above its altitudes, that if he is loyal in some ways and disloyal in others that is because of the laws of his gods formulated in remote antiquity and of the laws of those who combated those gods with alien gods of venality. I have to answer for what the British did in the Indian subcontinent on their own two centuries ago. One does not find oneself in a world of one's own making; one finds oneself a Britain in some Indian subcontinent. One is always with a Sherpa youth on some expedition.

5. The Time of Responsibility

The responsible subject presents itself, strives to take hold of what has come to pass in itself and in others, addresses futurity. In his analysis of responsibility in subjectivity Levinas is led to formulate the meaning and the movement of presence, pastness, and futurity in new terms.

Heidegger had desubstantialized the now; *the present* is produced, he showed, by the ecstatic movement in our existence by which it sets itself forth and arrays a world about itself. Presence is the pure thrust which makes what is to come come to what has come to pass, delivers what has come to pass to what is to come. The present has to be conceived not as de facto givenness but as this transport. Levinas, on the contrary, sees in the present a movement of closure and innocence—the insistence of an instant. By making itself present subjectivity stands in itself as though not deriving from the layout of a past or required by the fatalities of a future. An instant forms in the beginningless, endless flow of the becoming in which one's substance drifts; in existing there forms an *existent*. An existent is a term that assumes existence, makes itself its support, takes responsibility for it, standing in itself as though existence were its attribute or its property.[22] To stand as though one were not suspended on the forward thrust of the past, as though the content and significance of the past awaited one's actual initiatives; to stand as though no future devolved from this position, to envisage a future for oneself by resolve and by projects and by obedience to a voice come from afar, from alterity—this is that being-with-oneself that is consciousness. Consciousness forms in, and as, an instant.

The past affects one, weighs. It is not what has passed into nothingness, but what has come to pass, become definitive and irrevocable. The passing of the past is this passing into passivity. Subjectivity is laden with its past, all its initiatives turning into determinations. It can retain their meaning, re-present their content and their form, but it can do so because they are there and beset it. Subjectivity increasingly burdened with all its acts, encumbered with it-self—ages.[23] There is a lassitude in subjectivity by which one feels the reach of one's own life slipping away and becoming a weight laid on one. In this inner lassitude one feels one's presence passing into passivity without being re-presentable; one feels the falling away, the lapse of time.

What requires that the present take up and bear the burden of the past, what awakens it[24] from its natural forgetfulness of what passes, is not the nothingness of the possible but the demands of alterity. The alterity of the other concerns one's presence as something that passed without having been presented or re-presentable. One is thrown back upon one's own past, one's passivity, and upon the world that has come to pass, by the imperative to answer to the passing of alterity. The taking up of what has come to pass is an effort to catch up with[25] the demands put on the present—as put on a source or on resources.

Levinas contests Heidegger's identification of futurity with death, the pos-sibility or the eventuality of impossibility which gives actuality a depth or a dimension of possibility. As the *real future* is not a conceptual variant of the actual (Husserl's *und so weiter*, which prolongs the lines of the actual—and which gives only the logically possible), so it is also not produced by the compounding of nothingness with being. For the actual to have a future is not for it to be affected by the oncoming of an imminent dissipation into nothingness but for it to be affected already by the approach of *something else*. The to-come is not deducible from the present and its past; its promise affects the present through and through: The present itself will be reborn but elsewise.[26] My future is something else promised my sensibility and my responsiveness, in a world in which something else will be possible and required. It is brought to me with the approach of the other that calls my present out of its sufficiency and its contentment.

It is true that for Heidegger too my own future, as a vortex of potentialities addressed to me, is manifested by the deeds of others. The concrete figure of the being-to-come to me, the singular potential I have to become in a possible configuration of the world envisaged through that future presence, cannot materialize simply out of the anxiety that senses the approach of death. "Those possibilities of existence which have been factically disclosed are not to be gathered from death."[27] It is then in the perception of others—who are per-ceived as others, authenticated ones—that my authentifying anticipation dis-covers the figures drawn of my own possible existence.[28] For the others in devoting themselves singularly to what was possible for them also circumscribe and make visible possibilities that are for-others—for me.

Yet Heidegger's thinking here is similar to Kant's. For Kant the other is the schema, the type, of the law. Law becomes visible in the words and deeds of others, which affect me with the same imperative they obey. But for Kant this a posteriori recognition presupposes an a priori understanding of law which thought first finds within itself. In a parallel way in Heidegger, the potentialities sketched out for others by authentic lives count not as alternatives delineated in the past but as futurity for me—because my existence is inwardly affected with the absolute futurity of death. The ineludible oncoming of the black night of nothingness unerringly closing in on my singularity is what supplies every destining for me of that which, as but possible, belongs to the realm of nothingness. The a priori understanding of the possible impossibility of death destined for me makes possible understanding possibilities left in the world by others *as* destined for me.

But, Levinas objects, the power of the future to invoke the present, to summon it, to order it, could not issue out of the nothingness and the impossibility that for Heidegger is its essence. That which calls an existent out of itself, into something else, that which calls the present into another time, is not nothingness but alterity. Responsibility before the other, not the drift of anxiety in a nothingness already everywhere imminent, is the original protension of futurity.

Responsibility gives dimensions of time beyond the span that anxiety extends from one's birth until one's dying. In every response one answers for the failings and the irresponsibilities of others now dead. The passing away into death of the face of another does not efface his solicitation or his contestation. Always when he faces he faces as one already passed, not present under my scrutiny nor captured by my comprehension, not representable, trace of what passes irrevocably. One is born hostage for the faults and the irresponsibilities of others who have passed on. One occupies one's post by taking the place others have vacated, in order to bear their burden for them. And one answers to them. In actualizing one's own potentialities one maintains present the validity of the appeals and demands formulated by the passing of the others.

And each word and deed that responds to the other commits the future, answers for the future and to the future. Responsibility is not measured by the consciousness of the consequences which the agent possessed nor by his presence directing their course as they ensue. To be responsible for my enterprise or for my child is to take measures to safeguard their course when I am no longer there.

6. Alterity and Infinity

For Levinas the sense of infinity has its origin not in a formalization and idealization of the spatial sense of horizonal openness and in the absolutization of the idea of truth—as Husserl had set out to demonstrate—but in the inapprehendability of alterity and the unsatisfiability of the ethical exigency. In fact in Husserl already the passage from the idea of a particular and pragmatic truth to the idea of absolute truth incorporates a recognition of the universal contestation and unrestricted claims of the other point of view—which Levinas takes to be first an ethical exigency. While Husserl had located a power to engender a horizon of infinite time in the subject and then a power to locate the objects of the world in an infinite space-time which the infinite horizons of subjective time make possible, while Nietzsche had located an unrestricted will for the present in the most powerful life and conceived an eternally cyclic cosmic time in which such a life locates its own nature and all nature, Levinas locates the dimension of the unfinished, the unsatisfiable, *infinition*, in the position and the exactions of alterity. He correspondingly removes infinity both from oneself—on the contrary, to be responsible is to find oneself too late on the scene, wanting before the demands put on one—and from the world. For him "being's move" which unfolds or extends as a world is to present, re-present, synchronize, integrate, totalize. The approach of alterity to one who finds himself in the world comes as disturbance, transcendence, infinition.

Alterity remains other in being not interchangeable with me, even if finally my whole subjective reality consists in substituting myself for him. The dimension of irreversibility, that by which alterity unendingly withdraws, Levinas names *illeity*.[29] The you is *ille*, that one, by what exceeds the concepts with which the I is conceived. There can be command, obligation, contestation put on me only if the other is not derivative from me and cannot become equivalent to me in any maneuver.

Levinas does not seek to give of illeity, of irreversibility and infinition, intuitive evidence—the kind of *idealizing intuition* Husserl has claimed for a subjectivity that intuits its inner time-horizon as infinite. He also does not credit, as does Nietzsche, a will and a joyous love whose veracity would be to the measure of their illuminating comprehensiveness. But he claims to find testimony for the irreversibility and the infinition of the other's position, the illeity in the you, in the first moves of language.

The first person singular enters language with the utterance "Here I am." This entry into language is not an act of self-presentation or self-representation; it is the passivity of an exposure. The words do not record exposedness, and represent or signify it; they effect exposure. With them the exposure to another is expressed or exposed. They are, Levinas says, a sign given of the giving of signs—more exactly, they are a sign given by which one becomes this giving and this signifying.

Through their passive expositional sense, the words bear witness to unending withdrawal and transcendence. This transcendence beyond being that contests and judges being, this Good that calls unto being and to expiation for the wants and faults of being, Levinas names God.

Yet even these phrases already thematize God and already dissimulate or transpose his incidence in human discourse. God, the infinite, is properly neither designated by words nor even indicated or named but borne witness to by the "Here I am." He approaches as a pure saying that calls forth my response, a saying inconvertible into something put forth, said.

It is then in my own words, saying "Here I am," that the infinite touches discourse. God is not a voice that addresses me and becomes thematizable; God enters language only in the witness I formulate in words that do not put forth my presence but expose my exposedness. The infinite is there in the order that orders me to my neighbor. But it is in my words inasmuch as they formulate obedience to this order that the order is first decreed. Levinas does not express this situation according to the Kantian typology, as a veritable constitution of autonomy out of the inaugural heteronomy of the law—where I must act as though it is I myself that gives myself the law to which I am subject. Yet he calls the Kantian formula remarkable and reinterprets it to mean that the law I recognize is first formulated in my own words of obedience—"Here I am." I speak as the author of an order put in me despite myself and unbeknownst to me.

Not only is God invisible, infinity not manifest in the cosmic order, but his command is inaudible, or audible only in my own words. There is not even really a belief in God, which would supply for the inadequate evidence. The proximity of God can be completely repudiated. It is even always dissimulated in the movement by which the saying itself converts into, is fixed, in a said. All saying, which says being, dissimulates this *beyond*. It is only referred to—more exactly, addressed—retrospectively or reductively by a critical movement back from the already-said. This reduction is not a phenomenological reduction, for it does not issue in a pure intuition, does not come upon the given origin or principle from which the discourse advanced. Unlike in the Kantian moral deduction, God is not attained in the demand for moral intelligibility that postulates him, for the demand for immanent coherence in the total fabric of the said already dissimulates the disturbance or the disruption to which the first utterance bears witness.

7. The Self in Itself

The effort to formulate our existence not only as responsive to being and to nothingness but as responsible to alterity and to the infinity in alterity, leads us into the paradoxical theses of a heterology.

Before the destitution of alterity, I am singled out as the rich one, from whom something is required, from whom a response is always possible and always required. I exist in the midst of a nourishing medium, enjoying the elements. My existence finds itself a substance, resources under requisition.

To be responsible is to answer for the wants and failings of the other; it is to put oneself in his place, to bear his burden. It is to be in every place, a support for the whole universe. It is to ex-ist desituated, without a sphere of one's own, in expropriation.

But responsibility is also finding oneself under accusation. There is no taking up of responsibility without taking up a situation that did not emanate out of oneself nor according to one's intention. Responsibility is finding oneself already under claims, too late on the scene to have helped. The more responsibilities one takes up the more one finds oneself laden with.

How could the structure of such subjectivity be formulated—the one that is singularized in finding that no one can answer in my place but that exists in occupying any and every place, put from the start in place of another, to answer to and for alterity? What is this singular being without the haecceity of being? What is this ex-isting in the world everywhere expropriated, "exiled in oneself"? What is the self in itself? Levinas has formulated the structure of, and the movement that produces, the self differently in his different works.

If it is true that the being that is, or that one makes, one's own is *being*—the being with which the universe of what is is—then the existential interpretation of our being as ex-isting finds in it not just the ec-static movement out of *one's own* state of being; this thrust out of one's own determinate form or state of being is a thrust out of being *simpliciter.* Thus, for Heidegger, our being exists casting itself toward nothingness. But while Heidegger identified this nothingness with the world as the very clearing in which entities are arrayed, Levinas from the start understood our existence as a thrust out of the world— evasion, according to the title of a 1936 essay.[30] Existence as ex-stasis is a movement of escape from the definitive. But it is not a movement toward the final termination, that which fixes its itinerary irrevocably with the wall of nothingness. Existing, as movement out of the definitive, is not a quest for ends and for ending but postponement of dying.[31]

This movement is unto itself a term; it breaks with, breaks out of, the horror of anonymous participation in existing. It makes itself an *existent,* according to the conception Levinas elaborated in *Existence and Existents*—that which does not exist only but relates to its existing, takes up a position with regard to it, arises in *hypostasis* to take on or assume its existence as its own property. It is then a term, not in that all its activities would consist in terminating—as in Heidegger's conception, where the existent that can terminate itself, that casts itself unto its dying, is that which can determine what is really possible for it. For Levinas an existent is rather what determines because it makes itself a starting point; it initiates. It is the focal origin of a perspective, a point from which there is a view, the source of lines of perspective and currents of efficacity that then go on to die away on the horizons. The determining efficacity of an existent does not consist in its power to die but in its power to come to birth, to begin, to take on existence as something it initiates and bears.

But an existent as a commencement is not *in* being; it breaks with the beginningless, endless force of be-ing (the "there is," *il y a*), and rises out of it. In *Totality and Infinity* Levinas had found this exceeding in the most elementary movement of sensibility: to sense is indeed to be immersed in the sensuous element and to find this concordance agreeable, a pleasure, but the enjoyment in enjoying its enjoyment rises out of existence—over and beyond existing enjoying existing. The circuit of ipseity, the egoism that first forms in sensibility, is this "over and beyond."[32] One can, Levinas observed, judge one's existence in the name of one's enjoyment, one can sacrifice one's life to one's enjoyment.

The analyses of *Existence and Existents* and *Totality and Infinity* explained the structure of a subject as a movement forming an *instant* in the flow of anonymous time, a positing of itself by itself in *posture*, resting on the support of the elemental earth, and finally as an *existent*, a term that assumes existence as its own. It was out of this consistency, as a closed instant of presence, a *here* that posits itself, an existent, that subjectivity would be then contested in all its self-sufficiency and appealed to for all its resources, by the a posteriori encounter with alterity. Levinas was then very concerned to avoid the dialectical logic that makes of the self a counter-position to the position of the other. Forming a system, from within as much as from without, they would be reintegrated into the totality of being, where alterity is reduced by identification. It seemed to Levinas that the position of the ego in itself, complete in itself, indeed maintaining itself the same by appropriating everything external to it by possession and comprehension, was required so that the other that then affects it remain genuinely other.

But *Otherwise than Being* takes as a first evidence—or rather as that which is borne witness to with the first words of speech—the axis of sacred infinity, the illeity, the proximity to God in which the other abides. Levinas now presents the relationship with alterity as constitutive of all sensibility; apprehensiveness before the approach of the other does not come second, to disturb a closed and contented sensibility for the world. The self "in itself" is what is singled out, isolated from the anonymous passing of be-ing in which "one" participates, in the exposure to alterity. Once it is thus exiled in itself, it can ex-ist out of itself into the world and disclose a world. Levinas now argues that ipseity is not constituted in the tide of phenomenality, with which being returns upon itself. Before the self is the axis of the ontological process whereby being becomes an apparition, it is in relationship with what is other than the world and does not present itself in a phenomenon.

The subjectivity that forms as one's own is now no longer conceived as the pivotal or archetypal existent; now Levinas sees the self finding itself thrown back upon itself by another, exiled in itself, finding itself in deficit, born too late to answer to what is demanded, arising in an effort to catch up to what is demanded. To be responsible is to find oneself always exceeded by what is required of one's being. It is to be without a stock of one's own, to be in the incessant emptying out of one's resources. It is to be without a place of one's own, to exist in incessant desituation, displacement.[33] It is to exist in putting oneself in the place of another, to bear his burden and answer to and for his failings.

There is personal identity, to be sure, the work of a self-identification, a maintaining oneself the same throughout one's acts and states, effecting temporal syntheses. But this identity with which one presents oneself functions not to make appear to conceal the fundamental ipseity. The selfsameness one identifies covers over an ipseity produced by passive genesis. This persona is a mask, the pro-noun with which is named what is without identity, the pseudonym by which what is unique is classified among beings. Ipseity is not only unity but uniqueness, the first person singular is what cannot be replaced. This not being able to let another answer in one's place throws one back into oneself in such a way that one cannot contemplate oneself, cannot express oneself, cannot identify oneself. One finds oneself mired *in oneself*.[34]

Very early Levinas sought to catch sight of the fundamental movement of ipseity in corporality. Corporality is self-movement, but this initiation of movement is not a force that spontaneously projects itself against the inertia of obstacles; it is a burden and an obstacle to itself. Its very thrust weighs on itself. Fatigue is the inner sense of this weight of the effort, which has to overcome itself, overcome its own resistance to the launching of itself into position. Once launched the movement continues but also relapses, has to be continually launched anew, does not prolong itself like a rhythm. Indolence is the repugnance before the non-rhythmicity of labor, repugnance before the prospect of having to undertake existing. What was launched or conceived, what had come to pass, definitive and irrevocable, in oneself, lapses, is not fully appropriated or re-presented in the present, has to be reinstated with effort. Indolence is not pleasure but torment; those who live for distractions are fleeing indolence as much as labor.

There is anxiety in indolence. Anxiety—*angustia*—is not finding oneself adrift in the indeterminate and the insubstantial but being thrown back upon oneself. This is already the case in Heidegger where the sense of the world receding and nothingness gaping open about one is boredom and vertigo; the anxiety is being left clinging only to oneself. The force of existing, which naturally flows out upon a world, is now thrown back upon itself, upon the plenum of its own being, and experiences this being hemmed in being, this definition, as suffocation. Here definition, which as form, *formositas*, is beauty, perfection, and epiphany, is also strangulation—*angustia*. Being and its phenomenality are felt disproportionate.[35] But in Levinas's analyses the situation of finding oneself cast adrift in the emptiness or clearing in which beings are suspended, or in the indeterminate, the *apeiron*, does not mire one in one's own determination; it brings about depersonalization, it reduces one to an anonymous vigilance without object. It is being thrust back into oneself by the exactions of alterity that produces the anxiety by which a being stifles in its own form.

Finding oneself mired in oneself is not something produced by the thrust of spontaneous existence that dies and that now anticipates its dying; it is produced in aging. The inability to put oneself back at one's beginning, to find oneself once again at the commencement of one's initiatives, to recuperate and re-present again what one had begun, which is the inner diagram of the fatigue in effort, is, across time, the condition of a subject that forms by aging. Senescence is the process of one's initiatives turning into habitus, into weight, by which time is irreversible. One *has to* be what one has come to be; one retains one's past but does so because one is held by one's past. Our endurance then is not that of a passivity, which reacts with a force equal to what acts on it, but that of a patience. Levinas understands patience as the mode of enduring through time in an exposedness to what one cannot assimilate or appropriate— one's own initiatives, the death whose blow is always violence, or the demands of alterity.

The I that exists thrown back upon itself by the demands made on it, that finds itself backed up to itself by the alterity that afflicts it, exists in the effort to receive, to take hold of, an event that has come to pass and has passed, that did not make itself present and proves to be unre-presentable. The I finds itself unable to put itself at the beginning of the contact and unable to take itself up, to convert its weight into force. The responsibility answers for a debt contracted before freedom arises, before consciousness begins to exist for itself, before there is a present present to itself.

Negatively, this condition by which subjectivity exists subjected is described as being inessential, a nonexistent, a non-quiddity, a non-identity, that is, a movement that does not identify itself of itself, a non-existent that does not stand on its own beneath its deeds, in possession of its own existence, a term that discovers itself not in the plenitude of being but in the want of failing and offense, an insubstantiality that does not contain its own resources but knows them only in the exposure to another. The metaphysical terms of sovereignty— autonomy, spontaneity, activity, quiddity, identity maintaining itself identical, identifying itself, one or totality, self-positing position, *Da* or *here* that posits itself, term and telos and ideal unto itself—all this conceptual apparatus built to express subjectivity as cognition and as agency Levinas repudiates as masking the ethical substructure of cognition and praxis.

Positively, in *Otherwise than Being* subjectivity is ontologically—or hetero-logically—conceptualized as *exposure* and as *signification*. One's own existing forms with the trope the-one-for-the-other.[36] Its existing is then meaning or signifying. The one that exists exposing its exposedness to another or signaling to another is not a term within existence. It "otherwise than is." This passive genesis of the self outside the sphere of light and of objects, outside of the play of being and nothingness, is not an event in a transcendental sphere; it is the structure of sensibility. The voice of alterity strikes a being that is passive, corporeal, vulnerable, a being whose efforts weary, whose time lapses, whose presence is senescence. It is not in our ideal constancy, our apathetic self-satisfaction, our resoluteness, our power and our will to power, but in the frailty of our flesh that we are responsible for the other and before the other.

The one whose existing is signification speaks—in signs. And assigns himself a sign. What is the relationship between the-one-for-the-other as the structure of existence and the indicative, imperative, and vocative force of its signs? How does the pro-noun mask the fundamental ipseity it designates? How does the face double up with its own caricature?

VII

THE SIGN OF THE SUBJECT

Subjectivity gives itself a sign. It says I; *I* think, therefore *I* am. As *significant*, it stands for, represents an ideal term, the signified, anywhere, anytime representable—a term which here refers to the very subject that utters it. As a semiotic *value*, it stands for, represents, other signs for which it can be substituted. It is because the subject acquires a sign of its own that one can speak. One enters speech only as an element of language.

Certainly the sign of the subject acquires neither its signification nor its value all at once. A sign has an ideal meaning, in Husserl's explanation, inasmuch as what it refers to is not a *hic et nunc* reality, but a term that can be presented anywhere, anytime, can be represented ad infinitum, is situated in a dimension of infinity. But the dimension of idealization, of infinity, along which the index that is associated with a reality comes to represent an ideal signification, opens progressively, and is open to a genetic analysis on our part. And the constellation of other signs in which its semiotic value is determined is not the totality of the language (languages, if we admit that the kinship systems and the economy are also communication systems)[1] that would have to be there all at once, exposed to intuition, in order for any sign to be determinate in it. The semantic value of a sign is determinate in a field of signs close to or far from its use, and whose confines are horizons.

How does the subject acquire its sign? How does that sign acquire its significance and its value? How does the subject acquire significance and value by procuring its own sign? What is the relationship between the idealization and valorization the subject invests in the sign with which he presents himself in the exchange system of language, the persona with which he presents himself in the kinship systems and the field of labor and the market, the economies of production and of reproduction, and the idealization and valorization with which he comes to be a subject, autonomous, on his own, one that can be singled out and addressed, one that can respond in his own name? For is he not singled out with a sign, and does he not respond with signs?

1. The Idealization of the Sign of the Subject

Within civilization an infant is significant before he is. Before he was born, perhaps even before he was conceived, the infant already figured in the parental discourse. What functioned as the material substrate of the signifier of the infant in the parental discourse was not the real fetus but an image, the "imaged body" of the infant, imagined especially by the mother.[2] The doubling up was possible first because the real fetus is invisible and because its movements, its kickings, form a fragmented body, fragmented in space and also across time. There was an urgent vital reason to produce this imaginary body. It is what will enable the mother to experience the childbearing as a birth, an increase, rather than as a fragmentation of her body, a dismembering, a loss of part of her substance, or a threat to her whole existence.

The infant screams with the pain of being born. It is held against the maternal breast, and there draws in the vital fluids in which it was immersed when it was steeped in the uterine broths. The fluids flow, are held, flow again, in the tubes, the coils, the veins, the tide pools of the inner, functional organism, and flow on, out of his orifices and pores, into other channels of the deltas and estuaries of surrounding nature. The soft vesicle of the infantile organism, warm sack full of content, of milk, blood, and biles, fills with contentment. What is most infantine in the infant face, which even in the second infancy of senility will never swell again, are the infantile jowls, so admirably muscular and strong, bellows contrived to suck in the milk, and whose form so strikingly mirrors the form of the milk-swollen maternal breasts, with lips and gums perfectly engineered to couple on to the maternal teats.

But this admirably fitted coupling leaks, the infant drools, slobbers, utterly without professional conscience. It will take years to teach him the satisfactions of a neat job. He is discovering another pleasure—the pleasure of slavering, of smearing the saliva and the milk, of spreading a surface of warm pleasure. Through this foamy warmth extending the surfaces and discovering the pleasure of surfaces. Life learns to use the energies generated in the biological functioning of the organs to produce pleasure, a pleasure of surfaces, a pleasure of having surfaces, a pleasure of being outside, of being alive. This pleasure extends interference against the craving to return to the womb, to quiescence, to the fluid equilibrium of inorganic nature; it functions to block the death drive. Freud identified it: the libido.

The genetic analysis does not, like the phenomenological intentional analysis—with which a consciousness, driven by a cognitive motive, examines its own structure—take as given sensations that are intentionally structured, that is, sense data that are givens of sense, indicative and informative. Jean-François Lyotard, and Gilles Deleuze and Félix Guattari have especially emphasized this, in their reformulation of the metapsychology of psychoanalysis against Jacques Lacan.[3] The infantile sensibility is a production. And one must distinguish the infantile production of closure and plenitude, that which Deleuze and Guattari call the employment of the organs to produce an unreceptive closure, a "body without organs"—from the production of an *erotogenic surface*. In both cases that which drives the sensibility is a death drive, but it is not to be identified, as Freud did, as a drive to return to the equilibrium and quiescence of the inorganic. The closed plenum of an organism with closed organs, which Deleuze and Guattari take to constitute the id as a state of the body, produces and reproduces itself. It functions by repetition. Deleuze sees in the primary repression which constitutes an unconscious in the organism not an organism that repeats because it does not remember—because memory has been suppressed—but rather a system that does not remember, that is, represent its past, because it repeats it. It does not reinstate its past in the nonactuality of representation but in the actuality of its repetition.[4] This system is productive not of representational sensations, givens of sense that would function as intentional traces of what inscribed them, but of affective sensations, the opaque, plenary affects of contentment. The contentment that simmers in the closed organism without organs functions to seal it in its torpor.

On the other hand, by what Freud called an anaclitic deviation, the functional organ coupling, deviated or perverted from its machinic use, produces an erotogenic surface. Then the organ uses the energy sources to produce unbound intensities Freud called *excitations*. These excitations are filtered through the "partially deadened outer layers of the infantile corpuscle"—lest massive invasions of stimulus crush it. Samplings of outside forces, they are representational—representatives of them. But of themselves they are forces, intensities—and unbound, freely mobile across the closed surfaces of the body and its organism functionings now sated and closed to the outside. They collide, polarize, intensify by reciprocal induction and irradiation. They do not send messages and directives to the central coordinators of the body motility. They are not rays emanating from the central ego or appropriated to it as predicates of a subject. They are consumed, in surface nodes of egoism, in discharges of pleasure. They are not signs signaling to another. They are indeed produced on a surface which is a surface of exposure, but on contact with other surfaces—that of the maternal breast over which the infantile drool spreads, that of the flannels of the mattress which extends his excrement and retains its warmth and pleasure for him—that of the radiant sunlight, the tepid water, the hum, or the lullaby that caress him. These multiple surface eddies of egoism do not aim at objectives across distances, do not seek to maintain themselves; they discharge in spasms of pleasure, which Freud conceives after the model of orgasmic pleasure. They also do not address themselves to the other as absence, as alterity only signaled across distances; the original relation with the other is contact, is embraces and kisses and caresses. We must then indeed maintain the Freudian term excitations—they are not sensations, not signs. This sensibility, identified with libido, with life-force, is not signifying, is not intentional; it is a contact phenomenon. It is not a lack or a negativity aiming at an objective; it is a production. It is not addressed to another; it engenders an erotogenic surface where the pleasure that simmers is indistinguishably that of the infant and of the mother. The slavering, the buzzing, and the babbling of the infant give pleasure, as an entity given and giving in nature—as the sun, hub of nature, which squanders it warmth and its light, its excess energies, without thinking, without demanding recompense.[5]

But the mother has other concerns. She extracts herself from the affective mists the baby extends over her. Her absence teaches the baby anxiety. The arbitrariness, the capriciousness, of her absences give rise in the infant to phantasms of omnipotence. Alterity begins to figure in the infantile consciousness in the form of maternal omnipotence. The mother satisfies the infant's needs and departs—satisfies the infant's needs in order to depart. The infant is given the bottle and put to sleep. The satisfaction of need in a particular moment functions as a refusal of the demand for love, the demand for the pure gift of total satisfaction. Each time the mother satisfies the infantile need, in order to frustrate his demand for absolute love, she reinforces the phantasm of her omnipotence in the infantile consciousness; she reawakens the demons she frustrates. The infant is given the bottle and put to sleep, but the demand for love does not cease being formulated in the sleeping organism. The language, or, more exactly, the inscription, the hieroglyphics and the rebuses,[6] of the infantile dream continues to formulate the demand still addressed to the other.

How will this demand, how will this infancy now addressed to alterity, be able to break outside, leave the closure of its somnolence and its dreams, in order to speak? One can enter language only as an element of language, a sign. How will the infantile life, this primary process libido, this surface production exhilarating in itself and discharging without demand for recompense or response, come to be doubled up with a sign for itself or turn into a sign?

Civilization is equipped with reflection. A mirror offers a child a representation of himself, at a distance. But this representation is not a copy, a replica, or a facsimile; the infant knows himself as a core of motor vectors and feelings, excitations, and the mirror puts in front of him a visual pattern. This colored cut-out is recognized by an infant beginning at the age of six months, an achievement which the higher apes seemingly never attain, but an achievement which they do not have the same kind of biological interest in attaining, as Lacan has explained.[7] Bolk describes the human mutation as that of a primate with greatly slowed-down metabolism, with nonetheless the same nine-month intrauterine existence, born premature, then, unable to coordinate neurologically and without motor integration, existing in dependence and anxiety.[8] In this situation the identification of the mirror-image as himself is not merely a predicative and judgmental synthesis—"That is me!"—it is an affective and projective identification. Not an identification of it but an identification with it: The infant is alienated into the image, captivated by it. For the mirror image will function vitally as a factor of integration: It presents the infant with an anticipated composition of the fragments of his body into a subsistent totality. It presents the infant with an ideal version of himself. In pleasure the infant identifies with this ego ideal. A pleasure which is both the tearing asunder, the rending of an ec-static pulverization of himself, and a swelling up of himself into the anticipatory totality—an ecstatic contentment. The stage of fascination with the mirror image is also the stage of the original narcissism. For it is also a suicide, a losing oneself in the stagnant element of the image. The infant is alienated from the Heraclitean flux of his own experience of himself and of viscous nature, to identify himself with this specular object posited at a distance, fixed, identical and substantial.

There is already something of a linguistic structure in this identification. For from now on there is a material element—the mirror image—which can be referred to, by the child as by others, as the signifier of the subject. The parent that watches says: That is you! And in saying that, the parent pronounces an alchemical order, one that fuses the mirror-image the child now sees with the imaged body of the infant the parents conjured up before he was born to function as the signifier for him in their discourse, one that fuses the anticipatory phantasm now given to the infant with the archaic image he was for them before his emergence into his own life. The mirror image, this signifier, can be set forth, displayed, paraded about, presented to others; it can discourse with others. It has a metonymic form: A signifier for a part of the child (the future totality) has been substituted for the actual and present reality, the physiological and experiental reality of the infant—which had no signifier.

With this metonymic signifier the child himself enters into the discourse in which he had already figured. The imaged body that figured in the parental discourse to signify him before he was born he can now identify, project himself into, make it speak. Make it bear his demand to the other.

But once the child enters into the parental discourse he finds himself subject to its law. The parental law requires that the infant detach himself definitively from his physical reality as a pleasure surface, to identify himself with the signifier that bears him into discourse. The law requires that the child's body as a pleasure surface be taken out of his hands, requires renunciation of masturbation, requires castration.

The law is the word of the father. The father intervenes to counter the phantasm of maternal omnipotence with the potency of his word. Its force is not that of the pain of a real fear effectively produced. Subjection to the word of the father is not equivalent to the maintenance of a real threat of castration whose reproduction in memory would produce the inhibiting fear.

To see this, one would have to recognize, with contemporary philosophies of language, that speech acts are not only representations, representing an ordered reality. Speech is not only indicative but also imperative; speech itself orders. The outcome of the Oedipus complex will be that the demand put to the other will be diversified, deviated, multiplied, articulated in the byways of language, of symbolism, of culture. The infantile libido is not suppressed by a real castration threat; it is deviated, extended, formulated, as the law allows, as the law directs. The word of the father does not have its effect as the physical reproduction of a gesture that produces fear; it is a word of law, the first instance of an ordering, ordaining word. It functions to put a sign in the place of reality—the phallus in the place of the penis. It makes the infantile substance and surfaces into signs.

The paternal word will be taken seriously when the infant discovers the castration of the mother. The paternal decree has already been executed; it speaks with the power to vacate the place of a reality. Melanie Klein reported that the infant, who has no perception of the vagina as the recipient of genital penetration and thereby itself a pleasure object, originally perceives the mother as containing a penis within the fragmented image of her body that forms in the infantile consciousness.[9] Castration phobia in boys and penis envy in girls does not originate in real threats of castration addressed to the child by the real father (more often in fact formulated by the mother) but in the discovery that the penis is missing in the mother. Missing at the place from which the child has come to understand he has himself issued.

In the foreboding horror before the discovery of the maternal mutilation, the child feels then both the seriousness of the eventuality with which he is himself threatened—and the chance he is. For he now also understands the voracious intensity of the ardent eyes the mother turns on him, understands why all this time she has been holding him close to herself, drooling over him, understands he is the missing part of which she has been castrated. The object of her longing is invisible with the invisibility for him of his own only kinesthetic, only affective, only feeling substance. There thus arises the *phallus*—as what is signified by the desire of the mother, that which is addressed in the voluptuous desire of the mother the infant has felt by feeling it turned in his direction. There arises in him the voluptuous idea of being a phallus for the mother. In order to be able not only to torment her with his importunate cries for the satisfaction of particular needs but to be able to demand of her the absolute gift of love.

The seriousness of the word of the father is engraved on the body of the mother, in the castration of the mother. It designates the phallus, pure signification and original absence, as that to which the libido of the mother has always been addressed. If the child can will to subject himself to the law of the father, if he can will the castration of his penis from his body as immediate pleasure object, if he can will the excoriation of all his erotogenic surface, it is because he wills to be the signified which the word of the father designates on the perceptible body of the mother. He invests in the phallic form of his specular ego the libidinous gratification prohibited in his immediate body. He renounces his hedonic substantial *hic et nunc* condensation in reality, in order to invest himself wholly in an image no longer functioning as a spectacle, now functioning as a signifier addressed to the appeal of the other, addressing a demand to the other. He makes himself a sign. He has idealized himself. He has repudiated the haecceity of his reality in order to function as the correlate of the insatiate craving of the other, as that whose immediate presence is effaced and which represents itself to the absolute, indefinitely reiterated because insatiable, demand of the other.

But in appropriating the paternal law, in himself pronouncing upon his own body the law that requires castration, the child puts himself in the place of the father. What wills in him is the desire to identify himself with the phallus the other lacks, but what speaks in him is the word of the father. The *yes* with which he designates his phallic ideality is insinuated in the *no* pronounced on his substantial reality. The phallic phantasm is henceforth that which is always designated but passed over in silence whenever the law of the father speaks in the child. All the objects that turn their surfaces to him from their distances his libido designates, names, appropriates—like a sacred sovereign, according to Nietzsche, with the lordly right of giving names, sealing every thing and event with his seal and taking possession of it.[10] But his libido appropriates them as the accouterments, the array of his own phallic exteriority; by their visibility they stand in for its invisibility. Beyond the kaleidescopic surface patterns that caressed him as they passed, in them, his desire now seeks *objects*, the inapparent cores, objectives that signal the unpronounceable phallic absence. Thus all the surfaces of things become signs, addressed to the appeal of, laying his demands on, others. The signs regulated by the law of instinctual renunciation, as the child will set them forth in discourse, are metaphors for the phallus.

This phallic idealization of the world is distinctively different from the idealization that would be worked by the Nietzschean love. Nietzsche imagines a state of integral affirmation, in which a living system would be able, would have the power, to affirm all its internal chaos, all that which is riddle, fragment, dreadful accident in itself; such a will would make necessary too, and turn an unrestricted, unending affirmation upon, the moment of nature in which it arises. Psychoanalysis claims to bring to light the libidinal force and function of the idealization of objects, the idealization that constitutes them as objects. It seeks the explanation not in a conversion from the natural attitude to the theoretical attitude committed to the idea of infinity, to subjection of the understanding to an imperative for universality and necessity, but in a fundamental change in the state of the body receptive to the exterior. The pivotal distinction is between the preoedipal state and the postoedipal body, between the preoedipal state of the body—biologically functional, coupling its organs upon the sources of its sustenance, veering into the closed state of a body without organs, and producing an erotogenic surface that relates to the surfaces it makes contact with as zones of excitation—and the postoedipal body— castrated, excoriated of its surface zones of immediate pleasure, now stationed before the other as appeal addressed to the other, demand put on the other— wholly a sign. The things are now appropriated as the accouterments of such a phallic visibility. It is as such that they become objective, not just for-me, correlates of my wants or prolongations of my pleasures, but appropriated to appropriate the demand of the other, lures addressed to the others. Their determination as *objects* is not simply effected cognitively, by situating what is perceivable from one's own perspective in the field of a space where there is an infinity of real and possible other perspectives to be annexed to each thing. They are determined first as objects of the *desire* of others, and this desire is recognized as insatiable, infinite, because it is desire for the inaccessible, for an integrity from which the other, the mother, has been removed by the castration which is my own phallic birth. One is then relayed from aspect to aspect and from term to term without end because what one seeks in objects is not excitations, immediate surface gratification, and not sustenance, but the means to captivate and capture the desire of the other. It is as symbols of the phallus, as lures for a desire that is everywhere in the others, that constitutes the others in their alterity, as objectives for a desire that is total and thus insatiable, that sensory surfaces are constituted as, idealized as, objects.

The infant and his wants are outcries; the libido that speaks speaks in the name of the father. The libido that is articulated, that has interiorized the law, has taken the place of the father, speaks in the name of the father. The Oedipus crisis is resolved when the child finds himself, makes himself, capable of being a father, reproducing a family, when the voice of his libido legislates castration. It is resolved when he presents his reality to the other, the woman—not the symbiotic reality of the mother of infancy, from which he has severed himself, but her representative—when he presents his reality not in order to make contact with his real penis but to use his penis now as a phallus, as an instrument of derealization, of idealization, of castration. He will not use it to extend the erotogenic surfaces but to engender an alterity, a libidinal exteriority, another infancy, to be castrated.

2. The Value of the Sign of the Subject

Economics as a science begins when Ricardo distinguished, in value, the apparent, the phenomenal, from the real. Goods enter economics as values, use-values. Use-value is not utility; water and air are prime elements of utility, but that does not make them have economic value. The use-value of a good represents its use for releasing its possessor of time, so that he can participate in social production and commerce. If I buy shoes rather than make them myself, they represent so many hours of labor with which I can devote myself to productive or commercial occupations. Thus what makes the utility of a good a measurable value, hence exchangeable according to a reckoned exchange, is the quantity of labor that went into it.

However, this real value of the possession of a commodity by a *Homo oeconomicus* is latent, hidden. What makes goods be recognized, in consciousness, as values, is exchange-value. The exchange-value is the measure of a commodity inasmuch as it can be exchanged, not for useful time but for other commodities. There are four forms. One commodity can be exchanged for another specific commodity—a coat for shoes, what Marx names the elementary, isolated, or accidental form of exchange value. It can be exchanged for any of an indefinite series of different commodites—the nomad who has found salt goes to the market and perceives his salt as something that can be exchanged for any of the goods on the market. This Marx calls the total or extended form of exchange value. Third, the exchange-value of all commodities may be expressed in terms of one commodity of the series—as in pre-Columbian Guatemala, where the exchange-value of all goods was expressed in terms of coca beans, or in Bolivia, where coca leaves were used. In the eighteenth century English merchants on the banks of the Monomotapa and the shores of the Gulf of Guinea expressed the value of all commodities in terms of human beings. Thus four ounces of gold, thirty piasters of silver, three quarters of a pound of coral, or seven pieces of Scottish cloth were, according to Father Labat, worth one slave.[11] In the fourth form of exchange-value, the money form, gold, which has no use-value, is that in terms of which the exchange-value of all commodities is expressed. Here between the living currency of the eighteenth-century British traders on the Gulf of Guinea and the inert currency—true money—the difference lies in that the human being used as currency is the most useful of commodities, whereas in the true monetary economy the currency is itself the most useless of commodities.

Marx distinguishes use-value from exchange-value in terms of content and form, the real and the phenomenal. But the phenomenal form here does not function to make the real content manifest in consciousness but to conceal it. The exchange-value is variable whereas within any given stage of productive methods, the use-value is constant. Exchange-value, the phenomenal form of value in consciousness, functions to conceal the value-content, the quantum of human labor a good contains when it figures in human intercourse as a value. It hides man's own substance, which, when organized for regular postures and operations, as an organism, is the archetype of and organizer of useful goods and is potentially useful to other men. It thus hides man from himself, conceals the value-creating character of human activity and the social character of individual labor.

Value appears as an arithmetical perception of goods. But in reality the value-ascription A = nB, which appears as a quantitative predication, is based on something qualitative, the judgment that A is equivalent to nB, or A is worth nB. "Paris vaut bien une messe." Value is a meaning that falsely appears to simply formulate real quantitative properties of the goods evaluated; in reality it is a surplus transferred on to them by the evaluation. Value, as a phenomenon given in consciousness is an increment, a transcendent excess, for which Hayden White has analyzed the rhetorical forms.

The elementary form of exchange-value, where one good is judged exchangeable for another good, is constituted in a metaphorical operation. "The metaphor," White says, "provides the key to the understanding of how purely material or quantitative entities come to be endowed with spiritual or qualitative attributes."[12] In its second form, the total or extended form, exchange-value is formulated metonymically. Here the relationships among commodities are conceived on the basis of the apprehension of their placement in a series that is indefinitely extendable: "A = B, B = C, C = D, D = E . . ." In the third form, the generalized form of exchange-value, each of the commodities is held equivalent to one of them—coca beans, coca leaves, or human beings. Here the meaning is constituted in the rhetorical trope of synecdoche, where entities are characterized by using a part to symbolize some quality presumed to inhere in the totality. Fourthly, in the trope of irony, entities are characterized by way of negating on the figurative level what is positively affirmed on the literal level. The figures of the manifestly absurd expression (catechresis) such as "blind mouths" and of explicit paradox (oxymoron) such as "cold passion" are types of this trope. The Marxist analysis of monetary value understands its meaning to be constituted in the rhetorical trope of irony. For in monetary economy each good is evaluated in terms of its equivalent in gold. The judgment makes goods, of real use-value, to be equivalent to the least useful of available substances, less useful than dirt and rocks. Gold is the most useless metal both by its properties and by its scarcity. Were it abundant one could plaster one's walls with it, for though it is too soft to use in implements, it is as good a nonconductor of heat, cold, and sound as lime.

It is in Marx's discourse that monetary value appears constituted in a trope of irony. But the discourse of political economy is not the discourse of ordinary consciousness; there is need of science because ordinary consciousness is dissimulating. In monetary economy for consciousness to perceive the value of goods is to perceive gold, and not labor, in them. Marx explains: "As a use-value the linen is something which to our senses is obviously different from gold; as a value it is the equivalent of gold, and therefore looks like gold. . . . [I]t acquires a value form different from its bodily form. The essence of its value is manifest in its likeness to the gold, just as the sheep nature of the Christian is manifest in his resemblance to the Lamb of God."[13]

The gold is in the linen as the sheep-nature is in the Christian. For exchange-value does not only cover over man's value-creating activity harbored in useful goods; his organism, the first useful commodity, is perceived through value. To recognize a man is to recognize the worth of a man. Marx writes: "It is with the human being as with the commodity. Since the human being does not come into the world bringing a mirror with him, nor yet as a Fichtean philosopher able to say 'I am myself,' he first recognizes himself as reflected in other men. The man Peter grasps his relation to himself as a human being through becoming aware of his relation to the man Paul as a being of like kind with himself. Therefore Paul, with flesh and bone, with all his Pauline corporeality, becomes for Peter the phenomenal form of the human kind."[14] The four basic forms of society are primitive communist, slave, feudal, and capitalist. In the first or elementary form, the individual appraises his value in the constituting meta-phor Peter = Paul. The servile evaluation is in the trope of metonymy: he is evaluated as equivalent to any of the infinite series of others, equivalent to and interchangeable with just anyone, as anyone with him; servility is this valuation of being completely dispensable. In the feudal society, valuation is according to the trope of synecdoche; the whole indefinite series of individuals are measured in terms of one individual as the standard of value. In the capitalist society, the individual is valued in terms of his monetary worth and values himself in terms of gold. He constitutes his worth in selling himself, in prostitution—trope, irony.

Marx called gold a fetish. A fetish is constituted in a libidinal economy, whereby some entity, useful for the production of voluptuous feeling by reason of its properties and its scarcity, its absence, is put in the place of, valued over, the organ most useful for the purpose of voluptuous discharge, and then over the whole series of organs that can be exchanged for this purpose.

There is thus an inner economy in the man that participates in political economy, the economy of the polis. It is by reason of his organism-structure that man is *Homo oeconomicus*. There are operations, whose rhetorical tropes we have to exhibit, by which man constitutes a value for himself in consciousness—an exchange-value that functions to hide the use-value.

The infant is tubes disconnected, corpuscle full of yolk put out of the fluid reservoir of the womb, grasping, gulping air, pumping circulating fluids. The tubes have orifices that couple on to the breasts, the mouth, the elbow of the mother, draw in flows of milk, as also flows of air, light, tone, sustenance. An organ fitted in the composition of an organism is susceptible of several usages. A mouth is a coupling that draws in the fluid but can also slobber or vomit it out forcibly, that babbles or cries, that can pout, smile, spit, and kiss; so the anus is an orifice that ejects the segments of flow but also holds them in, that ejects vapors and noise, can pout, be coaxed, refuses, defiles, and defies. And spreads the flow, produces a surface of waste, and surface effects of pleasure. Pleasure of making oneself a fetid viscosity, spreading over any surface contiguous with it, erotogenic continuum. The excrement is waste and gratuity and gift, the archetypal gift, which is transfer without recompense not of one's possessions, one's things, but of one's substance, oneself.

Now the other intervenes: The reluctant corpuscle is cornered into an exchange. It is done with words, with signs, which already have tangible physiological effects, organizing a semiotic field, the organism. The symbiotic couple now draw apart behind closed doors to strike a deal, bargaining to extend the time of the transaction in order that the quality and substance of the merchandise can be brought out in detail for suitable appraisal. Come on, do it in the potty! Let Mummy see! How pleased Mummy is! The inner sludge is not to be given freely, spread around on all the surfaces; it is to be retained, held back, hidden, covered up, privatized, constituted into private property, in order to be then given over not freely but in exchange. The golden baby feces are to be exchanged for maternal love on the installment plan. Human commerce begins, the libido is economized, capitalism is established in the men's room. And in the infantile soul.

The outside agitator seduces the infant with the lure of primitive communism; he is induced to give of his own substance in exchange for the presence of the other, the omnipotent one. In exchange for love, that is, for an absolute of gratification. Elementary form of exchange-value, trope—metaphor. Yet what is given are but signs of this absolute: How pleased Mummy is! Come sit by Mummy! Mummy will give you some candy!

Tokens for tokens. In fact she is not interested in what he can contribute to the potty and only wants to buy time for herself. The baby for his part no longer gives himself; he holds back for this transaction, holds back now in this transaction. He builds up a reserve of capital. He gives signs, tokens only, of himself. After much badgering and coaxing, he wryly gets off the potty after having left some ridiculously fraudulent measure of currency. Soon he will be only leaving a nickel, or a traveler's check, but the consumers will have to take what they can get. He puts some of his liquid assets into circulation at every lamp post, keeping hard assets in the cloacal vaults. He is building up character, that is, Freud says, compulsive orderliness, cleanliness, and parsimony. It is the extended form of exchange-value; trope—metonymy.

When does this inner servile economy get reorganized into a feudal economy—value trope, synecdoche? The change in the superstructure got prepared by developments in the infrastructure: the libidinal production shifted from anal to penile material. The penis, a detachable appendage, which appears as a sort of exterior prolongation of the column of feces felt hardening within, acquires the value of the gold of feces. If each organ is susceptible to multiple uses, they can be exchanged for one another. But for the moment—for years yet—the infant does not realize the value of his own resources. No buyer for jism turns up; by himself the child discovers the pleasure of wasting his seed; he produces a surface of waste again, and surface effects of pleasure. He adheres to this pleasure, wills this waste, this nullity; his will actively participates in and wills this collapse of will.

But these developments are being watched. The other intervenes, the father. The father interdicts this sly infantile return to his, the father's wife. The son is ordered to castrate himself, that is, excise his penis as an organ for the production of pleasure, take it definitively out of anyone's reach. The child laughs at the paternal threat, empirically most frequently formulated by the mother, even as she fondles him. He will take the paternal word seriously the day he discovers the castration of the mother. In horror he learns that the father has appropriated her to himself in this mutilation.

This horror vacui offers its fascinations—and, like every separation from reality, its understanding. He comes to understand that he has been pulled forth from that gaping wound between her thighs; he comes to understand that he is the penis of which she has been castrated. Now he comes to understand that all that rhetoric of double-entendre is not disinterested on her part; now he catches on to the soft-sell campaign she has been conducting for as long as he can remember. He sees himself as the absent part severed from her—and separated from himself, reflected in the mirror surfaces of her eyes. He conceives the project of making himself be that phallus of which his mother has been mutilated, in order to hold on himself her narcissist love. He identifies himself wholly with this phallic phantasm in order to demand of her the absolute of devotion. He understands very well that she satisfies his needs in order to frustrate this demand for love. He will exchange them all for the phallic contours, phenomenal form of void. It is this total investment of himself in the phallus that makes it possible for him to effect the castration of a part, his penis qua immediate pleasure-object, the paternal word demanded, as well as the polymorphously perverse erotogenic surface production about it.

The phallus is the primary fetish, the structure of every fetish. It is the absent part, the part only signaled, signified in the eyes of the other, in the desire of the other, put in place of the whole. It is the value, exchange-value, phenomenal form of value, that occludes the carnal surfaces as sensuous flux utilizable for the production of pleasure. A meaning of his existence constituted in the trope of synecdoche.

It is in order to obey the paternal law, in order to be able to realize his self-castration, that the child has constituted himself as a phallic fetish. But in internalizing the paternal law as the law of his inner libidinal economy, in engendering a superego, the child engenders his own father, puts himself in the place of the father. The word of the father becomes incarnate, as superego enters into the infantile erotogenic substance, in order to castrate the penis through which the infantile subtance is squandered. And in order to be put to death. The father becomes incarnate in the son in order to be sacrificed and in order to put infancy to death with his death. For the son passage beyond the phallic stage to the genital consists in learning the power to effectively take the place of the father, become a father in his turn. That is, assassinate his father, castrate infancy in his turn. He will identify himself with law and prohibition and use his penis to produce an infant to castrate. His real penis is now put in the place of the phallus, becomes a phallic metaphor.

This means that when now the son of the father comes to the other, the mother and her representatives, with his penis, they will no longer meet in the market of a primitive communism, bartering for immediate gratification. They now meet in a monetary economy where non-reciprocity, love, is at stake. Inhabited by the mystical body of the father, the son will not one day exchange his phallic value for the unprofitable penile gratification, he uses his penis to produce an infant to castrate in the name of the father.

Investment at a loss? To be sure; deficit spending, as any modern capitalist knows, is what maintains the value of the currency. His phallic ideality is maintained as that which has no erotogenic use-value; its value is measured by the quantity of goods of use-value which are sacrificed to its uselessness. It must have the value of gold. Gold demands love!

That which is supremely usable for the production of pleasure, the ever available erotogenic surfaces one possesses gratuitously by natural endowment, is exchanged for the intangible phallic mirage playing in the mirroring eyes of another's craving, the least erotogenetically productive substance. Trope, irony, to be sure. But the supremely unproductive phallus is reproductive. A currency that, of itself, reproduces what it is.

For the virile, imperial, vindictive[15] West is on the gold standard. Gold, Aristotle wrote, "has been devised as a common measure, and, consequently, money is the standard to which everything is related and by which everything is measured."[16] "Even the fact that man excels the other animals in having understanding and can set up ends for himself still gives him only an external value for his usefulness, namely, the value of a man in preference to another animal," Kant wrote in *The Metaphysical Principles of Virtue.* "This is to say that he has a price as a commodity in the exchange of these animals as things, in which he still has a lower value than the general medium of exchange, money, whose value is therefore called preeminent."[17]

3. The Masks of the Ideal

The phallic identity and ideal is exhibited by psychoanalysis as the figure with which the insignificant and uneconomic infantile substance has become a sign. The substance of infancy has been transfigured from a core of immediate libidinal gratification into a signifier; now not only the child's coded words and gestures but all the positions and movements of life, of libido and of death drive, in him appeals to another, puts a demand on another. The sensuous surfaces of the outlying substances accessible for-him, in tangency with him, now become *objects*, objective, first significant for others—terms with ideal identity and value, inasmuch as they are metaphors and metonymies for the phallus.

The phallic identity is ideal in Husserl's sense—it is a term whose identity is identified, as selfsame, in an infinite, unendingly prolonged, time-horizon. This identity is no longer that which forms, ephemerally, in eddies of surface gratification. It is not that of a pleasure which vibrates upon, illuminates and affirms an intensity which is already discharging itself, already passing. The ephemeral and nomadic egoisms that form in the primary-process erotogenic zone form in closed moments of a now without memory and without expectations. The phallic identity is set forth in a horizon of time. That which inaugurates the process in which the infant will contract phallic identity is the approach of the castration threat, which afflicts the moment of masturbatory pleasure with a future, a death in the form of dismemberment. It disrupts the self-sufficiency of moments of pleasure and afflicts infancy with an adult destiny; it extends the libidinal time in a structure of prematuration. It induces an identification with the specular image of adult, reproductive and not only productive, sexuality. The castration anxiety, anxiety before the menace of death by dismemberment, does not throw the child back upon his ownmost erotogenetic potential but induces him to identify with an identity that has always already existed. For he abandons the penis and the masturbatory surfaces he has, castrates himself, in order to identify himself with the phallus the castrated mother had, and become for her what the father was. His phallic identity is ancestral, a recurrence of the same; he identifies himself with the name of the father. This ancestral paternal figure and role is at the same time his future. When one day he approaches the surfaces of a woman again, it will be not to sink into the closed present of pleasure but in order to father a child in turn, a child to bear his name, a child with which the name of the father can recur. The phallic identity subsists in a time-axis of unending recurrence. Life identifies itself, maintains this identity, not by the involution and self-affirmation of pleasure but by an ever-repeated operation of ascribing the diverse figures and positions of his libido to this abiding identity-term, by attributing his kinesthetic and affective movements each time to this specular identity, by narcissistically projecting himself into, losing himself in, its medusa-features. The phallic identity is constituted in the ideal or infinite time of signs.

The phallic figure is not only an ideal; it is an imperative. It is a figure of the universal and the necessary, the universally necessary. The figure of the father is a figure of law; the name of the father *(le nom du père)* is the No of the paternal voice *(le non du père)*.[18] In the phallic figure the particularity of libidinal impulses had been suppressed, the multiplicity of surface connections have been superseded by the unity of a desire demanding the absoluteness and absolute oneness of plenary satisfaction. The primary-process erotogenic zone is to be anesthetized, excoriated; the phallic splendor is exemplary as a figure of this mortification. Lacan opposes *to be a phallus* with *to have a penis;* the phallic identity is the schema or the type of the imperative dispossession of all pleasures immediately at hand, all pleasures in which the particular closes in on its particularity. This "type" is imposed upon libidinal infancy as an order put on categorically and not simply hypothetically—not simply as the compensation consequent upon prudence before a threat of pain and dismemberment.

The phallus is a value; in becoming a phallus the infant becomes an element in a libidinal economy. He makes himself into a substitute for the father; he will one day father an infant in turn as one that will take his place in the economy of householding *(oikonomia)*. Like gold that counts not for the pleasure of its soft glow but by reason of the quantity of commodities for which it can be exchanged, he counts not for the soft pleasures of his own sensuous substance and not as an end in himself, a dignity, but as a value, a currency to be exchanged for the place of the father, a place he himself engenders a son to occupy in turn. He makes himself, according to Klossowski's terminology, live currency.[19]

Could it be that, like the ideal types that have dominated the successive epochs of man's self-cultivation in Nietzsche's history of culture, the phallic identity and value is chosen not for its truth but for its splendor? Could it be that this telos—afflicted on our libidinal impulses to make them not processes formed in actual surface couplings which find their satisfaction and their discharge in the moment of their own intensity but a desire for the absent, an insatiable demand for the infinite, according to Lacan's insistent teaching, in order to make the libido pass from the real and the imaginary unto the realm of the symbolic—is in fact but the representation in the theater of the psyche of the *directing force* of libidinal drives? Could it be also that what *drives* the libidinal impulses in a certain direction is not the self-engendering force of this desire, that the real directing forces are masked by the phallic ideal? Could it be that the real *driving forces* of libidinal life are nowise accumulated and finalized by this objective? And how would one know that? What would bring this knowledge to the phallic and reproductive adult? What would bring this knowledge to us who question the psychoanalytic genetic analysis with a genealogical investigation?

The ideal is ideal, Husserl says, by repetition. It is not that which is outside time but that which recurs, anywhere, anytime, the same. It is that which presents itself, at a moment of presence, as that which recurs and that which can recur ever once more. Its presence is representation. In this sense every sign is a representation;[20] there is no inauguration of a sign in language and no terminal usage. If a word can be introduced into English, it must, upon its first occurrence, appear as already latent in the possibilities and grammar of English; and even if it is never uttered again, its de facto last usage does not terminate its signifyingness—every word now obsolete one comes upon in a text of Old English appears as being able to signify again. In this sense when the child stands phallicly before the figure of the mother, bearing the name of the father, he assumes an identity, he identifies with an identity that preceded his birth, that made his birth possible. He identifies himself with a figure that overcomes both death and that fear of death by dismemberment which is the castration anxiety.

For this ideality he sacrifices his sensuous and singular reality. The erotogenic primary-process zone of infantile reality is also a zone that maintains itself by repetition: it is a zone of the upsurge, discharge, and resurgence of intensities. But here repetition precedes and precludes representation. There is no memory, no constitution of a representation of the impulse in an inactual mode because the impluse really recurs. It is not the failure to remember the traumatic event, the fact that the primal scene has been repressed into the unconscious, Deleuze argues,[21] that produces its compulsive repetition; rather it is the real repetition of the impulses that prevent the projection of them into the mirror of consciousness. The pre-representational, infantile libido is a field of real events, real couplings, real productions, which discharge, of themselves, and resurge, of themselves. The return of each impulse is the oblivion of the last to occupy the theater of presence. The primary repression constitutive of unconsciousness is not a supplementary agency that would suppress a representation in consciousness that would otherwise occur and that would inevitably alter the primal scene. Rather, what drives out the prior impulse and prevents its being projected on the screen of representation is the repetition of that impulse. It is not that one repeats an impulsive stance because one represses; one represses by repeating. Thus the primary processes engender a time of presence and repetition; the phallic stage projects a time of unending representation. In this infinity life would situate its passing moments in being definitively, absolutely. Nietzsche projected on a dimension of time the infinite distance and the infinite power that metaphysics had since antiquity thought was necessary to move an entity from nothingness to being. The infinite theater of nature now replaces the infinite gaze of God as the theater in which the being, the significance, and the worth of each life is maintained unrestrictedly.

There are two problems intrinsic to this project and the means it has employed. By situating our life and our joy on the theater of the infinite time of nature and no longer on the theater of the infinite gaze of the supernatural, Nietzsche thinks he has affirmed life just as it is—not a moment that longs for an infinite prolongation but a moment that of itself passes, wholly devoted to dying. Inscribing such a moment on the infinite cycles of nature, Nietzsche believes he has found in it the unrestricted affirmation which invests it with definitive being, a significance for every other entity and moment of the universe, a currency never worn away by the movement of natural time. But can one use this representation of one's life to supplement each movement of one's will with unrestricted affirmation unless one can believe this representation is true? Cosmological criticism has not retained Nietzsche's argument: One can without difficulty construct a model with a finite number of parts or a finite number of processes, whose combinations can indeed be without limit.[22] And the actual physical universe of our contemporary scientific instruments of representation is such a model.

But one can then answer it does not matter, for Nietzsche's intentions: in any case the unending becoming he postulates dissolves every abiding identity— with them the identity of the self and its memory of any prior existence. The theory of eternal recurrence, Klossowski argued, undermines every possibility of any substantial identity of the ego; it engenders a pure multiplicity of personae and destinies. It excludes any possibility of synthetically uniting the life one finds oneself now living with its prior occurrence by memory; the real repetition of my whole life precludes its re-presentation as now inactual on the mirror of conscious memory. Nietzsche is "every name in history,"[23] each time one lives one lives with another name. Thus the cosmological hypothesis of a physical universe in which the same combinations and states of affairs never recur has de facto the same result, as far as the impossibility of a node of life to contract abiding selfsameness is concerned, as the Nietzschean hypothesis of a finite world in an infinite time that recurs. Both cosmological representations dismember the life one now lives from one's birth to one's death into a pure multiplicity of identities and destinies. Yet the first hypothesis does not seem to be able to impose that supplement of affirmation the Nietzschean hypothesis does. It undermines the possibility of idealizing one's existence by projecting it on an infinite dimension of existence. The universe as represented in contemporary physical sciences reduces my present life to a series and succession of combinations that can never recur; if one believes this representation to be true, one divests one's life from that horizon of infinite time with which one had operated its idealization: Is it not then reduced to itself—"an ill without prestige, a fatality without luster."[24] If one's existence is a series and sequence of riddles, fragments, dreadful accidents, that shall occur but once, can one still find in oneself, in the excesses of one's will, the supplement of will to affirm it and value it without reserve? And if one could, would not such a will be arbitrary, and impotent against a cosmological judgment declaring rather the infinitesimal significance and worth of one's existence in nature? Is not then the phantasm of the Nietzschean overman too—this phantasm that orders life to be master, master all the way to and over the limits of its death, making of that pure negativity its own unrestricted power—chosen for its beauty, the splendor of its infinite radiance, and not for its truth? Is not this idealization too a masquerade, covering over the real directing force that conducts it to its definitive end?

What Nietzsche must find from the most comprehensive understanding of all nature is that supplement of exultation that will yield the will to release oneself wholly in nature and to wholly pass. This will Nietzsche found immanent in one's own nature. Life is governed not by an internal coding for adaptation and survival but by the solar economy of squandering, of expenditure without compensation. What his thought must find then is not a dimension of infinity in which this life is itself affirmed and maintained as a significance and a value unto itself but a kind of thought that can affirm, and consecrate, this very dying that occurs in each moment. Is not this thought that which sees a frontier of unending alterity that holds it resolutely to its own limits?

Does the *libidinal destiny* of a man itself find such a truth and such a knowledge? The infant that has taken on a paternal identity one day engenders a son upon whom to inscribe his own name and his own law and finds this son arising to take the place of his father. In this alien figure of his own identity, bearing on a new substance his own form and his own name, the father sees his own ideal identity, his sign, immortalized—and is left with his own dying, only the more strange. His idealizing consciousness looks down upon his own flesh, upon the strangeness of its aging, the strangeness of its own death drive.

Ivan Ilych[25] found in the significance of the funeral ceremonies of his colleague an ideal consolation: Life goes on, the significance and value of life is undying, finding ever new carnal substance to bear it. But then, at home alone, he suffers the physical wound that progressively fills his body with pain. And he learns another death—that of the pain, of the progressive reduction of his own sensory-motor carnality to passivity and prostration. The pain in his own body little by little obtrudes the wills and the intentions that worked in the world, that inscribed their intentions and their values on the pyramids of external inertia. This pain brings him back to the substance of his own body and to the distentions with which his body itself produces the libidinal intensities that arise only in order to be discharged, to be released in ephemeral and voluptuous egoisms.

But is not aging, by which every flesh receives, in the form of the pain of exhaustion, the accumulating blows of the material world, this same wound and pain? Is it not the form in which life suffers the passing of each of its spontaneities into passivity that encumbers it, the form in which it receives its carnal death? And does it not bring the body back to the primary productions of carnality, its primary-process infantilism? With aging, the idealized phallic father, left with the aging body not of a castrated woman but a woman departing into her own alterity, returns to the infantilism of his own voluptuous particularities and turns to the contact consolations of infancy. An infant again, he makes contact with the consoling caresses of the woman, and in the contact his own tenderness and femininity reawakens. Under the phallic mask that represented the directing forces of his libidinal life, there is a return of the real directing forces of the infantile libido, the surfaces of contact that excite the primary-process erotogenic zone. In their return his aging and deathbound carnal libido recognizes as an imposture the idealized identity and value his phallic eros had pursued.

It is the skin, the infantilism, the pain and the voluptuous torments of the carnal surfaces spreading a zone of excitation behind the phallic identity that denounce it as false and as a mask. Beneath the eternally recurring phallic mask, the libidinal life returns to its own birth, to the infantilism of the aging father become mortal, in the arms of a mortal. The sensibility, which throughout its phallic career had sought to surpass itself, the particularity of its intensities, unto the inscription of a sign, a phallus of significance and value, an idealization, now falls back into infantile laughter, weeping, blessing, cursing.

Nietzsche wrote he learned as "one of my most essential steps and advances,"[26] that the real directing forces are accidents—external contingencies that befall a life charged with force from without. They are not intrinsic to a life; it does not contain a telos immanent to it, a libido is not an impulse engendered by its own objective. The real directing forces are external; they are the surfaces of exposure of exteriority itself, or, more exactly, the surfaces of exteriority with which alterity exposes itself, afflicts itself on us. What excites the excitations of the erotogenic zone are the hand, the kisses, the murmurs, the pulp and the down of sensible things, the caressing waves of the sensory elements, that by chance make contact with it.

This also means, in the Nietzschean learning, that the driving forces of a life cannot be deduced from the directing forces, still less from the representation of those directing forces in the sphere of ideality. The libidinal phantasms are not phenomena functioning to reveal the noumenal will. Nietzsche discovers the driving forces not by an intentional analysis of the objectives represented in consciousness but by a physics. Our own nature is an element of nature and circulates within the solar economy of nature, regulated by the laws of the sun, hub of nature, prime mover of the tide of energies in this sector of the cosmos— a sun which engenders its excesses only to squander them far from itself in an expenditure without recompense which is its joy and its glory.

The solar impulses Nietzsche finds in the strong essence of sensibility, the active and not reactive movements—those of weeping, laughter, cursing, blessing. The sensibility that the understanding looks upon as upon a receptivity for pleasure and pain sensations is reactive. It lends itself passively to the organizing, integrating, equilibrating operations of the understanding. But this purely receptive sensibility with the calm and impassive understanding constructed on it is not the primary sensibility; it is weak and servile, produced when the strong actions of laughter and tears, blessing and cursing which confront with their own forces the outside things is exhausted.[27] The primary and strong, productive, sensibility is the tragic sensibility, that of the ritual, participationist Dionysian culture that preceded the theoretical culture of impassive contemplation inaugurated by Socrates in Greek antiquity. The primary sensibility, that of infancy and of the infancy to which aging returns one, is driven by its own energies to make contact with the surfaces of alterity, and it discharges upon their fragments, riddles, and dreadful accidents the echoes of its own laughter and the light of its blessing, discharges upon what does not position itself before that life as its objectives and its complements its weeping and its cursing.

On the last day Ivan Ilych is reduced by pain to the helplessness of an infant. After the last trappings had fallen like masks he no longer had the strength to hold over the tenderness of his body; he feels on his hands the kisses of his son and the tears of his wife. Looking inward he seeks his former accustomed fear of death and finds no fear because there was no death; he feels his closed eyes flooding with an immensity of light.[28] The light with which exteriority greeted him at birth, the light that is the sign of the rebirth of the body.

We who contemplate the sign Oedipal life has made for itself, the phallic mask with which it has covered itself, do we not hear beneath that mask the laughter, weeping, blessing, and cursing with which the infancy that returns encounters the strangeness of the real carnal dying that had been covered over by the word of the father, which had formulated death as a castration threat? Do we not hear the laughter, weeping, blessing, and cursing with which the infancy that returns encounters the real other beneath the uniform of mother and that of father—the deathbound flesh of the other?

VIII

THE OTHER DEATH

The total explosives, conventional and atomic, unleashed on all the theaters of World War II, which left fifty-five million dead, did not equal three megatons; there have now been constructed single nuclear bombs with a destructive power of fifty-eight megatons; the present nuclear stockpile totals some fifty thousand warheads, with a total yield of one million six hundred thousand times that of the bomb that annihilated Hiroshima. If on each day of the forty some years since August, 1945, since Hiroshima, a warhead the size of that dropped on Hiroshima had been hurled upon a city somewhere on the planet, no doubt, as Jonathan Schell has written, some progress toward nuclear disarmament agreement would have been found possible.[1] But those forty some years of annihilation of human cities would have used up less than one percent of the nuclear weapons now stockpiled.

In the nuclear arsenals there are now more than enough weapons to make the earth uninhabitable for the human species and to destroy the ozone shield. Four hundred and twenty million years ago that shield allowed forms of life which had, for three and a half billion years, been secreting an atmosphere with oxygen about our planet, to emerge from the deep oceans and commence life on the exposed surfaces of the land. Were only five thousand megatons detonated—one-third of one percent of the existing stockpile—they would bring down a nuclear winter of $-23°$ Centigrade upon the only planet where life is known to exist.

Were this nuclear arsenal now to be destroyed, the science and technological knowledge from which it issued cannot be abolished, and any outlaw nation, or group, will henceforth be able to produce neurological, biological, chemical, and nuclear weapons in a short time. The existing delivery systems are able to reach targets from one continent to another, with an accuracy range of 300 yards, in six minutes. From now on, humans will exist with the power to bring total extinction upon the human race, as well as upon all evolution, in their hands; since the creation of these weapons was the result of the use of human consciousness and the consenting wills of human society, the power and the responsibility for weapons of extinction lie henceforth nowhere but in the understanding and will of each human being.

Humans have not been able to live, philosophers have understood since

176

antiquity, without a relationship with their own dying; henceforth humans will not be able to live without a relationship with the death of all, with extinction.

This relationship is not simply a quantitative extension of the relationship with one's own death, a relationship of anxiety. Heidegger says the dying of the other is radically inapprehendable: One sees only immobilization, the corpse which leaves no gap in the continuity of being. The death of all the future generations, of all the unborn ones, is yet more radically inapprehendable, unimaginable, beyond the powers of any feeling, which is only numbed by the inconceivable absence of any subsequent memory to mourn or to refuse to mourn.

Yet it is a relationship that each existing one now sustains; whether extinction be unleashed or postponed—for six minutes, for an hour, for six years—depends only on the lucidity and will of each speaker of language and participant in a civic order. Between each existing one and the incalculable multitude of the unborn ones there is now a bond which will have to be represented by thought, by a certain kind of thought without imagination or feeling, sustained by no force of instinct. If our species survives it will be only out of obligation, because a thought, cold, lucid, and efficacious, is produced in us commanded by an obligation to survive the unborn address to us, commanded by an imperative all the others, from their distances, their absence, their mortality, afflict on each one. What is this imperative that binds us to the inapprehendable absence of the others?

1. The Alterity of Law

For Kant, law, the universal and the necessary as an exigency, is first received by the faculty of understanding. The mind is subject to the exigency for law before the law is formulated in a representation. The faculty of understanding is constituted in this subjection. It is in obedience to law that the understanding can understand anything, can produce acts of understanding.

But in order for law to order me, in the particularity of my practical and instrumental field, this immanent exigency for the universal and necessary is not sufficient. A "type," that is, a general practical schema or model, must precede the action to show in advance how the particular can be realized not for its particular resolution but as an instance and exemplar of the universal. Such a type is for Kant the cognitive representation of empirical nature organized by speculative reason as a law-governed totality, or a nature; it is also the other whose words and deeds in a practical field are presented, in the sentiment of respect, as law-governed.

Respect for the other, Kant says, is respect for the law in another, which obliges me also. But the sense of the law in force in another is constitutive of my perception of him as other, that is, as an autonomous individual.

This *respect* then is not a cognitive act which makes the events dispersed spatio-temporally in the body of the other and the field of his activities intelligible for me because it supplies the formula their multiplicity is synthetically grasped. I can to be sure see the sensorially given events there as determined by, synthetically comprehendable in terms of, the laws of universal external nature, I can see his positions and moves as exemplifying physico-chemical and dynamical laws; I can also see them as determined by, synthetically comprehendable in terms of, the laws of his own nature, I can see his positions and moves as exemplifying psycho-physiological laws. As such I would comprehendably perceive him as another nature but not as an existing end in himself.

To encounter another is to perceive his positions and moves to have been determined by himself alone, autonomously. It is not to see in them positions and moves that result from the particular forces and lures of the external situation about him nor to divine them as resulting from the particularities of his internal natural impulses; it is to see them set forth as instantiations of the universal and the necessary which understanding—his understanding—represents first of its own power. It is to then see his positions and moves as put forth to diagram at a moment of space and time the universal, which binds me also.

I do not really *know* that law rules in the other. We do not perceive causality in general; we do not perceive—in ourselves no more than in another—the causality of the pure exigency for law to activate the musculature and nervous circuitry of the body. It remains forever possible that what seems to me to be words and gestures—in myself or in another—put forth as pure instantiations of the exigency for the universal and the necessary may be in fact produced by physico-chemical processes found throughout all nature, or psycho-physiological processes found in our nature—and which are inobservable by us.

But I believe—I *must*, I am obligated by the law, to believe, that my constitution is such that such words and deeds issued in pure obedience to law are possible. To perceive, to respect, the other, is to believe—with this obligatory belief—that his words and deeds can be put forth in pure obedience to the exigency for law, that the other I see is an autonomous one. To believe I see an *other* is to find myself bound by the order his words and deeds instantiate.

This sense I have of law ruling him, this sense that his words and moves are commanded by representations of law his mind arrays before his will, is not induced from observation of his positions and moves comprehensively grasped in their setting; it conflicts with that systematic observation. Rather, the initiative to comprehensively organize all empirical givens under universal and necessary laws obeys the categorical imperative I sense operating in him. That is why the sense of his words and deeds diagramming the law that binds me too comes most often in our experience upon an only very superficial perception of the other. In the measure that I inspect the other, itemize his particularities, integrate them comprehensively into the laws I invoke to apprehend a nature in the contingent forms dispersed about him and the laws I invoke to apprehend the psycho-physiological functions behind his surface, my perception draws over the divination of an *other,* an autonomous one, the image of a *nature,* another one of my nature. The divination of an other, an autonomous one, is a superficial perception—perception of skin only,[2] perception of the surface of exposure, not as enclosing the substance and causalities of a nature that is his but as pure surface functioning to schematize the exigency for the universal and the necessary. The surfaces of the other do not contour a substance for my apprehension or a nature for my comprehension; one's eyes touch them lightly, to be ordered by them.

In fact it is the other alone that can provide the schematic diagram necessary for practical judgment, the "type," that Kant's theory of the functioning of the faculties of a rational agency requires. I find the sense of the universal imperative within my own understanding, but the particular position of a composite human nature which is to be made an example of the law has to be inserted into the contingencies given in external perception. One will need a model to guide the practical judgment in advance. The model I need is a figure perceptible in a particular situation, but generalizable, not because it has certain traits that other situations could accommodate but because it has certain traits that other situations must accommodate themselves to. It is the other, and not myself projected in imagination, that fulfills these conditions. (Imagination could only vary the actual perception of my position, which I would be obliged to understand as determined by the laws of nature and of my own nature.)

What I divine, what I respect, in the figure of the other is death at work in him. He himself suppresses and does not affirm the particularities of his own substance, of his own natural forces, of his own sensibility and wants which attach him to the particularities of his contingent environment of sensuous means for natural satisfaction and for pleasure. "[A]ll inclination and every sensuous impulse is based on feeling, and the negative effect of feeling (through the check on the inclinations) is itself feeling. Consequently, . . . the moral law as a ground of determination of the will, by thwarting all our inclinations, must produce a feeling which can be called pain."[3] I sense the mortification with which the universal becomes a motive in his will and intercepts his sensuous attachments from their objects. What I divine, in seeing the surface of exposure of the other turned to me as a surface of inscription of the law, is this pain. Pain here is the subjective feeling not of the extirpation of the impulses and inclinations of our sentient nature but of their reduction to passivity. Mortification is the invasion of death, not in the Heideggerian sense of a reduction of existing to nothingness, annihilation, but in the sense of a reduction of impulsivity to passivity. One senses the pain with which the other rationally reduces his particular—irrationally impulsive—nature into the system of universal nature, that of the non-sentient, which Kant had set up as his first "type" (cf. supra, p. 54). This maintenance of the forces of carnal nature in the passive mode by the commanding drive of a rational agency we might, with Le Clézio,[4] name *extase matérielle*—an ecstatic thrust toward material nature. It is this death in the other, generated within and imposed on his own sensuous impulses, that makes his sensible inscription in the setting exemplary, makes it addressed to anyone as a type, makes it exposure. It is this death that makes our surfaces appear to one another not as contours enclosing chunks of subsistent substance but as surfaces of exposure to one another, surfaces that are afflictions upon one another.

In Heidegger the movement of thought is the reverse. Death is the pure exteriority, exterior with all the exteriority nothingness has from being. Anxiety senses it in the world, in the contingency of all things, in the nothingness in which all things are adrift now, without guarantees. Death is everywhere in the world, it is the world as pure exteriority, as axes of dispersion down which entities are spatially and temporally excluded from one another, the world as clearing. I find myself exactly at the core of this clearing, this death; death besets me from all sides, singles me out, as my personal future. For me to stand or to move is to die, to throw myself toward possibility, which cannot be real possibility without really containing the eventuality of impossibility, of my definitive and irreversible reduction to impotence.

But if anxiety divines death in all that is, movement divines possibility in all impossibility. The shadow of my death stalking me brings out into relief that zone of the earth, that crossroads of the open world, which is contingently there, there for now as possibilities. The incandescent world outlines for me a possible place and a possible standpoint ahead of me—my own possible being there. The anxiety that throws my forces, my potential, back from the gaping openness of the world as endless abyss of death, back upon themselves, leaves them clinging to themselves, clinging to a potential for existing another moment, which is oneself. Clinging to the being one has, one is, now, and which is condemned without appeal by the ex-isting that has left it already to anticipate entry into the absolute exteriority of death is different from clinging to one's very ex-isting inasmuch as it is revealed to be both a susceptibility of becoming nothing and a potentiality to become something else. In this difference Heidegger sees the summons to die turning into an imperative to be, in the voice of conscience. What calls, what is articulated in a figure that functions imperatively, is being—my own potential being. Being is an order and a command. What I am ordered to is first to be, to be myself, to be on my own. No order can be laid on me unless I am first constituted imperatively as one that takes up his own being and answers for it. It is being that binds us, that is the law and the destiny. Our being is not an object we envisage, a presence in us we represent before ourselves; it affects us, weighs on us, afflicts us. This possible being that the world's being outlines for us we do not engender; it is given to us, laid upon us. We are burdened by it, we have to bear it. It is not a substrate that supports us; our existing has to support it. It is not given that we are; we have to be. The possible before us is not a simple conceptual possibility; there is an imperative to exist—in order to answer for existence.

But this potential being laid upon us subsists in the realm of nothingness. The possible is not a given structure in the actual, nor a variant of the actual posited by and in the actual power of our representational faculty; it is possible by being possibly impossible. It is the nothingness that besets us that afflicts us with a being that is only possible. This possible can be destined singularly for me because the only nothingness that anxiety divines is not an annihilation of the beings of the world—whose being subsists unaffected by the evolution and eclipse of their forms—nor an annihilation of the others—whose demise is rather a reduction to the immobilized subsistence of a material corpse—but an annihilation of my own being that shows itself imminent at any moment. The fatality of a dying toward which I am thrown with all the forces of my own nature, the nothingness to come for me, harbors the destination to a potential being which I am imperatively summoned to become.

If the potential being-there held before me as my authentic and imperative future is to have imperative force, the imperative force of being, then it cannot simply be an outline exteriorized from my present actuality and projected on the screen of the world before me. It must be something the being of the world prepares for, calls for; the layout of the world must be such as both to make it possible and to await me, await that singular nexus of powers which can be no one but me.

As, in Kant, the type, the general model I need for practical judgment, cannot be derived from the pure exigency for the universal and the necessary which is the form of law, so, in Heidegger, the figure of existence to which I am called cannot be delineated by the pure abyss of indeterminacy that is death. My imperative existence in the world is delineated in the world. But the world is not the opaque mass of being in itself; it is already discursively articulated; the logos immanent to it exhibits it as a world.

The general lines of the world and of its recurrent events and states of affairs are articulated in the talk—the verbalized indications, the positions, and movements—that gets passed on from one to another—whose formulations are such that they can abide, can be passed on, can be the formulations of anyone. The singular one who finds himself in the world finds himself in a world already gridded in these anonymous forms and formulations.

But there are also those who say and who do what they alone have to say and can do—the authentic ones. By his positions and his movements each singularized one brings a singular situation out into relief. His resolute path, which decisively articulates the singular, is at each step a choice. Each being in the world can materialize a face of itself in the light only by enveloping other faces of itself in the darkness; so each life can articulate the thinker, artist, craftsman, lover he was destined to be only by sentencing to silence the parent, inventor, virtuoso, visionary he was also destined to become. In setting out to actualize a potentiality he alone can realize, he consigns to death other potentialities, other destinies, that he was also called upon to bring to birth into the world. With each step he brings out into relief a possibility that is for-him, refusing and leaving aside the possibilities that are for-anyone, and which his eyes fixed on the wall of death coming for him delineate. But with each option of a singular potentiality to which he gives his life, he also delineates the other singular potentialities he consigns to death—or to other singular ones. It is in this way that his itinerary draws into the course of the world the outline of singular and not only general or anonymous potentialities. It is in this way, Heidegger says, that, his existence is a good, that is, a force that makes authentic existence— the authentic existence of another—possible. His heritage, which he delivers over to singular ones, is not the treasury of his deeds which have come to pass and which terminate certain possibilities, which displace others from possible tasks, but the heritage of possibilities he brings into the world. It is these stillborn lives he gives to others by virtue of his failing, his guilt, his having been born, his mortality.

One looks for oneself, then, in the death-tracked figure of the other, the singular one. In the force with which he was able to determine, to terminate, a figure of existence, and in the traced-out paths of singular and unrealized possibilities his itinerary leaves as it passes through the world, I look for my own imperatives. I find the law inscribed, in the world of Kant and in that of Heidegger, in the same place—the figure of the other, the autonomous one, the authentic one. The decisive difference is that in Kant I look upon the other as one on whose surfaces of exposure the harrowing of death makes him the exemplary one, the imperative schema of the universal, whereas in Heidegger I look upon the other as one which death has singularized, and I look in the traces of the path from which his mortality barred him the vivifying possibilities for the singularity of my life.

Thus the death of the other concerns me; it is that in the other that makes the existence of the other concern me. In Kant it is the mortification at work in the autonomous one I divine in respect, the active work of an inner reduction of all particular impulses in his nature to passivity, the pain in which the universal is known in a particular nature, that afflicts me. In Heidegger it is the solitary itinerary of the deathbound other that traces out possibilities his departure leaves for me, possibilities which the approach of impossibility destines singularly for me. But in Kant, beyond the perception of the other as another particular in the empirical world I can divine the other as schema of the universal that binds me only because I have already discovered the imperative force of the universal within my own understanding. And in Heidegger, I can recognize in the possibilities left in the world by the departure of others imperatives addressed to me only because I have been called to seek in the being of the exterior the possible and future figure of my own being by my own conscience, whose articulating voice, silent and uncoded in the talk of others, the silence of death that closes in on me makes audible to me.

For Levinas the words and deeds of the other are not instantiations of a universal logos that first speaks inwardly in my own faculty of understanding nor indicatives formulated in the world of an imperative that first I hearken to in the silence of my own conscience. To establish this, we first argue, with Heidegger

rns me as the sole source of the possibilities which make my authentic
nce possible. But this also means that in finding, not in the blank abysses
thingness but in the articulation of the world, the possibility addressed to
he chance and the task that will make it possible for me to become myself,
in reality coming to the assistance of the other, I am putting my forces in
lace to take up the burden of an existence his own and excessive for him, I
utting myself in his place to answer for his wants and his failings and for his
responsibility. I substitute myself for him in his dying.

2. The Alterity of Death

ne use of human consciousness and human will compounded into cog-
e, productive, and civic organizations, a final kingdom, a kingdom of ends
invests each one that participates in language and in civic structures with
ower to decide the extinction of all the born and unborn others, would
a to be the most extreme distention of the movement of our ex-isting. Here
ing goes forth unto its extreme limit, unto nothingness, and converts
ossibility itself into a possibility, a power. Each one becomes an absolute
in himself. To be sure, the chemical, neurological, biological, and nuclear
ers that will bring about extinction will also bring annihilation to the one
holds these powers in his mind and his will. But is it not always death that is
power and the work in the spirit? One converts the drifting in one's forces
acts by determining, terminating, them and determining, terminating,
rior processes with them; one converts one's existing wholly into one's own
oy making the dying toward which one drifts into a movement one enacts.
mortality," Blanchot wrote, "if it is mine to enjoy by definition, is not mine.
rather my limit and my constraint. Then in this context my whole vocation
man consists in making of this immortality which is imposed upon me
ething I can gain or lose: hell or heaven. But immortality in itself, over
ch I have no power, is nothing to me. On the other hand, immortality might
ome one of science's conquests. Then it would have the value—beneficial or
—of a cure for sickness . . . Immortality, guaranteed by science, would have
weight in [Kirilov's] destiny unless it signified the impossibility of
th. . . . For a human race weirdly destined to be immortal, suicide would
stitute perhaps the only chance to remain human, the only way out toward a
nan future."[6]

eath is an eventuality whose certainty is apprehended in anxiety. But dying
a obligation. It is what each one has to do, for himself alone. Each one is not
ply condemned to recognize that the end is a fatality that he shall not
pe. This knowledge is wholly practical; each one forms the deeds of his life
uch a way as to consign them to this end—or to deny or defy this end, devote
present to working out his immortality.

he metaphysical thought that identifies dying with becoming-nothing also

and against Kant, that the imperative that affects me at the
constitution is not an imperative that the particular die befo
the universal but that the singular be. Then we argue, again:
the imperative that the other addresses to me is not an impera
possibilities, destinies, lives which were his but which his res
one task left aside; it is an imperative that I answer for his ta
for the wants and failings and the very responsibility of his e:

We have seen that it is only when one identifies law by
formal universality and necessity that the faculty of underst:
locus of receptivity and the other comes to be taken as a pa
under death sentence. But the formalizing understanding
properties of law from the universe ordered by speculativ
commanded by an understanding which understands that it is
putting that law, through a representation, before itself, that
law has been formulated. It would be possible to show, with
the exposure to the others, the being-commanded by the oth
the project of constructing, by speculative reason, a univers
objective, that is for-anyone. It is then the other, as an "existin
singular figure of alterity, that is the original locus of the
imperative is not the death-sentence which, in the struggl
Hegel sees the other engage with me in order to affirm his
moves would put on me. The struggle for recognition can on
affirmation of the other as my alter ego. His imperative
positively, as an appeal made to me, a judgment put on me
other not to be recognized but to be contested. The other
because he can appeal to me, and he singles me out, demand
imperative is first a demand that I be, that I stand forth to resp
own name.

For Heidegger it is the finitude of every authentic project of
that every projection of one's existence is a choice, that explain
the authentic other who pursues resolutely the tasks destined s
concerns me. The fatality of not being able to actualize the
craftsman, lover he was destined to be save by sentencing to d
inventor, virtuoso, visionary he was also destined to become
knows oneself as one that was born. That is, that was given one
did not invest oneself with one's potentialities, that cannot cor
receptivity for them into an active conceiving and elaborating o
explained, one were not born, given a being to be, but engende
would not have invested oneself with potentialities that one cou
that were not compossible. The other, then, in inscribing up
the world his own authentic itinerary, also sketched out on t
things those other destinies he was not able to realize, and he le
as the goodness of his own life, that is, that which makes authe
another authentic existence—possible.[5] The birth of each de

sees it as the becoming-nothing of whatever meaning and value a life was able to discriminate in the field of what is about it and whatever significance and worth it was able to give its own states and deeds. Life would be a struggle to set something aside, in the external field of what endures inertly or ideally, from the nothingness to which life itself is doomed. Man is afraid of time, says an Egyptian proverb, but time is afraid of the pyramids. Life consigns itself to be interred and monumentalized, held in reserve in the constructions of inertia. Life ex-ists, exteriorizing its intentions and its will in the abiding element of the State, history, language, or an ideal order it itself posits and sustains. Externalizing, alienating itself, it only leaves death, my singular dying, the more strange. Heidegger's identification of life's essence with ex-istence says that death is not an accident that befalls a life; life dies of its own nature, its own birth, life's essence is essentially mortal, life throws itself with all its own forces to its end. The movement in life is discharge, evacuation at a loss; one dies in and with each act, each actualization.

Heidegger can see this essential mortality not as the extinction without recompense of every significance and every value but as their condition for possibility, because the nothingness with which he equates death is also the essence of the possible and thus the clearing in which being is determinate. This impossible which is eventual and certain is what makes what is but possible and really possible. The really possible is not just put in beings by the mind, which envisages alternatives by imaginatively varying the real. It comes, of itself, and it comes in the being that presents itself to us and brings us what is as possibilities for us. Death then is nowhere else than in the world, and in throwing ourselves into the world we are casting ourselves into our death; death is the world as pure openness or clearing in which beings are distinguishable and phosphorescent, reservoir of possibility for beings and for nothingness. Death is both the indeterminate and the terminating. It is because our existence casts itself unto this ending that it directs itself toward ends, terminations, in general, and makes of its thrusts of force not dissipations in the indeterminacy but determinate moves.

Heidegger thus restores the ancient Greek sense of telos as the contours or boundaries that belong to a being's own nature and that are not merely the frontiers at which counter-forces circumvent it. These contours are then the figure of its accomplishment, its perfection; their decisiveness is what makes that being assemble its forces to be able to interact with other beings, to function. Its contours are then the very figure of its significance of the way it counts or has value. They are also the surfaces of its radiance, its apparition and its glory—*forma formosa*.

To be sure, our existence is at grips with mundane entities, and it itself reads its own form and itinerary from the traces it leaves in the spectacle of the world. But its own significance and worth do not derive from the extent to which these traces will extend their repercussions among things: It is in the decisiveness with which our existence assembles all that has come to pass in it, to project it toward all that is possible for it, that the contour of a life contracts orientation, sense, and its surfaces close in upon it as upon an end in itself, a dignity.

What menaces its significance and its dignity is not ending but the temptation to make itself a relay-point of the unending. Seeing itself as a moment in a movement of forms of conduct, diagrams of articulation, functions that exist already, in others, it fails to give its forces a form of their own. Existing with function, worth, and significance but without a dignity of its own and an orientation of its own, its own potential or its potential for ownness, for existing as its own being, is never actualized. At the core of a public existence fully functional, valuable, and significant, there is an existential insignificance and worthlessness. From which only the cold touch of faceless death can awaken it.

—The cold imminence of nothingness that touches *me*. Death, envisaged as a state, is anonymous and indeterminate, it is even indiscernible; one sees only the corpses, inert in their being, to which others are immobilized. Death can be an ordinance and a destination only in the measure that the line between it and me is unequivocal. Death as the possible impossible to elude, death as unerringly coming of itself unto me, closing in on me, singles me out and singularizes me. Before every station in being, I take my place by displacing others, and the place I occupy I yield to others; the station I occupy before the oncoming of nothingness is absolutely fixed and unsubstitutable, unrepresentable—no one can be present there for me. Every taking my place in the midst of beings is a movement of substitution designed to elude the singularization of my mortal destiny. The one that equivocates before his destination to his death finds the world a reservoir of equivalent possibilities and interchangeable positions. What alone distinguishes possibilities that are for-anyone, possibilities that are for-others, from possibilities that are singularly destined for my singular powers is the line of impossibility which my death draws about me.

It is true that of itself the premonition of the realm of death is but the intuition into unending impotence, and it cannot disengage the potential being I have to be. That is why for Heidegger conscience, which articulates for me the potential being before me, precedes and makes possible the anxiety which anticipates the nothingness to come for me and which separates me decisively from all that is possible for-others. Yet for Heidegger to project the being that has definitively and irrevocably come to pass in me into this singular figure of possibility is for me to release or discharge my forces, to die with my own forces, and it is this summons to die with my own singular powers that orders in the singular figure of possibility articulated for me by another in the world.

Maurice Blanchot has argued that death, the utterly indeterminate, the indeterminate moment and not only the zone of the unending and the indeterminate, cannot perform this singularization and this orientation.[7] Death hovers about me in *imminence*. It is not located at a moment of time to come, from which a line can be sighted, which would function as a singularizing axis of orientation for me. My death lies before me, and opens a depth of futurity, but its position is utterly indeterminable. It is imminent in every moment. The moment of death is an instant, instantaneous cut of the line of duration, but any moment may be the last instant. It is true that a certain death, by execution, by disease, by the foreseeable approach of a danger, can be sighted. Yet even in this case there is a non-adequation between the death that, of itself, comes to me and the moves with which I convert the passage of time into a distance I actively cross.

Blanchot distinguishes therefore between the act by which I actively synthesize the origin and the end of my time, actively enact the passage of time, actively make dying a movement propelled by the I, and the advance of death itself unto me. There is a diplopia in the gaze that resolutely turns to its end; each passage of time that is enacted, that is traversed by actively taking up all that has come to pass in me and projecting it into what is possible for me, also *drifts*, passively, unto the region of the utterly indeterminate, without being able to see or know in what direction one is going, without going any *where*. In *Thomas l'obscur* Blanchot explored this time of dying, this difference between the orientation toward the end assigned to one, this end which is one's own, on the part of a personage depicted as wholly occupied in this task of dying her death—and the finding oneself adrift in the interval, utterly indeterminate in span, before the point of encounter with the death that is absolutely other, from which one is separated by an impassable remoteness until it is there, to reduce the act and the actuality of the I to irrecoverable passivity.

Is not then the project to actively enact the passive synthesis, the passive passing of time, the groundswell transcendental illusion arising at the point of extreme distention of authenticity? Is not the death that my anxiety senses at the core of my potential being, which Heidegger takes to be the singular event that singles me out and singularizes me, rather the death of anyone and of no one, the death before which no individuality stands? Is it not this *other death*, that which no I can take hold of and that does not open to embrace any me, that each one now brings upon the other?

What possibility of dying on our own subsists for us today—we who have now invested in our knowledge and our will the power and the arsenal to send down a Hiroshima disaster upon a city every day for the next five hundred years? We who address one another not with exposed faces but neurological, chemical, and biological contagions?

3. The Most Extreme Distention

Nietzsche's diagramming of the weight of being on infinite cycles of time reinstates the ancient metaphysical conviction that between nothingness and being there is the longest distance, an infinite distance, that it requires infinite power, or infinite time, to posit something in being. The movement by which an entity casts or directs itself to the world is, for Heidegger, its extreme distention, a distention that consumes it wholly, for it is also the distance from the being in which it finds itself to the absolute exteriority of nothingness. Beyond, inaccessibly remote, comes of itself the other death, the night that no longer embraces any day. Is the concern with my own death the most extreme distention, the most extreme distress? Is not the most excessive, the most dissolute movement that which goes to join the other in his or her dying?

The other in his or her alterity is not, Merleau-Ponty wrote against Sartre, "an anonymous, faceless obsession, an other in general."[8] "For the other to be truly the other, it does not suffice and it is not necessary that he be a scourge, the continued threat of an absolute reversal of pro and con, a judge himself elevated above all contestation, without place, without relativities, faceless like an obsession, and capable of crushing me with a glance into the dust of my world."[9] The alterity of the other is that with which he or she faces me. The respect for the other is a superficial contact, tangency of surfaces of exposure. Across the surfaces of the other, everywhere exemplary, my eyes, my hearing, my touch make contact with the opaque seal of contentment with which this body itself produces the excitations that disconnect and close and close its organs and their couplings. The hand that touches the other touches surfaces across which spread not sensations, givens of sense, signals and informative bits which are fed into the inner functional organism, but excitations. The flash-fires, the bristling, and the murmur of the world's surfaces play across this surface of susceptibility, where torments of intensity surge. These seek and find their release in ephemeral eddies of pleasure, affected with themselves, consuming themselves, nomad surface egoisms.[10] This surface of susceptibility appeals to me, contests me. My sensibility is ordered into contact with this zone where laughter and tears gather and dissipate on the surfaces of alien libido. I touch that death drive; with the opaqueness of my blind caresses, my kisses spreading their torments of pleasure, I watch the body in my arms close into its mortal torpor.

One approaches the surfaces of alterity not as a surface of reflection upon which one can oneself be recognized but as a surface of susceptibility that orders me to come to its assistance, that alterity become possible, that it be able to depart. I am exposed to the dying of the other in approaching his or her surfaces upon which life produces its excesses and already consumes itself. What throws me most radically into question is the other that absents himself or herself in his or her dying. It is a relationship with that which moves away from every apprehension or comprehension on my part, from every appropriation, a relationship with that which cannot be confronted, that has no front lines and no contours—the utterly strange.

The relationship with the dying of the other is prior to language and to silence, insofar as silence among humans is a punctuation of, and invitation to, discourse. It is not a relationship that brings out something common, a common nature, or the common understanding which discourse both establishes and presupposes. For it is upon the evidence of his alterity that he is divined, is respected, as an other, an evidence which is not supported by but contests the perceptual evidences that rather integrate the events and states of his substance into the contexture of his nature and of universal nature. The relationship with the dying of the other is prior to every relationship with the other as an ideal, a positive law. For the death that commands me in him is his death, a consummation that consumes the singular discharges of his surface productions, and not a a universal or an indeterminacy that would subsist through the suppression of every particularity. The relationship with the dying of the other is not obedience to him or her as to a law, an obedience which, Kant's problematic demonstrates, constitutes me as an autonomy, a seat of powers and initiatives that answer for themselves. It is a passion, a contagion of nocturnal terrors.

For Levinas this singular other has imperative force when the absolute illeity of infinity positions the surface of another before me. Levinas names this axis which is not a fifth dimension in a world spread out in geometrical space-time or infinitely open horizons, God, and takes this name to cover the irreversibility of the relationship with the other, the unending demand the other's existence puts on me. Yet this illeity, this God, this infinity, is perhaps that of dying, or at least its transcendence to the world is manifest in me as the unending departure of the other.

Each movement to the other, unto his surfaces of exposure, to go where he or she goes, is a movement to touch this dimension of absence. This touch is not that of the apprehending hand that grasps him as an implement in the field of works. It is, Blanchot says, *désoeuvrement*, unoccupied, disarray, touch of the limit where alterity disconnects every project and every comprehension. Here, Jean-Luc Nancy says, the ecstasy, the exultation of our ex-isting touches the intangible. "Lovers touch one another, not fellow-citizens (save in the delirium of a fanaticized mass—or in the piling up of exterminated bodies, wherever the touch becomes a work). . . . [T]he touch, the immanence not reached but nearby and promised (no more words, no more looks) is the limit."[11] One does not touch the other in the field of production or of state power; not even in the handshake that seals a pact of collaboration for the works of economic production and civic enterprises. The touch of the other, the touch of a mortal alterity is a contact, a contagion, and not a communication of information or of understanding; it is the transmission of a trembling on the limits of beings.

"The caress of a consoler which comes gently in our pain does not promise the end of suffering," Levinas writes, "does not announce any compensation, and in its very contact, is not concerned with what is to come afterwards in economc time; it concerns the very instant of physical pain, which is then no longer condemned to itself, is transported 'elsewhere' by the movement of the caress, and is freed from the vise-grip of 'oneself,' finds 'fresh air,' a dimension and a future."[12] One does not die alone; the surfaces of exposure of the other— to the world, to death, to me—are also surfaces of exposure of his or her dying to me. Community among men, Kant wrote, is not due to the sphericality of the earth, as though, were the earth an infinite plane humans could be so distributed as to not be afflicted with one another.[13] We are indeed earthmen as a community, but it is not our common support on the earth that makes us exist the one before the other, the one for the other. It is rather because we are, each by his or her own existing, exposed to the surfaces of alterity that the perceptual arena of each will be, has to be, is obliged to be, assembled into the oneness of a universe in which the earth will be constituted as common.

What draws me to the other, in the necessity of being the neighbor of him or her that dies, is not the project or the will to heal, to deliver the other of mortality. It is rather the compulsion to substitute oneself for the other in his or her pain and dying. Our mortal community, our community in mortality more fundamental than every commonplace established by understanding, than every productive collaboration and every civic existence we can constitute, than every work we can externalize, has no purpose save to render present the serving of the other unto the abysses of his or her dying, in order that the other be not lost into solitude, into the night and fog. The hand that extends the touch of consolation to the other that suffers and that dies pursues him not in order simply to aid him in his dying but to share the solitude of an event that is simultaneously and unthinkably his own most proper possibility and his radical dispossession. It is not an act that *I* do; it is the passion which dispossesses me of my own citadel of selfhood yet more than does the anonymous and unconfrontable death that closes in on me.

Each one in coming to birth extends ever further the limit that exposes itself to my touch. For each one, in coming to birth, emerges a singularity. The surface of exposure where we touch one another is not a texture, flesh, substance, or spirit out of which I and the other arise by individuation. Individuation detaches closed entities from a formless ground; the commonness or communion of that ground extends as the being of those individual beings. But singularity is not a work resulting from an operation; singularity is not extracted, produced, or derived. Birth is not a production or an auto-position. It is not the contrary of death, for that which is born is already exposed to dying, and exposes us to it with him or her. The unborn ones, across the abysses of their extinction we have now appropriated as our supreme civic power, expose their surfaces as the most urgent imperative that afflicts us.

Nietzsche has identified love of the world with affirmation—the affirmation that a life utterly, excessively, affirmative of each of its own moments puts on the fragmentary, contingent, and enigmatic events outside itself as a blessing spread singularly over each. But these things concern one, and affect one, by distressing one with their mortality. *Sunt lacrimae rerum.* The love of each thing goes to join it in its own mortal contention, brings to it the support of one's own substance. It is not the overarching sphere of one ideality or heaven of light but a particular love for each particular, a proximity realized in the particularity of one's own substance. The Good, beyond the possible, beyond the wall of the death that besets the singular one, the other, imperatively requires the excessive substance, the goodness I have, I am, to give.

Then each natural thing—each thing that arises by birth—is located in the dimension of the infinity of the Good and insistently puts an imperative on me. This infinity is not external to it, not the outer horizons of the infinite space-time in which its aspects are reflected or the infinitely recurring time on which its passing is inscribed. The infinity of the Good is an unendingness of the appeal and the demand each natural thing makes in its continual withdrawal into its own infinitely inaccessible death. The joy in the goodness of the singular events and entities of the universe, the distress that goes to the assistance of their vulnerability, the affliction with which one exposes one's own substance to the dying that besets them, proceed from the passion with which one goes to be with another in his or her dying.

NOTES

Introduction

During the last two months that I worked on this manuscript, I read four newly published books that make me want to offer this book as a contribution to their grave and lucid conversation. They are *History as Apocalypse* (Albany: State University of New York Press, 1985) by Thomas J.J. Altizer, *Spirit in Ashes: Hegel, Heidegger, and Man-Made Mass Death* (New Haven and London: Yale University Press, 1985) by Edith Wyschogrod, *Erring* (Chicago: University of Chicago Press, 1984) by Mark C. Taylor, *Black Rain* (Tokyo and New York: Kodansha International Ltd., 1984) by Masuji Ibuse (trans. John Bester).

Part I. The Imperative Idealization

I. The Origin of Infinity

1. "The idealized world, then, is an ideal infinity of things, each of which is itself an index for an ideal infinity of relative exhibitings whose harmonious unity of identity—*idealiter*—the thing is." Edmund Husserl, *The Crisis of European Sciences and Transcendental Phenomenology*, trans. David Carr (Evanston: Northwestern University Press, 1970), p. 347.

2. "Knowing the world in a seriously scientific way, 'philosophically,' can have meaning and be possible only if a method can be devised of *constructing*, systematically and in a sense in advance, the world, the infinitude of causalities, starting from the meager supply of what can be established only relatively in direct experience, and of compellingly *verifying* this construction in spite of the infinitude [of experience]." Ibid., p. 32.

3. "Extrascientific culture, culture not yet touched by science, consists of tasks and accomplishments of man in finitude. The openly endless horizon in which he lives is not disclosed; his ends, his activity, his trade and traffic, his personal, social, national, and mythic motivation—all this moves within the sphere of his finitely surveyable surrounding world." Ibid., p. 279.

4. "Science is, after all, the most complete renunciation of the pleasure principle of which our mental activity is capable." S. Freud, "A Special Type of Choice of Object Made by Men" (Contributions to the Psychology of Love I), trans. Alan Tyson, *Standard Edition* (London: Hogarth Press, 1957), II, p. 163.

5. Husserl, *The Crisis*, p. 290.

6. It is true that Husserl's efforts, in volume VI of *Cartesian Meditations* to explicate the sense of alterity do not succeed in truly accounting for his experience of the other as force of contestation. His theory, accounting for the sense of the other by an analogizing perception, is wholly an effort to explicate how I can have an experience of an alter *ego*. It does not really account for the alterity of that ego. Levinas has seen this most keenly and has resolutely pursued its consequences.

In Husserl's own terms, we can say that *Cartesian Meditations*, VI, elaborates an explication of natural intersubjectivity, but its theory of an analogizing perception of the other does not account for the theoretical humanity, coexistence in mutual criticism, which arises when the other is taken as an instance of contestation of all my experience.

7. Edmund Husserl, *Formal and Transcendental Logic*, trans. Dorian Cairns (The Hauge: Martinus Nijhoff, 1969), p. 1.

8. Husserl, *The Crisis*, p. 284.

9. Ibid., p. 288.

10. Ibid., p. 283.

11. Ibid., p. 338.

12. Ibid., p. 341.

13. Edmund Husserl, *Ideen zu Einer Reinen Phänomenologie und Phänomenologischen Philosophie*, Erstes Buch (The Hague: Martinus Nijhoff, 1950), §§67–69.

14. Ibid., §81.

15. Emmanuel Levinas, *Existence and Existents*, trans. A. Lingis (The Hague: Martinus Nijhoff, 1978).

16. By "spontaneous generation." Edmund Husserl, *Zur Phänomenologie des Inneren Zeitbewusstseins* (The Hague: Martinus Nijhoff, 1966), Beilage IX, p. 100.

17. Ibid., §31.

18. Ibid.

19. Ibid., §32.

20. Husserl, *Ideen.* . . , Erstes Buch, §82.

21. Husserl, *Zur Phänomenologie des Inneren Zeitbewusstseins*, Beilage IX, p. 118.

22. Husserl, *Ideen.* . . , Erstes Buch, §83.

23. Ibid.

24. Edmund Husserl, *Analysen zur Passiven Synthesis* (The Hague: Martinus Nijhoff, 1966), pp. 377–81.

25. Ibid., pp. 377, 378–79.

26. Maurice Merleau-Ponty, *The Visible and the Invisible*, trans. A. Lingis (Evanston: Northwestern University Press, 1968), pp. 148–49.

27. Husserl, *Zur Phänomenologie des Inneren Zeitbewusstseins*, p. 100.

28. "What arises first is the idea of continuation which is repeatable with unconditional generality, with its own self-evidence, as a freely thinkable and self-evident possible infinity, rather than the openendlessness [described above]: rather than finite iteration, this is iteration within the sphere of the unconditional 'again-and-again,' of what can be renewed with ideal freedom." Husserl, *The Crisis*, p. 346.

29. Ibid., p. 13.

30. Ibid., p. 137.

31. Ibid., pp. 340–41.

32. Ibid., p. 338.

II. Images of Autarchy

1. Immanuel Kant, *Kritik der praktischen Vernunft, Kant's gesammelte Schriften*, Band V (Berlin: Preussische Akademie der Wissenschaften, 1913), p. 47.

2. Ibid., p. 55.

3. Immanuel Kant, *Grundlegung zur Metaphysik der Sitten, Kant's gesammelte Schriften*, Band IV (Berlin: Preussische Akademie der Wissenschaften, 1911), p. 401n.

4. Martin Heidegger, *Kant und das Problem der Metaphysik* (Frankfurt am Main: Klostermann, 1973), §30.

5. *Kritik der praktischen Vernunft*, pp. 82, 95. Thus we cannot accept without reservations Beck's formulation that "Nature produced man but brought him to the stage where he can finally assert his independence of her." Lewis White Beck, *A Commentary on Kant's Critique of Practical Reason* (Chicago and London: University of Chicago Press, 1960), p. 125.

6. *Kritik der praktischen Vernunft*, pp. 73–74. "[M]en as rational natural beings . . . are

unholy enough to be influenced by pleasure to transgress the moral law, although they recognize its authority. And even when they do obey it, they do so without gladness (in conflict with their inclinations). . . ." Immanuel Kant, *Die Metaphysik der Sitten, Kant's gesammelte Schriften*, Band VI (Berlin: Preussische Akademie der Wissenschaften, 1911), p. 379. Trans. James Ellington, *The Metaphysical Principles of Virtue* (Indianapolis: Bobbs-Merill, 1964), p. 36.

7. Beck, *A Commentary*, p. 124.

8. "[A] kingdom of ends is possible only on the analogy of a kingdom of nature. . . ." *Grundlegung*, p. 438. Trans. H. J. Paton, *Groundwork of the Metaphysics of Morals* (New York: Harper & Row, 1956), p. 106.

9. For Beck the only alternative to the Kantian formal sense of the universality and necessity of law "anchored in the *res cogitans*" cogitating in accordance with the laws determined in formal logic can be "only an expression of feeling and history, of *Zeitgeist, Volksgeist* and *Schwärmerei*." *A Commentary*, p. 125.

10. *Kritik der praktischen Vernunft*, p. 99; *Grundlegung*, p. 407.

11. *Kritik der prakitschen Vernunft*, p. 73.

12. Ibid., p. 23.

13. Immanuel Kant, *Anthropologie in pragmatischen Hinsicht, Kant's gesammelte Schriften*, Band VII (Berlin: Preussische Akademie der Wissenschaften, 1917), §60.

14. This is so also of human beings as sensuous objects: "Skill and diligence in labor have a market value; wit, lively imagination and humor have fancy value. . . ." (*Grundlegung*, p. 435; trans., p. 102), a value that is measurable in terms of the universal means of exchange, money, whose value is preeminent. (*Die Metaphysik der Sitten*, p. 434.)

15. *Kritik der praktischen Vernunft*, p. 25.

16. Friedrich Nietzsche, *Zur Genealogie der Moral, Werke, Kritische Gesamtausgabe*, Abt. 6, Band II (Berlin: de Gruyter, 1968), p. 430.

17. *Kritik der praktische Vernunft*, p. 59.

18. "[I]n the idea of a will which is absolutely good—good without any qualifying condition (namely, that it should attain this or that end)—there must be complete abstraction from every end that has to be *produced* (as something which would make every will only relatively good). Hence the end must here be conceived, not as an end to be produced, *but as a self-existent end*. It must therefore be conceived only negatively—that is, as an end against which we should never act. . . ." *Grundlegung*, p. 437; trans., p. 105.

19. *Die Metaphysik der Sitten*, p. 246.

20. *Grundlegung*, p. 439.

21. Ibid., p. 437.

22. Ibid., p. 431, trans., pp. 98–99.

23. "But because it is absolutely impossible to give an example of it from experience, since no absolutely unconditioned determination of causality can be found among the causes of things as appearances, we could defend the supposition of a freely acting cause when applied to a being in the world of sense only in so far as the being was regarded also as noumenon." *Kritik der praktische Vernunft*, p. 48; trans. Lewis White Beck, *Critique of Practical Reason* (Indianapolis: Bobbs-Merrill, 1956), p. 50. Thus "the law commands only the maxim of the action, namely, that the ground of the obligation is to be sought not in sensible impulses (advantage or disadvantage) but wholly in the law; and so the law does not command the action itself. For it is not possible for man to look so far into the depths of his own heart as ever to be entirely certain, even in one single action, of the purity of his moral purpose and the sincerity of his mental disposition. . . ." *Die Metaphysik der Sitten*, p. 392; trans., p. 51. Cf. also *Grundlegung*, p. 407; trans., p. 75: "[I]n fact we can never, even by the most strenuous self-examination, get to the bottom of our secret impulsions. . . ."

24. Gerhard Krüger, *Philosophie und Moral in der Kantischen Kritik* (Tübingen: J. C. B. Mohr, 1931), p. 36.

25. *Grundlegung*, pp. 435–36.

26. Hermann Cohen, *Kants Begründung der Ethik*, 2nd ed. (Berlin: B. Cassirer, 1910). Martin Heidegger, *The Basic Problems of Phenomenology*, trans. Albert Hofstadter (Bloomington: Indiana University Press, 1982), pp. 135–37.

27. *Grundlegung*, pp. 58–59.

28. *Die Metaphysik der Sitten*, p. 430.

29. Ibid., p. 434.

30. Ibid., pp. 456–57.

31. Ibid., pp. 434–37.

32. *Kritik der praktischen Vernunft*, p. 74.

33. Ibid., p. 88; trans., p. 91.

34. *Die Metaphysik der Sitten*, p. 440; trans., p. 103.

35. Kritik der praktischen Vernunft, p. 118.

36. *Die Metaphysik der Sitten*, p. 379; trans., p. 36.

37. Ibid., p. 405; trans., p. 65.

38. Ibid., p. 380; trans., p. 37.

39. Ibid., p. 409. "One defeats his purpose by setting actions called noble, magnanimous, and meritorious as models for children with the notion of captivating them by infusing an enthusiasm for these actions." *Kritik der praktischen Vernunft*, p. 157; trans., p. 161.

40. Ibid., pp. 88, 75.

41. Ibid., p. 88; trans., p. 91.

42. Ibid., p. 84.

43. Ibid., p. 80; trans., p. 83.

44. Ibid., p. 81n.

45. Ibid., pp. 77–78.

46. Ibid., p. 76.

47. *Die Metaphysik der Sitten*, p. 352.

48. Ibid., p. 262.

49. For Kant, the "wit, lively imagination and humor" and the "talents and diligence in work" which produce art have their price, but "morality, and humanity so far as it is capable of morality, are the only things which have dignity"; "in default of these nature and art alike contain nothing to put in their place. . . ." *Grundlegung*, p. 435; trans., p. 102.

50. *Die Metaphysik der Sitten*, p. 246.

51. Ibid., p. 318; trans. John Ladd, *The Metaphysical Elements of Justice* (Indianapolis: Bobbs-Merrill, 1965), pp. 83–84.

52. Ibid., p. 455; trans., p. 129.

53. Ibid., pp. 232–33.

54. Ibid., p. 333; trans., p. 102.

55. Ibid., p. 332; trans., p. 100.

56. Ibid., p. 490; trans., p. 160. It will be recalled that the hope of immortal life can be justified not as a reward for virtue but as required for the infinitely long progress in virtue the imperative demands.

57. In his *Anthropology* we find Kant's desolate view that if the human race has an economic, political, and civil history, it is driven by the cold, rational, passions for wealth, for power, for status—and these passions can only make of the human coexistence a war of each against all. That if our species is being led through this savage history toward some resolution, only the obscure and incomprehensible wisdom beneath everything knows. The idea of fulfillment of our nature is to this day inconceivable for each individual; each effort to give it content can only take the form of a passionate invest-

ment of a partial gratification. It could then only be the race itself, through its very history, that is being obscurely led to dimensions of fulfillment unimaginable for us, and if it is being so led, it is only through this dreadful training by which each passion is unleashed to find, in its own defeat, its proper bounds. *Anthropologie*, §§80–86.

58. *Grundlegung*, p. 112.

59. *Die Metaphysik der Sitten*, p. 471; trans., p. 138.

60. Krüger, *Philosophie und Moral in der Kantischen Kritik*, p. 136.

61. Friedrich Nietzsche, *Nachgelassene Fragmente, Anfang 1880 bis Sommer 1882* (Berlin: de Gruyter, 1980) 15 [19].

62. "This is called the duty of religion, namely, that 'of recognizing all our duties as *(instar)* divine commands.' But this is not the consciousness of a duty to God. For since this idea arises entirely out of our own reason and is made by us in order, from a theoretical standpoint, to explain the purposiveness of the universe, or, for practical purposes, to serve as an incentive in our conduct, we do not hereby have before us a given being *to whom* we are obligated; for the actuality of such a being would first have to be proved (disclosed) by experience." *Die Metaphysik der Sitten*, pp. 443–44; trans., p. 107.

63. "[T]his is the Kingdom of God, in which nature and morality come into a harmony, which is foreign to each as such, through a holy Author of the world. . . ." *Kritik der prakitschen Vernunft*, p. 128; trans., p. 133.

III. The Vicious Circle of Mastery

1. Friedrich Nietzsche, *The Gay Science*, trans. Walter Kaufmann (New York: Vintage, 1974), §289: "Embark! Consider how every individual is affected by an overall philosophical justification of his way of living and thinking: he experiences it as a sun that shines especially for him and bestows warmth, blessings, and fertility on him; it makes him independent of praise and blame, self-sufficient, rich, liberal with happiness and good will; incessantly it refashions evil into good, leads all energies to bloom and ripen, and does not permit the petty weeds of grief and chagrin to come up at all." Friedrich Nietzsche, *The Will to Power*, trans. Walter Kaufmann and R. J. Hollingdale (New York: Random House, 1967), §714: "Value words are banners raised where a *new bliss* has been found."

2. Friedrich Nietzsche, *Thus Spoke Zarathustra*, trans. Walter Kaufmann (Middlesex, England, and New York: Penguin Books, 1954), Third Part, §13.

3. Friedrich Nietzsche, *The Genealogy of Morals*, trans. Walter Kaufmann (New York: Vintage, 1969), II, §17.

4. *The Gay Science*, V, §344.

5. *Thus Spoke Zarathustra*, I, §1; IV, §19, *4*.

6. *The Gay Science*, §110.

7. Ibid., §360.

8. Ibid.

9. *The Genealogy of Morals*, III, §1.

10. "For half of almost every human life, man is a decadent. And then the woman! One of the halves of humanity is weak, typically sick, changeable, unstable . . ." Friedrich Nietzsche, *Nachgelassene Fragmente Anfang 1888 bis Anfang Januar 1889* (Berlin: de Gruyter, 1972), 14[182].

11. Friedrich Nietzsche, *Nachgelassene Fragments Herbst 1887 bis März 1888* (Berlin: de Gruyter, 1970), 11[187].

12. On the complexity of the figure of woman in Nietzsche, cf. Jacques Derrida, *Spurs*, trans. Barbara Harlow (Chicago: University of Chicago Press, 1979). Derrida, strangely, does not take into account the maternal woman; identifying with this form of woman is the properly Nietzschean bisexuality.

13. Friedrich Nietzsche, *Beyond Good and Evil,* trans. Walter Kaufmann (New York: Vintage, 1966), §40.

14. *The Gay Science,* §§333, 359.

15. *The Genealogy of Morals,* I, §12.

16. Ibid., III, §5.

17. *Beyond Good and Evil,* §292.

18. *The Gay Science,* §§110, 113.

19. It is true that Nietzsche here writes, in contradiction with our exegesis: "The philosophic spirit always had to use as a mask and cocoon the *previously established* type of the contemplative man—priest, sorcerer, soothsayer, and in any case a religious type. . . ." (*The Genealogy of Morals,* III, §10). Yet the priest form described in the core of the essay, §§11–22, is the Christian priest, in complete contradiction with the officiant of pagan civic cults—or Dionysian rituals.

20. Friedrich Nietzsche, *The Antichrist,* trans. Walter Kaufmann in *The Portable Nietzsche* (New York: Viking, 1976), §31; *Beyond Good and Evil,* §40.

21. *The Antichrist,* §11.

22. Ibid., §27.

23. Ibid., §23.

24. *The Gay Science* (§10) presents this pathos of distance as pathos of temporal distance; the strong appear as the atavism of a people. They are ones in whom a recrudescence of obsolete instincts occurred, making excess power their sole defense against madness.

25. Neither religions—"Almost two thousand years—and not a single new god!" (*The Antichrist,* §19)—nor sciences are the work of the saved.

26. *The Genealogy of Morals,* III, §16.

27. Ibid., §28.

28. Ibid., §23.

29. Ibid., §24.

30. The exclusion of consideration of values is not decided by mathematization. Nietzsche does not exclude a quantitative expression of all values. *The Will to Power,* §710.

31. *The Genealogy of Morals,* I, §1.

32. Ibid., III, §25.

33. Ibid.

34. Ibid., §12.

35. Ibid.

36. *Thus Spoke Zarathustra,* II, §15.

37. *The Gay Science,* §357; *The Genealogy of Morals,* III, §27.

38. *The Genealogy of Morals,* III, §25.

39. Ibid.

40. Ibid., §24.

41. Ibid., §27.

42. Ibid.

43. *The Gay Science,* §357.

44. *The Genealogy of Morals,* III, §§14, 27.

45. Ibid., §13.

46. Ibid.

47. Ibid., §28.

48. *Thus Spoke Zarathustra,* I, §1.

49. Ibid., §15.

50. Ibid., §20.

51. *The Gay Science,* §109.

52. *The Will to Power,* §55.

53. *Thus Spoke Zarathustra*, II, §19; IV, §2.

54. Ibid., IV, §9.

55. *The Gay Science*, §341.

56. *Beyond Good and Evil*, §40.

57. Ibid., §22.

58. *Beyond Good and Evil*, §40.

59. Friedrich Nietzsche, *Die Geburt der Tragödie, Nachgelassene Fragmente 1869–1872* (Berlin: de Gruyter, 1972), 5 [115].

60. "And everything that could move Zoroaster, Moses, Mohammed, Jesus, Plato, Brutus, Spinoza, Mirabeau, I also was already alive to, and for many things what required several millennia to pass from the embryonic state to that of full maturity comes to light only in me." Friedrich Nietzsche, *Nachgelassene Fragmente 1880 bis Sommer 1882* (Berlin: de Gruyter, 1967), 15 [17].

61. *The Gay Science*, §337.

62. Ibid., §333.

63. Ibid., §337.

64. *Thus Spoke Zarathustra*, IV, §19.

65. Ibid., III, §§12, 13.

66. Ibid., §4.

67. Ibid.

68. Ibid.

69. Ibid., II, §20.

70. G. W. F. Hegel, *Phenomenology of Spirit*, trans. A. V. Miller (Oxford: Oxford University Press, 1977), p. 19.

71. *The Gay Science*, §301.

72. *Thus Spoke Zarathustra*, III, §4.

73. Hegel, *Phenomenology*, p. 19.

74. Friedrich Nietzsche, *Ecce Homo*, trans. Walter Kaufmann (New York: Vintage, 1967), p. 272.

75. *Thus Spoke Zarathustra*, IV, §19, 11.

76. *Nachgelassene Fragmente Anfang 1880 bis Sommer 1882*, 11 [202].

77. *Thus Spoke Zarathustra*, II, §20.

78. *The Will to Power*, §702.

79. *Beyond Good and Evil*, §56.

80. *The Will to Power*, §853.

81. *The Gay Science*, §299.

82. *Thus Spoke Zarathustra*, III, §13, 2.

83. *The Gay Science*, §337.

84. *Thus Spoke Zarathustra*, III, §14.

85. Ibid., II, §20.

86. Ibid., II, §10.

87. *The Gay Science*, V, §354.

88. Ibid., Preface for the Second Edition, §4.

89. Georg Simmel, *Schopenhauer und Nietzsche: Ein Vortrogzyklus* (Leipzig, 1970), pp. 250–51.

90. *Thus Spoke Zarathustra*, IV, §9, 11.

IV. The Work of the Masters

1. Friedrich Nietzsche, *Nachgelassene Fragmente Anfang 1880 bis Sommer 1882* (Berlin: de Gruyter, 1967), 11 [72].

2. Edmund Husserl, *The Crisis of European Sciences and Transcendental Phenomenology* trans. David Carr (Evanston: Northwestern University Press, 1970), p. 299.

3. Friedrich Nietzsche, *On the Genealogy of Morals*, trans. Walter Kaufmann (New York: Vintage, 1969), III, §12.

4. Friedrich Nietzsche, *The Gay Science*, trans. Walter Kaufmann (New York: Vintage, 1974), §333.

5. Edmund Husserl, *Ideas Pertaining to a Pure Phenomenology and to a Phenomenological Philosophy*, trans. Fred Kersten (The Hague: Martinus Nijhoff, 1982), §24.

6. *The Gay Science*, §130.

7. Friedrich Nietzsche, *The Will to Power*, trans. Walter Kaufmann (New York: Random House, 1967), §821.

8. *The Gay Science*, §301.

9. *On the Genealogy of Morals*, III, §28.

10. *The Gay Science*, §109.

11. Friedrich Nietzsche, *Thus Spoke Zarathustra*, trans. Walter Kaufmann (New York: Penguin, 1978), III, §4.

12. Ibid., IV, 19, §*10*.

13. Friedrich Nietzsche, *Beyond Good and Evil*, trans. Walter Kaufmann (New York: Vintage, 1966), §36.

14. *Thus Spoke Zarathustra*, IV, §10.

15. Ibid., III, §12, *19*.

16. *The Gay Science*, §337.

17. *The Will to Power*, §1067.

18. Georg Simmel, *Schopenhauer und Nietzsche: Ein Vortrogzyklus* (Leipzig: Duncker & Humblot, 1907), pp. 250–51.

19. Arthur Danto, "The Eternal Recurrence," in D. J. O'Connor, ed., *A Critical History of Western Philosophy* (New York: Free Press of Glencoe, 1964), pp. 399–401.

20. *Thus Spoke Zarathustra*, III, §13, *2*.

21. *The Gay Science*, §48.

22. *Thus Spoke Zarathustra*, III, §13, *19*.

23. See *The Gay Science*, §299.

24. *The Gay Science*, §55.

25. *K*, XII: part 2, §274.

26. *Thus Spoke Zarathustra*, IV, §10.

27. Ibid., II, §20.

Part II. The Subjection

V. Deathbound Thought

1. Martin Heidegger, *Being and Time*, trans. John Macquarrie and Edward Robinson (New York: Harper, 1962), p. 303.

2. Ibid., p. 115.

3. Ibid., p. 231.

4. Martin Heidegger, *On Time and Being*, trans. Joan Stambaugh (New York: Harper, 1972), p. 12.

5. *Being and Time*, p. 307.

6. Ibid., p. 346.

7. Ibid., p. 376.

8. Ibid., pp. 329–31.

9. Ibid., pp. 330–31.

10. Ibid., p. 354.

11. Ibid., pp. 441–43.

12. Ibid., p. 373.

13. Ibid., p. 291.

14. Ibid., p. 46.

15. Martin Heidegger, *What Is Metaphysics?*, trans. David Farrell Krell in David Farrell Krell, ed., *Basic Writings* (New York: Harper, 1977), p. 108.

16. *Being and Time*, p. 184.

17. Martin Heidegger, "The Origin of the Work of Art," trans. Albert Hofstadter in *Poetry, Language, Thought* (New York: Harper, 1971), pp. 22–31.

18. *Being and Time*, p. 213.

19. Ibid., pp. 477–78.

20. Ibid., §51.

21. Maurice Merleau-Ponty, *The Visible and the Invisible*, trans. Alphonso Lingis (Evanston: Northwestern University Press, 1968), p. 103.

22. *Being and Time*, p. 218.

23. Ibid., pp. 442–43.

24. *Poetry, Language, Thought*, pp. 149, 178.

25. *Being and Time*, pp. 434, 437–38, 442–43.

26. Ibid., p. 435.

27. Friedrich Nietzsche, *The Gay Science*, trans. Walter Kaufmann (New York: Vintage, 1974), §354.

28. Martin Heidegger, *On the Way to Language*, trans. Peter D. Hertz (New York: Harper, 1971), p. 61.

29. *Poetry, Language, Thought*, p. 132.

30. Martin Heidegger, "Letter on Humanism" trans. Frank A. Capuzzi and J. Glenn Gray in David Farrell Krell, ed., *Basic Writings*, pp. 198–99.

31. *Being and Time*, pp. 391ff.

32. Martin Heidegger, "On the Essence of Truth," in David Farrell Krell, *Basic Writings*, pp. 135–37.

33. *Being and Time*, p. 168.

34. Nathalie Sarraute, *Portrait of a Man Unknown*, trans. Maris Jolas (New York: George Braziller, 1958).

35. Jacques Derrida, "Speech and Writing According to Hegel," trans. Alphonso Lingis, *Man and World* 11(1978):107–30.

36. *Being and Time*, pp. 378–79, 476–79.

37. Ibid., pp. 408–15.

38. Ibid., pp. 408–12.

39. Ibid., pp. 96–97.

40. Ibid., p. 113.

41. Martin Heidegger, *Early Greek Thinking*, trans. David Farrell Krell and Frank A. Capuzzi (New York: Harper, 1975), pp. 26–27.

42. Martin Heidegger, *Discourse on Thinking*, trans. John M. Anderson and E. Hans Freund (New York: Harper & Row, 1966), pp. 52–53.

43. Martin Heidegger, *Nietzsche, Vol. IV: Nihilism*, trans. Frank A. Capuzzi (New York: Harper, 1982).

44. *Being and Time*, p. 289.

45. Karl Löwith, *Nature, History, and Existentialism*, trans. Arnold Levison (Evanston: Northwestern University Press, 1966), ch. 3.

46. *Being and Time*, p. 233.

47. Martin Heidegger, *The Question of Technology*, trans. William Lovitt (New York: Harper, 1977), pp. 34–35.

48. Ibid., pp. 6–12.

49. Martin Heidegger, *Hebel der Hausfreund* (Pfullingen: Neske, 1957), p. 37.

50. *Poetry, Language, Thought*, p. 28.

51. Ibid., p. 178.

52. Ibid., p. 168.

53. Ibid., p. 177.
54. Ibid., p. 179.
55. *Being and Time*, pp. 79–80.
56. *On Time and Being*, p. 19.
57. Martin Heidegger, *The Question Concerning Technology*, p. 32.

VI. Face to Face

1. Emmanuel Levinas, *Totality and Infinity*, trans. A. F. Lingis (The Hague: Martinus Nijhoff, 1979), pp. 175–193; "The Trace of the Other" in *Collected Philosophical Papers of Emmanuel Levinas* (The Hague: Martinus Nijhoff, 1986), pp. 102–107.
2. *Totality and Infinity*, pp. 48–52, 292–93.
3. Martin Heidegger, *The Question Concerning Technology and Other Essays*, trans. William Lovitt (New York: Harper, 1977), pp. 26–34.
4. *Totality and Infinity*, pp. 257–61.
5. Emmanuel Levinas, *Otherwise than Being or Beyond Essence*, trans. A. F. Lingis (The Hague: Martinus Nijhoff, 1981), pp. 85, 89–90.
6. *Collected Philosophical Papers*, p. 66.
7. Ibid., p. 104.
8. Cf. supra.
9. Cf. supra.
10. Martin Heidegger, *Poetry, Language, Thought*, trans. Albert Hofstadter (New York: Harper, 1971), p. 179.
11. Emmanuel Levinas, *Difficile liberté* (Paris: Albin Michel, 1963), pp. 255–59.
12. *Totality and Infinity*, pp. 130–34.
13. Cf. supra.
14. Maurice Merleau-Ponty, *The Visible and the Invisible*, trans. A. F. Lingis (Evanston: Northwestern University Press, 1968), p. 133.
15. Edmund Husserl, *Cartesian Meditations*, trans. Dorion Cairns (The Hague: Martinus Nijhoff, 1960), §44.
16. *Otherwise than Being*, pp. 81–82.
17. *Totality and Infinity*, pp. 234–36.
18. Ibid., pp. 209–10.
19. *Otherwise than Being*, p. 74.
20. Ibid., pp. 181–82.
21. Ibid., p. 118.
22. Emmanuel Levinas, *Existence and Existents*, trans. A. F. Lingis (The Hague: Martinus Nijhoff, 1978), pp. 17–18.
23. *Otherwise than Being*, pp. 52–53.
24. Emmanuel Levinas, *Discovering Existence with Husserl*, trans. Richard Cohen (Bloomington: Indiana University Press, 1986), pp.
25. *Otherwise than Being*, pp. 54–55.
26. *Existence and Existents*, p. 91.
27. Martin Heidegger, *Being and Time*, trans. John Macquarrie and Edward Robinson (New York: Harper & Row, 1962), p. 434.
28. Cf. supra, pp. 135–36.
29. *Collected Philosophical Papers*, pp. 70, 103–107; *Otherwise than Being*, pp. 147–48.
30. Emmanuel Levinas, "De l'évasion," *Recherches Philosophiques* V (1935/36), pp. 373–92.
31. *Totality and Infinity*, p. 235.
32. Ibid., pp. 118–20.
33. *Otherwise than Being*, p. 112.
34. *Existence and Existents*, pp. 24–36.

35. *Otherwise than Being*, p. 108, n10.

36. Ibid., p. 179.

VII. The Sign of the Subject

1. Claude Lévi-Strauss, *Structural Anthropology*, trans. Claire Jacobson and Brooke Grundfest Schoepf (New York: Basic Books, 1963), p. 83.

2. P. Aulagnier-Spairani, "Remarques sur la structure psychotique," *La Psychanalyse* 8 (1964): 57.

3. Jean-François Lyotard, *Economie libidinale* (Paris: Editions de Minuit, 1974). Gilles Deleuze and Félix Guattari, *Anti-Oedipus, Capitalism and Schizophrenia*, trans. Robert Hurley, Mark Seem, and Helen R. Lane (New York: Viking, 1977).

4. Gilles Deleuze, *Différence et répétition* (Paris: Presses Universitaires de France, 1976), pp. 138–39.

5. Friedrich Nietzsche, *The Gay Science*, trans. Walter Kaufmann (New York: Vintage, 1974), §337.

6. Jacques Lacan, *Ecrits*, trans. Alan Sheridan (New York: W. W. Norton, 1977), p. 57.

7. Ibid., pp. 1–7.

8. Louis Bolk, *Handbuch der vergleichenden Anatomie der Wirbeltiere* (Amsterdam: A. Ascher, 1967).

9. Melanie Klein, *The Psycho-analysis of Children*, trans. Alix Strachey (London: The Hogarth Press & The Institute of Psycho-analysis, 1949).

10. Friedrich Nietzsche, *On the Genealogy of Morals*, trans. Walter Kaufmann (New York: Vintage, 1969), I, 2.

11. Fernand Braudel, *Capitalism and Material Life 1400–1800*, trans. Miriam Kochan (New York: Harper, 1973), pp. 330–31.

12. Hayden White, *Metahistory, The Historical Imagination in Nineteenth Century Europe* (Baltimore & London: Johns Hopkins University Press, 1973), p. 291.

13. Karl Marx, *Capital*, trans. Eden and Dean Paul (London: Dent & Sons, 1962) p. 22. I have altered "coat" to "gold" in the first sentence, in order to extend Marx's proposition, which concerns the elementary form of value, to its monetary form.

14. Ibid., p. 23, n1.

15. Martin Heidegger, "Who is Nietzsche's Zarathustra?" trans. Bernd Magnus, *The Review of Metaphysics* 20(1969): 420–31.

16. Aristotle, *Nichomachean Ethics*, trans. Martin Ostwald (Indianapolis: Bobbs-Merrill, 1962), 1164a 1–2.

17. Immanuel Kant, *The Metaphysical Principles of Virtue*, trans. James Ellington (Indianapolis: Bobbs-Merrill, 1964), p. 97.

18. Lacan, *Ecrits*, pp. 67, 199, 217, 310, 314.

19. Pierre Klossowski, *La monnaie vivante* (Paris: Eric Losfeld/Terrain Vague, 1970).

20. Jacques Derrida, *Speech and Phenomenon*, trans. David B. Allison (Evanston: Northwestern University Press, 1973), p. 50.

21. Gilles Deleuze, *Différence et répétition*, pp. 138–39.

22. Cf. supra, p. 110.

23. Friedrich Nietzsche, *The Portable Nietzsche*, trans. Walter Kaufmann (New York: Penguin Books, 1959), p. 686.

24. E. M. Cioran, *Précis de décomposition* (Paris: Gallimard, 1949), p. 128.

25. Leo Tolstoy, *The Death of Ivan Ilych and Other Stories*, trans. Aylmer Maude et al. (New York: The New American Library, 1960). Heidegger cites this narrative alone—surely pivotal in the modern literature on dying—in his chapter on death and authenticity in *Being and Time*. It is striking that he refers only to the opening pages of this narrative, to vehemently contrast the tranquilizing spectacle of the death of others in the

world with the anxiety before one's own dying from the world. Heidegger does not seem to have credited the way Ivan Ilych's own death approaches him in the whole body of this account. His own death does not close in upon Ivan Ilych in the guise of the nothingness into which his anxiety tells him his own being is being cast already; it invades him in the guise of pain, not as transition from existing to nothingness but as a passage of activity to passivity and prostration.

26. Nietzsche, *The Gay Science*, §360.

27. Ibid., §333.

28. Tolstoy, *The Death of Ivan Ilych and Other Stories*, pp. 155–56.

VIII. The Other Death

1. Jonathan Schell, *The Abolition* (New York: Knopf, 1984), pp. 31–32.

2. Emmanuel Levinas, *Otherwise than Being*, trans. Alphonso Lingis (The Hague: Martinus Nijhoff, 1981), p. 85.

3. Immanuel Kant, *Critique of Practical Reason*, trans. Lewis White Beck (Indianapolis: Bobbs-Merrill, 1956), p. 75.

4. J. M. G. Le Clézio, *L'extase matérielle* (Paris: Gallimard, 1967).

5. Martin Heidegger, *Being and Time*, trans. John Macquarrie and Edward Robinson (New York: Harper: 1962), p. 435.

6. Maurice Blanchot, *The Space of Literature*, trans. Ann Smock (Lincoln: University of Nebraska Press, 1982), p. 99.

7. Ibid., p. 87–170.

8. Maurice Merleau-Ponty, *The Visible and the Invisible*, trans. Alphonso Lingis (Evanston: Northwestern University Press, 1968), p. 72.

9. Ibid., p. 82.

10. Cf. Alphonso Lingis, *Excesses* (New York: State University of New York Press, 1983), pp. 25–38.

11. Jean-Luc Nancy, *La communauté désoeuvrée* (Paris: Christian Bourgeois, 1985), p. 96.

12. Emmanuel Levinas, *Existence and Existents*, trans. Alphonso Lingis (The Hague: Martinus Nijhoff, 1978), p. 91.

13. Immanuel Kant, *Die Metaphysik der Sitten*, ed. Königlich Preusslischen Akademie der Wissenschaften (Berlin: Georg Reimer, 1914), p. 262.

INDEX

Abschattung (Adumbration), 87–88, 90–91
Absolute spirit, 77
Absolute truth, 2–3, 15, 35–36
Adumbration *(Abschattung)*, 87–88, 90–91
Aesthetic mind, 79
Aesthetic perception, 92
Affective sensations, 158
Affirmation, 94–96, 128; Nietzsche on, 73, 78–79, 80, 101–102, 103, 104, 162, 172–73, 190
Aging (Senescence), 154–55, 173–75
Alienation, 133
Alterity, 3, 8, 158–59, 174, 175, 188; of death, 184–87; for Husserl, 18, 193 n.6; of law, 177–84; for Levinas, 6–7, 135–41, 143–45, 149–51, 153, 154–55; and responsibility, 145, 148, 149, 151–52. *See also* Other, the
Anaclitic deviation, 158
Annihilation, 112, 181, 184
Anonymity, 110, 112, 119, 121, 133
Answerability, 19, 119, 128
Anus, infant's, 166
Anxiety, 154, 177, 184, 187, 203–204 n.25; infant, 159; for Levinas, 148, 149, 154
—in Heidegger, 128, 180–81; of conscience, 118, 125, 186; and dying, 112–14, 116, 117–18, 121–22, 142; fear of, 126, 129–30, 133
Apodictic freedom, 36
Apollonian, the, 67, 70, 74, 76, 79, 83
Appropriateness (Appropriation), 83–84, 111, 133
Aristotle, 95, 169
Art: Kant on, 196 n.49; Nietzsche on, 62–63, 72, 73, 79, 83, 85, 94
Artist, 64, 94, 103; as ideal type, 59–60, 62–63, 70
Artist communities, 53
Artistry, 78–80, 83–84, 92, 94
Asceticism, 61, 63, 64–65, 66, 69
Atheists, 59–60, 67–68
Atomic age, 129. *See also* Nuclear technology
Autarchy, moral, 49–52
Authentic existence, 111–12, 116–17, 119, 124, 126; of another, 182, 183–84
Authentic speech, 121
Authentic understanding, 118, 124–26, 130–34
Authenticity, 6, 50, 117, 129–34, 181, 183
Autonomy, 49, 50–52; of the other, 53, 55, 178–79, 182

Baudelaire, Charles-Pierre, 61
Beck, Lewis White, 194 n.5, 195 n.9

Becoming, 81, 97, 98, 101, 172, 184–85
Being, 104, 126, 187; Levinas on, 148, 151–53, 155; Nietzsche on, 71, 97, 172, 187
—in Heidegger, 12, 125, 152, 154, 180–81, 185, 186; and dying, 122, 123; and existence, 111–15, 118–19, 121, 129–30, 132; and nothingness, 117, 127
Being-in-the-world, 128, 133
Birth, 123, 152, 157, 190–91
Blanchot, Maurice, 8, 184, 186–87, 189
Body, 137–38, 143
Bolk, Louis, 159

Capitalist society, 165–66
Care, 84, 133
Caress, 189
Carnal materiality of the other, 137, 139
Carnal nature, 179
Castration, 61, 66, 69; of the mother, 161, 163, 167–68; required by word of the father, 160, 161, 162–63, 167, 170
Castration anxiety, 170, 171
Castration phobia, 161
Castration threat, 160, 169, 175
Categorical imperative, 3, 38, 178–79; death as, for Heidegger, 6. *See also* Imperative; Moral imperative; Types of law
Causality, 71, 93, 131, 178; and the will, 49–50, 195 n.23
Child to come, 68–70. *See also* Unborn ones
Christianity, 60, 67, 76
Circularity, 14, 27
Civil society, 53–56
Classicism, 102–103, 128. *See also* Greek antiquity
Cognition, 87, 155
Collage, 79–80, 96
Comic sentiment, 92
Command, 39, 41, 46, 180
Commerce, 163–64
Commodity, 163–65, 169, 170
Community, 8, 189–90
Conscience: for Heidegger, 113, 115, 118–19, 124–26, 180, 186; for Kant, 44
Consciousness, 17, 21, 24–26, 157, 163–64, 184; for Heidegger, 113, 118, 123, 124–25; for Levinas, 147, 155; natural time of, 31–34; for Nietzsche, 60–61, 62, 70, 84; and political economy, 165, 166; theoretical, 17, 35–36, 89
—in Husserl, 4–5, 21–22, 23, 28, 89, 144; natural "attitude" of, 15–16; now of, 30–31, 34–

35; presence as telos for, 96–97; sensibility as, 90–91
Consolation, 75, 189–90
Constituted speech, 119–21
Constitution, internal: analogy with constitution of a state, 49–50, 51
Content, 30, 99, 158; for Husserl, 22, 23, 25–26, 31–35, 88–89
Cosmic force, 101
Cosmology, 99, 172
Creation, 51, 57–58, 62, 74
Culture, 59–70, 73, 74–77, 97, 171

Danto, Arthur, 98, 99
Dasein, 111, 118, 126. *See also* Existence
Death, 74, 78, 168, 171; and aging, 154–55, 173–75; alterity of, 184–87; in form of dismemberment, 169–70, 171; Husserl's definition of, 27–28; Nietzsche on, 64, 68, 69, 106, 173; of the other, 179, 182, 187–90; portrayal in "Death of Ivan Ilych," 173–74, 175, 203–204 n.25
—in Heidegger, 6, 109, 112–15, 117, 120, 130, 133–34; and anxiety, 121–23; and conscience, 125; Dasein as place of, 118–19; and futurity, 148–49; and life, 185–86; as pure extremity, 180–82; as reciprocal of existence, 127; and sensibility, 142, 143; and the world, 123, 128–29, 131. *See also* Dying; Mortality
Death drive, 157, 169, 173, 188
"Death of Ivan Ilych" (Tolstoy), 173–74, 175, 203–204 n.25
Death sentence, 115, 183
Deeds, 116–17, 182
Deleuze, Gilles, 157–58, 171
Derrida, Jacques, 197 n.12
Dialectics, 6, 76, 78–79
Dignity, 50, 51, 186, 196 n.49
Dionysian, the, 67, 83–84, 85, 94, 95, 175; compulsions, 70, 73, 76; joy, 81, 86; rituals, 74, 79
Directing force, 60–61, 66, 68, 171, 174–75
Discourse, 160, 189–90; parental, 156–57, 160
Distention, extreme, 187–88
Divine, the/divinity, 49, 60, 67, 132, 197 n.62
Driving force, 60–61, 63, 66, 68, 70, 174–75
Duty, 52, 197 n.62
Dying, 28, 173, 177, 184–85, 187; Heidegger on, 6, 28, 112–13, 121–22, 129, 142, 177; Levinas on, 152, 154, 189; of the other, 8, 188–90; portrayal in "Death of Ivan Ilych," 173–74, 175, 203–204 n.25. *See also* Death; Mortality

Economic history, 54–55, 196–97 n.57
Economics, 163–66
Economy, 156, 170
Ecstasy, 116–18, 123, 130, 179
Ego, 28, 33, 159, 193 n.6

Egoism, 152–53, 158
Eidetic identity, 93
Eigentlichkeit, 111–12, 118, 133, 144
Elemental, the: for Levinas, 142–43
Emptiness, 112, 120, 123, 128, 142, 154
End, 46–49, 50, 60–61, 66, 184; for Kant, 44–46, 51
End in itself, 44, 46–49, 195 n.18
Entschlossenheit, 124, 129
Equipment, 131–32
Equivocation, 119–21, 122, 139
Ereignis, 83–84, 111–12, 133
Erotogenic surface, 157–58, 161, 162–63, 168
Erotogenic zone, primary process, 169–70, 171, 174
Essence, 27, 57; for Heidegger, 111–12, 116–17, 130, 132–33, 185
Eternal return, 71–73, 82–84, 93–94, 97–98, 104–105; as law of the circle, 80–82, 85–86; will for, 95–96
Exchange-value, 163–66, 167, 168
Excitations, 158, 162, 188
Excluded middle, logical axiom of, 84, 92
Excrement (feces), infant, 166–67
Existence, 21; for Levinas, 147, 151–53, 155; Nietzsche on, 71, 103, 104, 172–73
—in Heidegger, 109–19, 120, 128, 130–34, 180, 182, 185–86; and conscience, 125–26; as deathbound, 129; relationship to death, 122–24, 127
Existence and Existents (Levinas), 152, 153
Existent, 147, 149, 152–53
Existential analytic, 120, 127, 128, 129, 133
Existential hermeneutics, 28
Existentialism, 56–57
Existing, 154, 155, 184
Experience, 24–26, 31, 88
Ex-statis, 152
Exteriority, 180, 188
Extinction, 176–77, 184, 190

Face, 157, 181; of the other, 138–39; phenomenology of, 135–37, 145, 149
Father, 167–68, 170, 173; name of the, 163, 170, 171, 173; word as child's law, 160–63, 167–68, 170, 173, 175
Feces (excrement), infant, 166–67
Fetish, 166, 168
Fetus, 157
Feudal society, 165–66, 167
Final kingdom (Kingdom of ends), 53–56, 184
Finality, 1, 12, 13, 132
Finitude, 12, 121, 127
First person singular, 117, 119, 122, 145, 150, 154. *See also* "I"
Force, 136, 137, 158, 180, 184, 186; for Nietzsche, 59–62, 63, 71, 73, 81–84, 90, 91, 94, 95–97, 100. *See also* Directing force; Driving force; Imperative force; Vocative force

Form, 4–5, 31–34, 68, 136, 139, 154; distinguished from matter, 30, 31, 88–89; for Heidegger, 109–10, 118–19, 131; of the present, 22–26, 30; science of, 96, 97; of time, 34–35

Freedom, 40, 50–51, 109

Freud, Sigmund, 157–58, 167, 193 n.4

Future, 4–5, 99, 148–49; Heidegger on, 24, 112, 113–15, 116, 123–24; relationship to the present, 23–26, 30, 35

Futurity, 33, 35, 147–49, 186–87

Genealogical analysis, 171

Genetic analysis, 7, 36, 156, 157, 171

Gerede, das. See Talk

Gestures, 136–38, 139, 140, 146, 178

God, 13, 50, 68, 150–51, 153, 189

Gods, 48–49

Gold, 164, 165, 166, 169, 170

Good, the, 124, 132, 150, 190–91

Goods, economic, 54, 163

Greek antiquity, 42–43, 73–77, 100, 128, 175; mathematics, 2–3, 12, 88; philosophy, 2–3, 12, 63

Guattari, Félix, 157–58

Guilt, 64, 115–16

Happiness, 75, 76; for Kant, 38, 49, 50; for Nietzsche, 44, 77, 104, 105

Hegel, G. W. F., 76, 78, 79, 93–94, 103, 183

Heidegger, Martin, 1, 50, 83–84, 106, 180–84, 187–88; deathbound thought of, 6, 28, 109–34, 142, 177, 203–204 n.25; on Kant, 39, 141; on law, 40, 42–43, 109, 132, 141; on Nietzsche, 46, 98; on the present, 112, 114, 116–18, 147; on sensibility, 123, 142, 143, 144–45; on time, 6, 12, 34–35, 111–12, 116, 120, 122, 129, 133; on truth, 12, 118, 119, 127, 134; on Western history, 11, 12. *See also* Anxiety (in Heidegger); Being (in Heidegger); Death (in Heidegger); Existence (in Heidegger); Nothingness (in Heidegger); Will: Heidegger on; World (in Heidegger)

Hermeneutical phenomenology, 127

Heterology, 135, 151

Historians, 59–60, 62, 65

History, 11–12, 13, 54–55, 76–77, 89, 196–97 n.57; of culture, 59–70, 171

Horizon, 21–22, 29–30, 31–33, 36

Human beings, 164, 176–77

Human nature, 1, 19–20, 51, 124; Kant on, 38–40, 41, 44, 178; Nietzsche on, 69–70, 75, 175; of the other, 178–79

Humanity, 4, 18, 77, 196 n.49

Husserl, Edmund, 11–13, 96, 100, 120, 148, 171; on alterity, 18, 193 n.6; on classical Greece, 128; on constituted talk, 119; on imperatives, 39, 40; on infinity, 13–37, 105, 126, 149–50, 193 nn.1, 2, 3; objective world for, 144; sensibility for, 90–91, 143; sign of the subject for, 156; and speculative reason, 183; on subjectivity, 2–3, 4–5, 21–22, 89–90, 128, 150; on theory as idealization, 87–91, 95, 96–97, 98–99; on time, 4–5, 34–35, 98–99, 104–105. *See also* Consciousness (in Husserl)

"I," 20–21, 35, 150, 187; responsibility of, 145–46, 151, 155. *See also* First person singular

Id, 158

Idea, 26–27, 38, 87–88

Ideal, 2–3, 15, 169–73, 189

Ideal infinity, 28–31

Ideal types (Nietzschean), 59–70, 95, 171

Idealization, 7–8, 14, 90, 104, 156, 162; of nature, 95–99, 100, 105; of the sign of the subject, 156–63; of subjectivity, 2–5; theory as, 87–99; of time, 28–31, 34; and truth, 96–99

Identical, the, 14

Identification, 87, 159

Identity, 15, 111, 153–54, 171, 173; Husserl on, 35, 87–89, 96–97; Nietzsche on, 71, 81, 172

Identity, logical axiom of, 71–72, 84, 92

Illeity, 150, 153, 189

Image, 41, 157, 161

Imagination, 27, 47, 54, 179

Imagination, moral, 40–42, 43–44, 49, 56

Immanence, 189

Imminence, 114, 118, 181, 186–87

Immortality, 55, 184, 196 n.56

Imperative, 2, 170, 177, 183, 191; for Heidegger, 109, 180, 182; for Kant, 5, 38–40, 51, 140–41; for Levinas, 6–7, 139, 140–41, 145, 148; for Nietzsche, 5, 82, 92, 103–104, 106. *See also* Categorical imperative; Moral imperative; Types of law

Imperative force, 7, 136, 137, 140, 181, 182

Implements, 129, 131–32, 144

Impotence, 116, 118, 123

Impulses, repetition of, 171–72

Inauthenticity, 121, 122

Indices, traces as, 139–40

Individual, the, 57, 103

Individuation, 190

Indolence, 154

Infancy/infant, 7, 153–63, 166–70, 173, 175. *See also* Libido: infantile

Infantilism, 174, 175

Infinite distance, 187–88

Infinite space, 3, 14, 88

Infinite space-time, 14, 150

Infinite time, 3, 12, 14, 21–31, 88, 98–99, 126–29; Nietzsche on, 4, 71, 93–94, 172–73, 187

Infinition, 136, 150

Infinitization, 87, 90

Infinity, 1, 2–3, 5, 13–37, 156, 171; and alterity, 149–51, 189; of the Good, 191; for Husserl,

13–37, 87–88, 105, 126, 149–50, 193 nn.1, 2, 3; for Nietzsche, 5, 104–105
Instrumentality, 131
Intellect, 63, 66
Intentional analysis, 120
Intentionality, 26, 34, 142
Intentions, 139, 185
Intersubjectivity, 17–18, 144
Intuition, 22, 24–28, 90–91, 96
Ipseity, 152, 153–54
Irony, 165, 169

Joy, 73–75, 80–81, 86, 102, 104, 126
Judgment, 41, 50; practical, 41, 54, 179, 181
Justice, 55

Kant, Immanuel, 7, 38–58, 72, 100, 148, 169; on art, 196 n.49; on community of men, 189–90; concept of an idea, 26–27; on conscience, 125; sensibility for, 143. *See also* Law (in Kant); Types of law; Understanding (in Kant); Will (in Kant)
Kingdom of ends (Final kingdom), 53–56, 184
Klein, Melanie, 161
Klossowski, Pierre, 170, 172

Labor, 154, 163–64
Lacan, Jacques, 7–8, 157, 159, 170–71
Language, 7, 105–106, 126, 156, 159–60, 171; and the other, 7, 150–51, 188
Law, 4–6, 42–43, 56–57, 189, 195 n.9; alterity of, 177–84; Heidegger on, 40, 42–43, 109, 132, 141; Levinas on, 7, 106, 140–41; Nietzsche on, 57, 58; of the will, 100–106; word of the father as, 160–63, 167–68, 170, 173, 175
—in Kant, 38–45, 49–58, 104; alterity of, 177–80, 181, 182; and the other, 140–41, 148
Le Clézio, J. M. G., 179
Legislation, 51, 53–56
Levinas, Emmanuel, 22–23, 24, 135–55, 182–83; law for, 7, 106, 140–41. *See also* Other, the (in Levinas)
Libido, 7–8, 161–62, 166, 169–71, 173–75, 181; infantile, 157–58, 160–61, 163, 171–72, 174
Life, 19–20, 23, 26–27, 126–29, 185; Nietzsche on, 4, 68–69, 72–73, 97, 100, 172–73
Life-force (Vital force), 44–45, 74, 158
Living now, 23, 24–26, 30, 33, 34. *See also* Now; Present, the
Logical axioms of identity, non-contradiction and excluded middle, 71–72, 84, 92
Logico-mathematical principles, law as, 42–44
Love, 64, 75, 94, 102, 105, 109; infant's need for, 159, 168
Love of the world, 101, 190
Lyotard, Jean-François, 157

Man, 47–49, 66, 69
Manipulanda, 109, 131
Marx, Karl, 164–65
Masks, 60, 62–68, 70, 153–54
Master, 46–49, 59–62, 65–67, 70, 82, 84; imperative to be, 104, 106; overman as, 173
Master consciousness, 103
Masturbation: and the castration threat, 160, 169–70
Mathematics, 2–3, 12, 88, 92
Matter, 131; distinguished from form, 30, 31, 88
Meaning, 2, 78–79, 119, 120, 155, 185
Means, 53–54, 66
Merleau-Ponty, Maurice, 29, 143, 188
Metaphors, 167, 169
Metaphysical consolation of tragedy, 73–76
Metaphysics, 5, 72, 78–79, 84, 109, 131
Metonymies, 160, 165–66, 167, 169
Mind, 43, 95–96, 101
Mirror-image, 159–60
Moment, 24, 35, 105, 126, 172, 178
Money, 164, 165, 168
Monotheism, 141
Moral agent, 42, 58
Moral autarchy, 49–52
Moral imagination, 40–42, 43–44, 49, 56
Moral imperative, 38–41, 43–44, 50–52, 151, 194–95 n.6; and the will, 39, 44, 45–46, 47–49. *See also* Categorical imperative; Imperative; Types of law
Moral judgment, 41
Morality: Kant on, 38–58, 196 n.49; Nietzsche on, 59–60, 67, 92–93
Mortality, 6–8, 145, 190; for Heidegger, 109, 112–19, 123, 131, 133, 182, 185. *See also* Death; Dying
Mother, 157, 159, 160–61, 166–67, 171; castration of, 161, 163, 167–68

Name, 172; of the father, 163, 170, 171, 173
Nancy, Jean-Luc, 189
Nature, 1, 11, 14, 88, 103, 194 n.5; Husserl on, 15–16, 28; idealization of, 95–99, 100, 105; for Kant, 5, 39–40, 41–42, 47–48, 54; state of, 53, 54, 55
—in Nietzsche, 48–49, 65, 77, 93, 97–98, 173; and eternal recurrence, 4, 5–6; and human nature, 69–70, 175; imperative force of, 71–73; law of, 99, 104; truth of, 85
Necessary, the/necessity, 41–42, 49, 51, 170, 181; as property of law, 3, 5, 140–41, 177–79, 183
Negation, 95–96
Nietzsche, Friedrich, 4, 5–6, 125, 126, 129, 172–73, 187; on creation, 58; on human nature, 19; on idealization, 87, 90–99, 162; on love of the world, 101, 190; on mastery, 46, 48–49, 59–86; on value, 58, 59, 65, 66,

72, 79, 85, 103, 198 n.30. *See also* Affirmation: Nietzsche on; Force: for Nietzsche; Nature (in Nietzsche); Pain: Nietzsche on; Sovereignty (in Nietzsche); Will (in Nietzsche)
Nihilism, 11, 96
Nihilists, 59–60, 62, 67, 68, 70
Non-being, 113, 115, 118, 122
Non-contradiction, logical axiom of, 71–72, 84, 92
Non-present, the, 22, 23
Nothingness, 33, 147–48, 184; for Levinas, 137, 141, 151; for Nietzsche, 67, 69, 95, 104, 187–88
—in Heidegger, 142, 143, 152, 180–81, 185–86; and deathbound thought, 112–13, 115–16, 117–18, 120, 122–23, 127–28, 130, 132
Now, 22–23, 24, 31–35, 80, 88, 147
Nuclear (atomic) technology, 1, 129, 176, 187

Obedience, 38, 51, 177–78
Objects, 14, 16, 25, 29, 162–63, 169
Obligation, 177, 184
Oedipus complex, 7–8, 160
Oedipus crisis, 163
Ontology, 71, 84, 97
Open-endedness, 28–31
Openness, 28–31, 56, 128, 131–32, 149
Other, the, 6, 8, 177, 187–91; Heidegger on, 144, 182; Husserl on, 18, 193 n.6; Kant on, 53, 140–41, 148, 177–80, 182; mother and her representatives as, 163, 166–67, 168. *See also* Alterity
—in Levinas, 135–40, 144–45, 150, 153, 182, 189; alterity of, 6–7, 148; responsibility for, 145–47, 148–49, 151
Other death, the, 6, 8, 187–90
Otherwise than Being (Levinas), 153, 155
Overman, 60, 70, 173. *See also* Master

Paganism, 141
Pain, 44–45, 49, 51, 174; Nietzsche on, 64, 66, 70, 71, 91, 93, 100–101, 175; of the other, 179, 182, 189–90
Parental (paternal) law, 160–63, 167–68, 170, 173, 175
Particularity, 14, 141, 145, 177–78, 182, 183
Passions, 196–97 n.57
Passivity, 100, 123, 147–48, 150, 155, 179
Past, 112, 115–16, 147–48, 154; relationship to the present, 23–26, 30, 33, 35
Paternal (parental) law, 160–63, 167–68, 170, 173, 175
Pathos of distance, 64, 198 n.24
Patience, 155
Penis, 161, 163, 167–68
Perception, 90, 92–93, 96–97, 142–43, 144; of the other, 145, 178–79
Phallic identity, 7, 169–71, 174

Phallus, 7–8, 61, 161–63, 168–71, 174, 175
Phenomena, 93–94, 139, 140
Phenomenological intentional analysis, 157
Phenomenology, 2–3, 4–5, 89–90, 119, 127; of the face, 135–37
Philosophers, 59, 62, 63, 198 n.19
Physico-chemical laws, 178
Platonism, 13–14, 60, 67, 76
Pleasure, 145, 152, 159–60, 169; infantile, 157, 158, 166–67, 169; Kant on, 44–45, 49, 51; Nietzsche on, 66, 74, 91–92, 93, 175
Pleasure principle, 193 n.4
Pleasure surfaces, 157–58, 160, 162–63, 166–67, 169
Poetic moment, 44
Poetics, 74
Poetry, 125, 130
Political economy, 2, 165–66
Political history, 54, 196–97 n.57
Possibility, 113–15, 116, 118, 129–30, 180–82, 185–86
Potentiality, 149; for Heidegger, 115–17, 124, 129–30, 180–82, 183
Power, 34–35, 50–51, 178, 184, 196–97 n.57; of existence, 115–16, 117, 129–30; Nietzsche on, 61–65, 77, 104, 172–73
Practical judgment, 41, 54, 179, 181
Practical life, 126, 128–29
Praxis, 128–29, 130–34, 155
Presence, 126, 147–48, 153, 171–72; for Husserl, 22, 35, 96–97, 171
Present, the, 22–26, 30, 99; for Heidegger, 112, 114, 116–18, 147; for Husserl, 4, 23–24, 31–35, 88, 99
Priests, 59, 62, 64–65, 198 n.19
Primitive communism, 165–66, 167
Psychoanalysis, 2, 7, 157, 162, 169
Psychoanalytic genetic analysis, 171
Psycho-physiological laws, 178

Rational agent, 47, 53–54, 58, 100
Rational faculty. *See* Reason
Rational man, 51, 55
Rational will, 100, 101
Rationality, 18, 20–21
Reality, 12, 13–14, 74–75, 156; representation of, 67, 87, 88, 93, 95
Reason (Rational faculty), 36–37, 39–40, 41, 43–44, 50
Recurrability ad infinitum, 87–88, 93–94, 98, 173. *See also* Eternal return
Religion, 13, 67, 197 n.62
Repetition, 158, 171
Representation, 46–47, 89, 127, 158, 159, 171–72; Kant on, 45, 53, 177, 178, 183; Nietzsche on, 60–61, 62, 95, 100, 102, 104–105; of the other, 135–36; of reality, 67, 87, 88, 93, 95
Repression, 158, 171–72

Respect, 38, 47, 51, 54, 67, 182; for law, 52, 53, 140, 177–78; for the other, 53, 177–78, 188
Responsibility, 145–49, 151, 153, 155
Retention, 25, 26, 31–32, 34–35
Ricardo, David, 163
Round, the, 14, 27

Sage-magi (Sages), 59, 63, 70. *See also* Philosophers
Saints, 59, 63–64, 68
Sarraute, Natalie, 127
Sartre, Jean-Paul, 183
Satisfaction, 52, 159
Schell, Jonathan, 176
Schopenhauer, Arthur, 68
Science, 11, 14, 18–19, 20, 42, 88, 193 nn.2, 4; Nietzsche on, 66–67, 70–71, 73, 81–82, 96, 97–98; representation in, 89
Scientism, 89
Scientists, 59–60, 62, 65–67, 68, 70
Self, 151–55
Self-determination, 39–40
Self-responsibility, 21, 35–37
Senescence. *See* Aging
Sensations, 44–45, 77, 91–92, 157–58
Sense organs, 84–85
Sensibility, 90–91, 157–58, 174, 188; for Heidegger, 123, 142, 143, 144–45; for Levinas, 135, 141–45, 152–53, 155; for Nietzsche, 91–93, 98, 100–102, 175
Sensuous will, 100, 102, 103
Sensuousness, 91, 92, 100, 102, 121, 131; Kant on, 44–45, 49, 51–52, 179; Levinas on, 136, 142, 145, 152
Servile (slave) society, 59, 165–66, 167
Sign of the subject: idealization of, 156–63; value of, 163–69
Signifier, 2, 157, 160, 161–62, 169
Signs, 2, 7–8, 159, 169, 171; for Levinas, 136–40, 150, 155
Simmel, Georg, 98, 99
Singularity, 82, 103–104, 190–91; for Heidegger, 111, 120, 122, 124, 125, 181–82
Slave (servile) society, 59, 165–66, 167
Social history, 54–55, 196–97 n.57
Socratism, 75–76
Soul, 80, 95–96, 101–102, 103, 111
Sovereignty, 19, 21, 36–37, 47–54, 56–57, 102–103
—in Nietzsche, 58, 61, 73, 84, 86, 100, 106; and consciousness, 70; phantasms of, 48–49; of subjectivity, 90; and survival imperative, 72–73
Space, 12, 98–99; infinite, 3, 14, 88
Space-time, 12, 88, 97; infinite, 14, 150
Speculative reason, 177, 183
Speech, 7, 122, 125, 156; and alterity, 135–37, 139; and equivocation, 119–21
Speech acts, 59, 160

Spirit, 68, 77, 78, 102, 109, 128
Spirituality, 11–12, 20–21, 76–77, 90, 102
Strauss, Leo, 62
Strong, the, 63, 64, 91–92, 100, 198 n.2
Subjectivity, 1–5, 7, 11–12, 14, 20–21, 28–31, 35–37; for Husserl, 2–3, 4–5, 21–22, 89–90, 128, 150; for Levinas, 147–49, 151–55; for Nietzsche, 90, 92, 95, 99; sign of, 156–69; and speech, 121
Suffering, 69–70, 83, 100–101
Suicide, 45, 160, 184
Surfaces: of the other, 135–36, 138, 179–80, 188, 189–90; as sources of pleasure, 157–58, 160, 162–63, 166–67, 169
Susceptibility, 91, 142, 143, 144, 188
Synecdoche, 165, 166, 167, 168

Talk *(das Gerede)*, 119–22, 145–46
Technology, 1, 129, 133
Teleological analysis, 21, 36
Teleology, 12, 51, 71, 96–97
Telos, 12–13, 60, 89, 96–97; Heidegger on, 111, 131, 185. *See also* End
Theoretical attitude, 15–20, 29
Theoretical consciousness, 17, 35–36, 89
Theoretical life, 16–17, 128
Theory, 15–20, 129–30; as idealization, 87–99
Time, 163–64, 169, 172, 185, 187; of consciousness, 31–34; Heidegger on, 6, 12, 34–35, 111–12, 116, 120, 122, 129, 133; Husserl on, 4–5, 34–35, 98–99, 104–105; Levinas on, 147–49, 153; Nietzsche on, 98–99, 104–105. *See also* Infinite time
Totality and Infinity (Levinas), 152–53
Touch, 188, 189–90
Trace, 139–41
Tragedy, 73–76, 92, 175
Transcendence, 127, 150, 189
Transcendental analysis, 21–28
Transcendental ego, 28
Transcendental phenomenology, 13, 36
Transcendental subjectivity, 98–99
Truth, 3, 12, 13–14, 60, 67, 102; absolute, 2–3, 15, 35–36; Heidegger on, 12, 118, 119, 127, 134; Husserl on, 89, 149; and idealization, 96–99; Nietzsche on, 60, 66–68, 70, 72, 78, 81, 84–86
Types of law (Kantianism), 41–42, 43–44, 51, 52–53, 177, 179–80, 181; imposed on libidinal infancy, 170; in kingdom of ends, 54–56; Levinas on, 151; and the other, 140. *See also* Categorical imperative; Imperative; Moral imperative

Unborn ones, 68–70, 177, 184, 190
Uncanniness *(Unheimlichkeit)*, 123, 130
Unconscious, 158, 171–72
Understanding, 79, 122, 130–34, 145, 175; deathbound, 118, 123–24

—in Kant, 3, 5, 38–40, 47; and the law, 43–44, 50, 140, 141, 148, 177–78, 179, 183
Und so weiter, 26, 29, 110, 148
Uneigentlichkeit, 110
Unendingness *(Unendlichkeit). See* Infinity
Unheimlichkeit (Uncanniness), 123, 130
Universal, the/universality, 40, 41–42, 49, 51, 103, 170, 181; in existentialism, 56–57; as property of law, 5, 56, 140–41, 177–79, 182–83
Universal agent, 102–103
Universal imperative. *See* Categorical imperative
Universal mind, 103
Universal nature, 72, 84
Universe, 3, 4–6, 58, 172–73; idealization of, 88–90; Kant on, 54, 72, 101; Nietzsche on, 65–67, 71–73, 93, 97–98, 101
Univocity, 119–20
Use-value, 163–64, 165–66, 168–69

Value, 57, 127, 156, 163–66, 169, 185; Nietzsche on, 57, 59, 65, 66, 72, 79, 85, 103, 198 n.30; phallus as, 168, 170; of sensuous object, 45, 169, 195 n.14; of the sign of the subject, 163–69
Vital force. *See* Life-force
Vocative force, 7, 136, 140
Void, 112–13, 130, 142

Wagner, Richard, 63
Weak, the, 63, 91–92, 100–101
White, Hayden, 164–65
Will, 1, 20, 43, 45–46, 47–49, 126, 184; existentialism on, 57; Heidegger on, 111, 117, 120–21, 128; and its law, 100–106; scientific, 18–19
—in Kant, 45, 52, 72, 100, 101, 178; and kingdom of ends, 53–56; and the moral imperative, 39, 44, 179, 195 n.18; relationship to act and law, 40–41, 49–50
—in Nietzsche, 45, 46–47, 57–58, 72–73, 100–106, 162, 173; to castrate, 66; and the driving force, 61, 63; and the law of eternal return, 80, 82, 99; to life, 69; and nihilist action, 68; to nothingness, 67, 69; for the present, 150; to responsibility, 70; to self-negation, 95
Will to power, 46, 64–65, 82–84, 91, 94
Women, 60–61, 197 nn.10, 12
Word of the father, 160–63, 167–68, 170, 173
Words, 171, 178; for Levinas, 136–37, 138, 146, 150–51, 182
World, 129, 144; for Kant, 40, 47, 141; for Levinas, 135–36, 141, 145, 152
—in Heidegger, 109–10, 112, 127–28, 130–31, 142, 144; death as, 180; and existence, 122–23; and law, 141

Yes-saying, 63–64, 68, 70, 80–81